CONTAGION, TECHNOLOGY AND LAW AT THE LIMITS

This open access book explores law, politics and inequality in fights against infectious diseases. Guided by a theoretical framework called 'governing through contagion', the studies in this book analyse how past and present governments have tried to combat contagious diseases, such as the bubonic plague, cholera, HIV/AIDS and COVID-19.

They examine how these governments used law and other technologies, including waste management, mask-wearing, quarantine stations, house inspections and the burning of entire neighbourhoods, to achieve their aims of protecting populations and ensuring productivity.

Although the studies recognise the power of the state, they simultaneously emphasise the active roles of technologies and creatures, drawing attention to the often-taken-for-granted workings of the non-human in public health governance. They also consider the implications of strategies of control on marginalised communities and democratic politics. Collectively, the studies in this book bring attention to the connections between COVID-19 responses by governments and their historical antecedents, shedding light on the role of capitalism, colonialism and geopolitics in circulating contagions and the strategies used to control them.

Contagion, Technology and Law at the Limits

Edited by

Lynette J Chua
and
Jack Jin Gary Lee

•HART•
OXFORD • LONDON • NEW YORK • NEW DELHI • SYDNEY

HART PUBLISHING

Bloomsbury Publishing Plc

Kemp House, Chawley Park, Cumnor Hill, Oxford, OX2 9PH, UK

1385 Broadway, New York, NY 10018, USA

29 Earlsfort Terrace, Dublin 2, Ireland

First published in Great Britain 2024

Open access was funded by Singapore Ministry of Education Academic Research Fund Tier 1 [WBS: A-8000923-00-00].

A catalogue record for this book is available from the British Library.

Library of Congress Cataloging-in-Publication data

ISBN: HB: 978-1-50997-070-4
ePDF: 978-1-50997-071-1
ePub: 978-1-50997-072-8

Typeset by Compuscript Ltd, Shannon

For my mother
– Lynette J Chua

To the memory of my mother-in-law, Heng Sok 香財喜
– Jack Jin Gary Lee

ACKNOWLEDGEMENTS

The central idea for *Contagion, Technology and Law at the Limits*, 'governing through contagion', originated with a paper that we were writing for a volume on the legal and policy responses to COVID-19 in 2020. At the time, the two of us, one under a nationwide lockdown in Singapore and the other a Stay-at-Home Executive Order in Chicago, palpably felt the impact of law and the SARS-CoV-2 virus. As we exchanged drafts of the paper that would form the theoretical backbone of this volume, we decided to start a project to investigate whether and how governing through contagion played out in different periods and contagious outbreaks. On the one hand, we began a historical ethnography of colonial and contemporary Singapore, drawing from archival materials, interviews and other qualitative data to connect macro-historical contexts and structures to the micro-sociolegal frame of action and practices involved in the processes of governing through contagion. On the other hand, we held an open call for papers, invited other scholars to engage with our concept and convened a workshop, 'Governing through Contagion: Perspectives across Time and Space' in hybrid format – in true pandemic form – from 19 to 21 April 2022. All nine chapters by our contributors came from that workshop.

We are extremely grateful to be able to work with our contributors to produce this volume while we were all navigating different degrees of pandemic conditions. The online conversations and e-mail exchanges about each chapter enriched the volume as a whole, as well as our thinking for the ongoing historical ethnography on Singapore. In addition, we want to thank our past and present research assistants, Cameron Gan Enyu, Elizabeth Koh Yuan, Ethan Leung, Jasmine Goh Xuanlin, Liu Yulin, May Wang, Wu Lingxin and Xie Yihui; and Wendy Wee and Kris Zhao at the Faculty of Law, National University of Singapore (NUS Law), for their administrative support. We are also grateful to receive funding for the research and writing of this project from the Singapore Ministry of Education Academic Research Fund Tier 1 [WBS: A-8000923-00-00] and Yale-NUS College Special Pocket Grant, as well as for the April 2022 workshop from the Centre for Asian Legal Studies, NUS Law.

Lynette J Chua and Jack Jin Gary Lee
September 2023

CONTENTS

EDITORS AND CONTRIBUTORS

Stephanie Burkhalter is Professor in the Politics Department at California State Polytechnic University, Humboldt in Arcata. She holds an MA in public policy and women's studies from The George Washington University, an MS in political science from the University of Oregon and a PhD in political science from the University of Washington. Her research focuses on small-group deliberation theory, design and outcomes, deliberative pedagogy and civic engagement, collaborative governance and deliberation in the US Congress.

Lynette J Chua is Professor of Law at National University of Singapore. She is the author of *The Politics of Rights and Southeast Asia*, *The Politics of Love in Myanmar: LGBT Mobilization and Human Rights as A Way of Life* and *Mobilizing Gay Singapore: Rights and Resistance in an Authoritarian State* and co-editor of *The Asian Law & Society Reader*. She was also President of the Asian Law & Society Association (2022–2023).

Lee Godden is formerly Professor at Melbourne Law School, Australia, and now Dean, Faculty of Law, Victoria University of Wellington. Her research sits at the interface of environmental law, resource and waste regulation and technologies of bodily control and brings a postcolonial lens to questions of governing the environment. Her current research focuses on public health and environmental regulation in pandemics.

Daniel WS Ho is a clinical psychologist at the Institute of Mental Health in Singapore. Outside of work, he volunteers extensively with marginalized communities and stigmatized minorities. He obtained his Masters in Clinical Psychology from National University of Singapore. His current clinical and research interests lie in the fields of youth, trauma and stigmatised minorities.

Nolan Kline is Associate Professor in the Department of Population Health Sciences at the University of Central Florida College of Medicine. He is an applied, medical anthropologist whose research areas broadly include immigrant policing and health, LGBTQ+ Latinx legal mobilisation and the politics of vaccination. He is the author of *Pathogenic Policing: Immigration Enforcement and Health in the US South*.

Jack Jin Gary Lee is Assistant Professor of Sociology at The New School for Social Research and Eugene Lange College of Liberal Arts. His scholarship explores how race and law shape the social logics and processes of governance in modern empires and (post-)colonial states. He is working on a book on the significance of law and race in the making of 'direct rule' in the modern British Empire.

Dhiraj Nainani is a Postdoctoral Fellow at the Asia Research Institute, National University of Singapore. He received his LLB and LLM from the London School of Economics and PhD in law from the University of Hong Kong. His current research focuses on reframing the relationship between the law and urban space in Asia.

Robert C Richards Jr is Assistant Professor at the University of Arkansas Clinton School of Public Service. His research centres on participatory governance, democratic deliberation and public dialogue. He is the co-editor of a special issue of the *Journal of Deliberative Democracy*, entitled 'Psychological Phenomena in Democratic Deliberation' (2022).

Sharyn Roach Anleu is Matthew Flinders Distinguished Professor of Sociology in the College of Humanities, Arts and Social Sciences at Flinders University and Fellow of the Academy of the Social Sciences in Australia. She is the author of *Law and Social Change* and four editions of *Deviance, Conformity and Control*, co-author of *Judging and Emotion: A Socio-Legal Analysis* and co-editor of *Judges, Judging and Humour.*

Christopher Roberts is Assistant Professor of Law at Chinese University of Hong Kong. His research focuses on the historical evolution of public order legality in nineteenth- and twentieth-century Britain, the British Empire and the British settler colonial world; on the evolution of ideas of workers' rights in the early to mid-twentieth century; and on comparative institutional and procedural issues in human rights bodies.

Sebastian James Rose is a History PhD student at the University of Greenwich and recipient of the John Charles Maynard Scholarship. His current research analyses the construction, operation and maintenance of the Indo-European Telegraph Department (IETD) in Iran and the Persian Gulf, with a specific focus on telegraph stations, workers and networks.

George Sarantoulias is a PhD candidate in the Literary and Cultural Studies Graduate Research Program at Monash University, Australia. He holds an Australian Government Research Training Scholarship and teaches social and political theory as an Assistant Lecturer in the School of Social Sciences, Monash University. He is Managing Editor of *Colloquy: Text Theory Critique*. His research centres around social imaginaries, citizenship and democracy.

Mark Sidel is Doyle-Bascom Professor of Law and Public Affairs at the University of Wisconsin-Madison. He is a long-time consultant on law and civil society for foundations, UN agencies, government donors and NGOs in China, India, Vietnam and elsewhere in Asia and a board member of the Washington-based International Center for Not-for-Profit Law. He earlier served with the Ford Foundation in Beijing, Hanoi, Bangkok and New Delhi.

Rayner KJ Tan is Assistant Professor at the Saw Swee Hock School of Public Health, National University of Singapore, where he obtained his PhD in public health. He also holds a visiting appointment at the National Centre for Infectious Diseases in Singapore. His current research broadly addresses social epidemiology and the social determinants of health.

Nathaniel Webb is a PhD candidate at the University of North Texas Health Science Center. His research lies at the intersection of public health and the criminal justice system with a focus on the influence of policing on health and health equity. He plans to utilize systems-level thinking to research the impacts of law enforcement actions on the health, health outcomes and healthcare utilisation of minoritised populations.

Daryl WJ Yang is a lawyer in Singapore. He holds an LLB from National University of Singapore, BA from Yale-NUS College and LLM from University of California, Berkeley, where he was a Fulbright Scholar. He has published in the *Australian Feminist Law Journal* and *Singapore Law Review* and has contributed to edited volumes on gender and constitutionalism, disability studies and queer Asia.

Introduction

Governing Through Contagion: Perspectives across Time and Space

LYNETTE J CHUA AND JACK JIN GARY LEE

> When I was first diagnosed, I actually wanted to be on medication, just to be like everyone else … when I came to know about [the law], it made me feel very small and very vulnerable.
>
> The law is quite sound, but unhappily it is systematically resisted … For one case of evasion detected, half a dozen may be successful, and from each evasion scores of new cases may arise.
>
> 'Protect Your Community': an LED traffic sign by the roadside.

These statements sound familiar, as though we might have encountered them during the COVID-19 pandemic, which continues to leave imprints in our lives – a crumbling poster exhorting the virtues of 'safe distancing', a forgotten mask by the kerbside, a lingering cough or memories of a loved one who succumbed to the virus. Yet, the above observations originate from different eras and different contagious diseases. The first quote comes from a HIV/AIDS patient in Singapore; the second a colonial newspaper editorial on the evasion of quarantine during an outbreak of smallpox; only the third is about COVID-19.[1] The familiarity of these expressions highlights our motivation for publishing *Contagion, Technology and Law at the Limits*: governmental responses to the COVID-19 pandemic are not entirely novel but emerge from existing technologies and infrastructures. By bringing attention to the connections between public health governance of COVID-19 and those of earlier contagious episodes, we hope this volume can inspire new avenues of inquiry that shed light on the role of capitalism, colonialism and geopolitics in circulating contagions and the strategies targeted at controlling them.

In other words, *Contagion, Technology and Law at the Limits* concerns a subject matter that is ever present and timely in all eras and societies, namely, the relationships that humans develop with contagions, law and other technologies. Unlike recent books that have focused on the legal and policy responses to the

[1] The first and third examples are based on Chapters 5 and 4, respectively, of this book. The second comes from 'Hospitals and Isolation: Reasons Why Natives Hide Smallpox, Miseries Suffered in Hospital and Camp', *The Straits Times* (Singapore, 27 July 1911) 7.

COVID-19 pandemic,[2] *Contagion, Technology and Law at the Limits* considers a variety of contagious diseases, temporalities and territories, and connects the past and present by bringing into view the historical formation of strategies of controls against contagion. While some chapters in *Contagion, Technology and Law at the Limits* feature COVID-19, others analyse such diseases as the bubonic plague, cholera, HIV/AIDS and the 'social contagion' of vagrancy. Collectively, these chapters examine how governments have used law and other technologies, ranging from waste management, mask-wearing, quarantine stations and the burning of entire neighbourhoods, to achieve their objectives of protecting populations and ensuring economic productivity. They also consider the implications of such strategies of control for questions of social inequity, justice and democracy.

The analyses in all the chapters are guided by the theoretical framework of 'governing through contagion' or GTC. We first sketched out GTC in an earlier paper based on our study of colonial and post-colonial Singapore.[3] With *Contagion, Technology and Law at the Limits* we offer the first book-length collection of papers that refine and advance the GTC framework. The collection brings together scholars from law, socio-legal studies, history, sociology, anthropology, geography, politics, medicine and public health, who conduct research on Asia, North America, Australia, Europe and the Middle East. Taking up our invitation, these scholars drew from their own original research – including archival work, discourse analysis, ethnography and interviews – to engage and develop GTC's theoretical themes.

We elaborate on GTC in the rest of this chapter. We situate the framework in relation to the relevant literature and distinguish it from other paradigms that also seek to understand contagious outbreaks, ensuing government responses and their effects. We also introduce the subsequent ten chapters and explain each chapter's distinctive engagement with GTC.

Contagion, Technology and Law

As governments and people interact with contagions, law and other technologies, they recursively produce relationships that constitute GTC. As an individualised mode of power, GTC directs social conduct, conditions moral sensibilities and aims to preserve the health of populations. Capable of minimising medical costs

[2] See, eg, V Ramraj (ed), *COVID-19 in Asia: Law and Policy Contexts* (Oxford, Oxford University Press, 2021); MC Kettemann and K Lachmayer (eds), *Pandemocracy in Europe: Power, Parliaments and People in Times of COVID-19* (Oxford, Hart Publishing, 2021); D Cowan and A Mumford (eds), *Pandemic Legalities: Legal Responses to COVID-19* (Bristol, Bristol University Press, 2021).

[3] LJ Chua and JJG Lee, 'Governing through Contagion', in V Ramraj (ed), *Covid-19 in Asia: Law and Policy Contexts* (Oxford: Oxford University Press, 2021). Subsequently, we refined GTC in our article analysing smallpox vaccination in Singapore and other parts of the Straits Settlements: JJG Lee and LJ Chua, 'Smallpox Vaccination and the Limits of Governing through Contagion in the Straits Settlements, 1868–1926' (2023) *Law & Policy* 43(3): 331–52.

and maintaining economic productivity, GTC is deployed as part of a political regime's economic strategies and therefore essential to legitimacy. This distinctive formation of power, while pervasive in modern societies, is not singular or all-encompassing: it operates alongside, or even in tandem with, other forms of power and social regulation oriented towards objectives unrelated to public health.

At the same time as our formulation of GTC, other scholars issued critical analyses of the public health controls directed at limiting the transmission of SARS-CoV-2, the virus that causes COVID-19.[4] Their critiques derived from, or resonated with, Foucault's view of law as a repressive mode of juridical power,[5] and they focused on the use of emergency powers and regulations in the prohibition of movement and the control of social interactions. In *Where Are We Now?* Agamben examines the relationship between COVID-19 strategies of control and democracy, focusing on the exercise of emergency or expansive legal powers to curb the rise of COVID-19.[6] He echoes Foucault's position on law as a repressive force tied to the sovereign, and is critical of the ways in which public health authorities reshaped politics and even human life through undemocratic measures. Another recent publication, *Pandemocracy in Europe*, is also concerned with the potentially undemocratic modes by which governments have rolled out strategies of control to fight COVID-19 and the threat of expanding state powers during and potentially after the pandemic in Europe.[7] From such perspectives, the crisis of the COVID-19 pandemic has provided cover for the creep of autocratic power.

Our approach is different. Contagious diseases and epidemics do not, as a matter of course, result in authoritarian rule or eventuate in totalising forms of power. Drawing also from Foucault, we identify how biopower, or the body of regulations aimed at security, channels, contains and controls human and nonhuman relations to obtain goals linked to the collective welfare; the underlying target of control, population, is thus a distinct reality composed of individual subjects and their relations.[8] However, in a departure from Foucault, we approach law as infrastructure, as technology and as a component of biopower – not just a tool of juridical power and sovereignty. Indeed, the studies in *Contagion, Technology and Law at the Limits* show that while the regulatory power of the state may be expansive, the state does not dictate the terms and processes of social life, being dependent, as it were, on human and nonhuman agents. For example, the inescapable human generation of material waste (Godden, Chapter 3), interpretations of ambiguous regulatory language (Yang, Ho and Tan, Chapter 5) or even the

[4] See, eg, S Thomson and EC Ip, 'COVID-19 Emergency Measures and The Impending Authoritarian Pandemic' (2020) 7(1) *Journal of Law and the Biosciences* 1–33; G Agamben, *Where Are We Now? The Epidemic as Politics* (Lanham MD, Rowman and Littlefield, 2021).

[5] M Foucault, *Security, Territory, Population: Lectures at the Collège de France*, 1977–1978 (London, Picador, 2007).

[6] Agamben, *Where Are We Now?* (n 4).

[7] Kettemann and Lachmayer, *Pandemocracy* (n 2).

[8] Foucault developed the concept of security in his lectures (n 5) after *The History of Sexuality* (New York City, Vintage Books, 1990), in which he used 'regulatory controls' instead of 'security' to refer to power concerned with regulating the life of populations.

structures that make up public infrastructures of communication can aid, reconfigure or trouble GTC (Rose, Chapter 1; Roach Anleu and Sarantoulias, Chapter 4; Burkhalter and Richards, Chapter 7). As a result, GTC is not static, for it grows, declines and transforms in accordance with the complex of human/nonhuman relations that constitute it.

In addition to our critical engagement with postmodern perspectives on security, we draw from the interdisciplinary field of science and technology studies, which has well theorised the active roles of technologies and creatures in shaping the fates of humans and their projects. A key contribution of GTC, therefore, is that we emphasise the oft-overlooked role of nonhuman agents and things including, but also extending beyond, law in the governance of public health. Critically, this intersection between theoretical approaches allows us to map and better understand the limits of human agency. Despite the central role of official and other human actors in the regulation of contagious diseases, nonhuman creatures – for example, dogs, cows and viruses – and the non-living – legal frameworks, medicine, communication and other technologies and even soil (for example, Nainani, Chapter 2; Roberts, Chapter 6) – also figure into the workings and failures of GTC. Regardless of whether readers have any interest in the empirical context of each contribution in *Contagion, Technology and Law at the Limits*, they may find this emphasis instructive.

Based on our historical-ethnographic analysis of colonial and postcolonial Singapore, GTC possesses the following three inter-related characteristics. Although the case studies in Chapters 1 to 9 contain, to varying extents, imprints of all three features, here we highlight one in each chapter for the purposes of illustration.

Centralisation and Technology of Law

The manner and extent of the centralisation of state legal infrastructures strongly influence policy approaches to contagious episodes and the uses of law in regulatory strategies. Law, as a technology and infrastructure of control, shapes the development of GTC. The more centralised legal infrastructures are, the more totalising governing through contagion can become even though human and nonhuman agencies may limit its reach. For instance, British rule occasioned the development of legal technology to deal with contagious diseases in the colonies, responding to the recursive relationships among humans, critters and germs. In turn, postcolonial states typically maintained and enhanced their colonial legal infrastructures of public health governance, modifying their approaches according to the nature of the contagion at hand.[9]

One such case is Hong Kong, which Nainani examines in his chapter to show how the development and centralisation of legal and other infrastructures by the

[9] Chua and Lee, 'Governing through Contagion' (n 3); Lee and Chua, 'Smallpox Vaccination' (n 3).

colonial and contemporary governments enabled their swift, targeted actions against the bubonic plague and COVID-19, respectively (Chapter 2). In Chapter 7, Burkhalter and Richards suggest a complexity to the relation between legal centralisation and the reach of GTC in the US state of Oregon, highlighting the role of participatory governance in enacting strategies of control in a settler-colonial context. Focusing on statutory law-making in his intriguing, productive extension of GTC to 'social contagion' in Chapter 6, Roberts shows that the form and ideologies of what he calls the 'vagrancy law model' remain influential within contemporary postcolonial legal orders. Furthermore, as Sidel reminds us with his study of China, even when the state already exercises a high degree of supervision and surveillance over its citizens, strategies of control against contagion can still significantly enhance the reach of an authoritarian regime (Chapter 9).

Normalisation and Technologies of Moralisation

When implementing strategies of control, governments try to render populations into a disciplined body of subjects conducive to defeating contagion. They do so through law and other technologies, such as vaccines, masks, contact-tracing apps and social media, that convey state-sanctioned notions of appropriate conduct. At its most potent, GTC can moralise and shape behaviour to the point of normalisation, where the state's regulatory power dictates the discourses, imaginaries and rules underlying social action. In such cases, those subject to GTC comply without needing to be told by officials or others, even policing the behaviour of others. For example, honing in on a ubiquitous phenomenon during the pandemic, masks, Roach Anleu and Sarantoulias find that infrastructures and information about the effectiveness and methods of mask-wearing recalibrated what was 'moral' behaviour in Adelaide and Melbourne and altered the assumptions, understandings and frames of social interaction (Chapter 4).

Inter/dysconnectedness and Rearticulation of Difference[10]

GTC could also reinforce, perhaps exacerbate, existing social inequalities. Thriving on interconnectedness, contagion spreads through the technologies and practices that enable social life: for example, eating together; travelling on buses, trains,

[10] Formulated independently, our term, *dysconnectedness*, runs parallel to Stephan, Friston and Firth's work on the causes of schizophrenia: KE Stephan, KJ Friston and CD Frith, 'Dysconnection in Schizophrenia: From Abnormal Synaptic Plasticity to Failures of Self-monitoring' (2009) 35 *Schizophrenia Bulletin* 509–27. In their view, the term 'emphasizes the notion that there is *abnormal* (rather than decreased) functional integration among brain regions in schizophrenia' and while *dis-connectivity* implies the loss of connection, *dys-connectivity* denotes the 'bad' or 'ill' nature of connection (510, emphasis added). The significance of this term in medical discourse on states of mind mirrors our emphasis on the moral implications of dysconnected social relations like those found in colonial contexts, namely the different realities and judgements experienced by colonisers and the colonised.

cruise ships and aeroplanes; clearing or excavating land for agriculture, mining or construction; and building agglomerated structures for urban living. GTC, on the other hand, seeks to counteract interconnectedness, utilising technologies of physical isolation, immunisation and communication to disconnect, separate and, importantly, contain contagious matter from humans and the sick from the healthy. Such controls compound dysconnectedness – inequities and social divisions that often worsen existing inequalities along such lines as race, class, legal status, gender and age. Furthermore, resistance to GTC's strategies of control risk infection and possibly death through contact with contagion, even becoming dysconnected from compliant subjects due to the stigma attached to misbehaviour and sickness. For example, in Yang, Ho and Tan (Chapter 5), when their interviewees resisted the Singaporean state's strategies of control against HIV/AIDS, their actions inadvertently reproduced dysconnectedness by othering members of their own social group, gay, bisexual and other men who have sex with men (GBMSM).

These three characteristics of GTC point to the foundational, but also moderated, role of law in the protection of public health against contagious outbreaks. Central to GTC, law can aid or hinder governmental efforts to stave off threats to human life, sometimes doing so inadvertently. When the three features of GTC are analysed as a whole, we can also establish how the centralisation of law and its infrastructures facilitates the deployment of legal and other technologies to normalise social conduct that keep (privileged) members of a community 'safe'. However, such projects of legal ordering can also be mediated and undermined by the actions and effects of human and nonhuman agents. As Rose suggests in Chapter 1, despite reinforcing the dysconnectedness of the empire's emergent racial order, British attempts at building enclaved quarantine stations to guard against cholera in the Persian Gulf were not only undermined by uncooperative human behaviour but also by the fluvial nature of these stations' jurisdictional boundaries. Similarly, the tendency of nonhuman agents to elude strategies of containment looms large in Godden's chapter (Chapter 3). She focuses on how the global problem of waste, heightened by the accelerated production of medical waste and lack of protection for waste workers in the COVID-19 pandemic, has confounded and overwhelmed international and national efforts to manage and maintain the distinction and distance between the infected from the non-infected. In an extreme case in the opposite direction, in Chapter 8, Kline and Webb demonstrate how politicians took advantage of heightened fear and moralisation during the pandemic to employ law not to combat contagion but deliberately exacerbate inter/dysconnectedness.

Chapter Outlines

Our contributors come from a variety of backgrounds in terms of gender, career, institutional affiliations, disciplinary training, research contexts and geographical locations. Although we are unable to represent every continent in the volume, we conducted a worldwide call for submissions to the workshop that preceded this book. At the workshop, held on 19–21 April 2022, we featured twice the number of papers and scholars from far more diverse research sites and backgrounds. Ultimately, we moved forward with our slate of contributors based on the ways their respective scholarship elaborated on, challenged and advanced the GTC framework. To illustrate, one of the issues that emerged from our workshop discussions was the need to specify the limits of GTC in relation to its purported aims and its impact on political life – a theme that several chapters in this volume engage with. Another was the role of nonhuman agency. While all chapters have been organised around the concept of GTC, each contributor to this book focuses on a different period, geographical location or contagious episode to offer their unique take on the framework. They do not elaborate on GTC's fundamentals but delve into their case study to draw out a particular theme or argument connected to GTC.

Part I: Technologies of Governing Through Contagion

Chapter 1: 'British Quarantine and Telegraph Stations in the Persian Gulf, 1864–1928: Governing Through Contagion, Entanglements and Enclaves'

Sebastian James Rose

This chapter explores the material and spatial organisation of British Indian quarantine stations and the Indo-European Telegraph Department's telegraph stations in southern Iran and the Gulf in the late nineteenth and early twentieth centuries. Analysing the overlaps between telegraphy, quarantine, mobility and the subsequent rise of contagious diseases, Rose argues that this quarantine network sought to manage the contradictions between the interconnections and dysconnections of networked imperial power. He shows how enclaves and human and nonhuman entanglements emerged from such inter/dysconnectedness. In addition, by examining the practices of enclaving and the reality of entanglement at the Faw telegraph station, he shows how the empire's racial and microbial anxieties produced the station's boundaries. At the same time, he demonstrates how humans and nonhumans continually challenged quarantine, confused the station's boundaries and undermined enclaving. Such human and nonhuman entanglements consequently limited the reach of governing through contagion.

Chapter 2: 'Wastewater Surveillance in Colonial and Present-Day Hong Kong: Governing Through Contagion from Below'

Dhiraj Nainani

This chapter compares two events in Hong Kong: the arrival of the bubonic plague in Taipingshan in 1894 and the emergence of COVID-19 in Yau Tsim Mong in 2021. Nainani traces both the 1894 quarantine and the 2021 lockdown to show

how the state uses the legal regulation of space to control bodies, borders and objects. He also evinces how sewage infrastructure evolved with responses to contagious diseases to govern inhabitants 'from below,' thus suggesting that the state governs through contagion by using infrastructure technology. In addition, he points out differences between the two cases: the quarantining of Taipingshan in 1894 reinforced a racialising logic that linked the plague to 'filthy' (racialised) bodies and their habits; whereas wastewater surveillance in 2021 resulted in the temporary suspension of existing power dynamics, offering an opportunity to transform relations between the state and certain populations.

Chapter 3: 'Regulating Pandemic Wastes: Governing Through Contagion via Disciplining Modalities'

Lee Godden

This chapter examines the ubiquitous phenomenon of wastes and their regulation in the COVID-19 pandemic through a survey of World Health Organisation (WHO) protocols, guidance and national legislation. Godden shows how laws on the regulation of COVID-19 infected wastes produce both human and contagion-based 'subjects' in a pandemic. Furthermore, she demonstrates how the exponential growth in infectious wastes in the pandemic exposed the material vulnerability of human populations. In the legal framings for COVID-19 waste regulation, contagion assumed an agency that was co-dependent on human populations. Meanwhile, contagion's materiality, manifest in burgeoning wastes, threatened to undercut the regulatory and social order. 'Populations' in the COVID-19 pandemic became heavily reliant on technologies of waste management but also the 'willingness' of designated workers to carry out the tasks of managing contagious wastes so that others avoided contagion. Godden thus highlights the extent to which human populations risk being subsumed by contagion despite the disciplining modalities of laws and protocols designed to avert 'danger'.

Chapter 4: 'Instruction and Information, Images and Icons: Governing Through Contagion, Social Regulation and Public Health'

Sharyn Roach Anleu and George Sarantoulias

This chapter examines a visible component in the complex processes of governing through contagion during the COVID-19 pandemic: the communication of information and instructions on mask-wearing. Analysing mask-wearing posters and signs located in publicly accessible situations across two Australian cities, Adelaide and Melbourne, and their surrounding suburbs, Roach Anleu and Sarantoulias show how these visual images rely on legal and medical-scientific authority as well as appeals to collective wellbeing, and sometimes individual self-interest to convey new norms, recalibrate ordinary social activities and cast previously non-problematic, even expected behaviour as deviant. They also demonstrate that the signs and posters contain the assumption that individuals will (be able to) interpret instructions correctly and then have the capacity and motivation to align their behaviour with the directives and advice in a manner that enables ordinary social interactions to continue with minimal disruption.

Part II: Inter/Dysconnectedness of Governing Through Contagion

Chapter 5: 'Intimacy, Queer Men and the Law on HIV Risk Disclosure in Singapore: Governing Through Contagion at the Margins'

Daryl WJ Yang, Daniel WS Ho and Rayner KJ Tan

This chapter explores governing through contagion at the margins in Singapore's use of criminal law to combat the spread of HIV and its effects on the lives of GBMSM. Yang, Ho and Tan focus on Singapore's Infectious Diseases Act, which makes it an offence (i) for a person with HIV to engage in sexual activity without having obtained the informed consent of their sexual partner; and (ii) for a person at 'significant risk' of contracting HIV to engage in sexual activity with others without first taking certain measures. Based on qualitative interviews with GBMSM, they demonstrate how the totalising effect of governing through contagion operates at the margins via law's 'strategic ambiguity'. They call attention to how GBMSM conceive of and resist legal and non-legal modes of control of the most intimate parts of their lives. Yet, echoing our caution that such resistance performs complicity with governing through contagion, Yang, Ho and Tan's findings reveal that the dysconnectedness of the law is reproduced by GBMSM themselves through a cascading chain of othering.

Chapter 6: 'The Vagrancy Law Model: Governing Through Social Contagion in the Anglo World, 1824–1932'

Christopher Roberts

This chapter conceptualises vagrancy as a socially transmissible ill and explores how governing through *social* contagion is even more fundamental and widespread than health crisis-related forms of governance. Focusing on the development of the 'vagrancy law model' over little more than a century in Britain, the British Empire and the British settler colonial world, Roberts analyses the connection between four different regimes of vagrancy law – anti-poor, anti-immorality, anti-criminal and anti-migrant measures – and the public rhetorics and ideologies that helped justify the adoption of even more extreme policies by the early twentieth century.

While such extreme policies as forced sterilisation have since been condemned, many of the more mundane approaches from which they developed have only faced modest challenges and remain deeply embedded in contemporary legal orders. Overarchingly, Roberts' chapter underscores the importance of paying greater attention to anti-contagion strategies, both social and biological, in governance.

Chapter 7: 'The Oregon Citizen Assembly Pilot on COVID-19 Recovery: Participatory Governing Through Contagion'

Stephanie Burkhalter and Robert C Richards, Jr

This chapter explores patterns of governing through contagion in three periods of pandemic to show how the decentralisation of state institutions affects the extent to which governing through contagion is totalising. Burkhalter and Richards focus on the US state of Oregon, which has a decentralised government and a well-established and unique culture of participatory governance, and analyse how Oregonians participated in an online 'citizens assembly' to deliberate about the potential state responses and protective measures during the COVID-19 pandemic. Through this process, participants were granted a sense of agency, acquired a systemic understanding of complex policy issues and succeeded in experiencing connectedness across social differences. Nonetheless, these moments of connectedness also exposed embedded forms of dysconnectedness, such as legacies of settler colonialism and division along class lines. Burkhalter and Richards find that when state centralisation and enforcement of legal technologies are relatively minimised, techniques of normalisation and moralisation become more important to a state attempting to limit the impact of contagion on its population.

Part III: Authoritarianism and Governing Through Contagion

Chapter 8: 'Advancing a Politics of Social Division and Governing Through Contagion in Texas, USA'

Nolan Kline and Nathaniel Webb

This chapter examines how lawmakers took advantage of a public health crisis to advance their politics of exclusion and exacerbate existing forms of inter/dysconnectedness. Governmental approaches toward the COVID-19 pandemic have varied across US states. Focusing on the state of Texas, Kline and Webb argue that political leaders failed to address the COVID-19 crisis and instead increased social exclusion, passing bills that constrained the rights of lesbian, gay, bisexual, transgender and queer-identifying (LGBTQ+) individuals; limited reproductive rights; restricted political representation; and promoted xenophobia. The populations targeted by these laws – women, minorities and migrants – are also those who already suffer more from inter/dysconnectedness as a result of the pandemic and governing through contagion or, as this case shows, the lack thereof.

Chapter 9: 'Governing Through Contagion in the Authoritarian Context and the Case of China'

Mark Sidel

This chapter explores governing through contagion in authoritarian Asia, focusing on China as a case study for how COVID-19 regulation has worked alongside the authoritarian governance that long preceded it. In China, as in some other parts of authoritarian Asia, the authorities did not need the processes of governing through contagion to take and maintain strict control of their societies. Nevertheless, Sidel details how even in such authoritarian environments as China, COVID-19 strategies of control have significantly enhanced the state's supervision and surveillance of both domestic and overseas civil society and nongovernmental activity. Sidel also details how such strategies, layered upon existing, broader authoritarian governance, have led to different forms of resistance: citizen resistance against harsh COVID-19 rules; overseas support for attempts to provide legal aid to COVID-19 victims and families in China; and the cautious emergence of carefully worded suggestions for less harsh and more facilitative civil society regulation in the future.

Chapter 10: 'Governing Through Contagion and the Limits of Law'

Lynette J Chua and Jack Jin Gary Lee

Reflecting on previous chapters and our research on vaccination in colonial and post-colonial Singapore, this concluding chapter examines the relations between contagion, power and law in governing through contagion, highlighting law's mediated role and the limits to its reach. We focus on two intertwined dynamics: first, law's collaboration and dependence on a range of human and non-human agencies; second, the compounded negative consequences of resistance to law and other technologies deployed in governing through contagion, generating what we call endemic inter/dysconnectedness – that is, the continual re-enactment of existing inequities and unequal power relations. Through GTC's theoretical frame, we identify points of continuity and congruence between the colonial government's struggles to implement mandatory smallpox vaccination and the post-colonial nation-state's efforts to encourage COVID-19 vaccination. Law does not dictate the unfettered expansion of state power, but the overall power of governing through contagion is significant to marginalised human (and non-human) populations who bear the brunt of both contagion and the state's exercise of law and other technologies.

PART I

Technologies of Governing Through Contagion

1

British Quarantine and Telegraph Stations in the Persian Gulf, 1864–1928

Governing Through Contagion, Entanglements and Enclaves

SEBASTIAN JAMES ROSE

> [A]ll intercourse with the outer world was suspended. Merchant vessels from Europe, which had sailed for the Gulf before the epidemic broke out, arrived in the roads and signalled in vain for a pilot; every one who could leave the town fled to the interior, and men could not be found to bury the dead.[1]

In 1876, Captain Prideaux, the British Political Resident in the Persian Gulf, recalled the horrors of the 1832 cholera outbreak in the southern Iranian port of Bushehr. His written recollection was part of a letter to the Government of India (GoI) on the status of British quarantine arrangements in the Gulf. Prideaux aimed to convince the colonial government that his Residency should prepare for the next inevitable wave by arranging a fixed point to temporarily relocate. He argued that the success of relocating was dependent on a strict maintenance of quarantine that would stave off infection and enable 'a link of communication between India and such portions of the Gulf as are more immediately under British influence'. Prideaux's *cordon sanitaire* envisioned connecting these enclaved sites through telegraph and quarantine networks. In doing so, British naval bases and consulates, Prideaux argued, would be free to implement rules 'of precaution and surveillance' without external interference.[2] These plans were predicated on the Indo-European Telegraph Department's (IETD) network, whose Persian Gulf Section (PGS) had been successfully in operation since 1864, connecting ports in southern Iran and Iraq to British India. It was this network with its new infrastructural idiom of sea cables and landlines that undergirded Prideaux's plan of connected British space. A few months prior to

[1] Letter from Captain WF Prideaux to Secretary of the Government of India, Foreign Dept, Bushehr, 7 September 1876. Establishment of a quarantine station at Bassidore [Bāsa'īdū] May 1875–March 1877. British Library, India Office Records (IOR)/P/1003.

[2] Prideaux to Bushehr (n 1).

Prideaux's letter, the Qajar government had called on Britain to enforce maritime quarantine in the Gulf as bubonic plague spread from Arabia and threatened Iran's southern ports. Despite Prideaux's plan, the measures eventually implemented by British and Iranian authorities proved unsuccessful in halting the spread of plague in 1876. However, Prideaux's vision, together with Iranian calls for British assistance in enforcing quarantine, inaugurated the emergence of an imperial quarantine network, which would draw upon and intertwine with the established IETD network.

This chapter focuses on the spatial and material organisation of the GoI's quarantine and IETD telegraph stations in southern Iran and the Gulf. Drawing on this comparison, the chapter offers insight into the process of imperial boundary making through quarantine and telegraph stations at the periphery of Britain's Indian Empire. To understand this process and the relationship between stations and their localities, this chapter develops Chua and Lee's idea of 'inter/dysconnectedness' from their concept of governing through contagion. It traces how imperial interconnections produced through trade and communication were coupled with attempts to disconnect peoples and things, particularly during the spread of contagious diseases. As Chua and Lee have argued, strategies to control contagious diseases often invoked dynamics of inter/dysconnectedness as states sought to link humans with technologies, such as vaccinations, quarantine measures and protective gear, while also disconnecting them from other potentially contagious humans and spaces. These efforts consistently resulted in the exacerbation of existing social divisions and inequalities.[3] This chapter extends Chua and Lee's analysis by arguing that quarantine and telegraph stations were crucial components in managing 'inter/dysconnectedness' and aiding the British in governing through contagion in southern Iran and the Gulf.

By exploring the inter/dysconnectedness of telegraph and quarantine networks, the chapter highlights the lacuna between imperial desires to create telegraph and quarantine stations as enclaves and the reality of local entanglements.[4] While the British imagined enclaves as technologies for cordoning British networks and spaces from external intrusion, they also imagined them as connective tissue, binding imperial nodes over great distances. In practice, attempts by British officials to produce enclaves with these desired interconnections and disconnections were never realised. As imperial officials on the ground learned, enclaves remained disappointingly enmeshed in local space, dependent on and sometimes in direct opposition to local human and non-human actants.[5]

[3] See JJG Lee and LJ Chua, 'Smallpox Vaccination and the Limits of Governing through Contagion in the Straits Settlements, 1868–1926' (2023) *Law & Policy* (online first DOI: 10.1111/lapo.12221); LJ Chua and JJG Lee, 'Governing through Contagion' in V Ramraj (ed), *Covid-19 in Asia* (Oxford, Oxford University Press, 2021).

[4] Robert Peckham makes a similar point arguing that a contradiction existed between British emphasis on 'unrestricted commerce' and 'the naming and fixing of categories, the imposition of immobility and the production of enclaves'. R Peckham, 'Spaces of Quarantine in Colonial Hong Kong' in A Bashford (ed) *Quarantine: Local and Global Histories* (London, Palgrave Macmillan, 2016) 68.

[5] Actant as a concept emerged from STS to understand forces and networks among actors and describe non-human agency. S Jackson, 'Toward an Analytical and Methodological Understanding of

As such, the terms *enclave* and *entanglement* have been used to describe imperial practice and the organisation of quarantine and telegraph stations at various junctures. British enclaves in Iran and the Gulf developed out of the establishment and construction of diplomatic, military and infrastructural buildings, such as Consular sites, naval bases, coal depots and, later, telegraph and quarantine stations.[6] As British influence grew in the region throughout the nineteenth and early twentieth centuries,[7] enclaves were frequently sought and protected in treaties as 'concessions'.[8] Legal documents were often vague about the specificities of local buildings with boundaries and rights of repair undefined. This led to the British engaging in practices of boundary making to shore up the material and spatial porousness of enclaves, defining micro-borders and solidifying contested internal space.

Entanglement, by contrast, has two meanings. Firstly, the term points to the impossibility of realising the totality of enclaving. Attempts to produce neatly delineated enclaves in contested space were continuously challenged and stifled by unintended ecological, legal and political entanglements. Shorelines shifted boundaries, while actants hindered British juridical and material interventions in and around quarantine and telegraph stations. Secondly, entanglement as practice refers to a specific shift in imperial policy during the 1920s as the British consciously moved towards imbedding quarantine stations into the fabric of urban spaces as political and etiological consensus shifted.

Despite the inter/dysconnectedness of quarantine and telegraph stations, existing scholarship has largely ignored this relationship.[9] Literature on contagious diseases and telegraphy in the region in the late nineteenth and early twentieth centuries primarily focused on the rise of 'modernity' in Iran through the creation of national health institutions.[10] In these accounts, quarantine and telegraph

Actor-Network Theory' (2015) 4 *Journal of Arts and Humanities* 29; B Latour, *Science in Action: How to Follow Scientists and Engineers through Society* (Cambridge, MA, Harvard University Press, 1987).

[6] Dane Kennedy's history of British Indian Hill Stations demonstrates that enclaving had been a colonial practice formed in India. Like the enclaves in Iran and the Persian Gulf, concerns over health, space and race defined these enclaves. D Kennedy, *The Magic Mountains: Hill Stations and the British Raj* 1st edn (Berkeley, University of California Press, 1996).

[7] Despite an increasing British presence in southern Iran and the Gulf in the late nineteenth century, the region remained largely outside formal control.

[8] For example, the Treaty of Paris signed in 1857 between Britain and Iran stipulated 'the establishment and recognition of Consuls-General, Consuls, Vice-Consuls, Consular Agents'. The IETD telegraph concession was granted in 1862, while the private Indo-European Telegraph Company Concession was granted in 1868. CU Aitchison, *A Collection of Treaties, Engagements and Sanads Relating to India and Neighbouring Countries: The Treaties, &c., Relating to Persia, the Arab Principalities in the Persian Gulf, and Oman*, vol XII (Calcutta, Superintendent Government Printing, 1909) 78, XXI, XXX.

[9] Except for Robert Peckham, 'Panic Encabled: Epidemics and the Telegraphic World', in R Peckam (ed) *Empires of Panic: Epidemics and Colonial Anxieties* (Hong Kong, Hong Kong University Press, 2015); and Heidi JS Tworek, 'Communicable Disease: Information, Health, and Globalization in the Interwar Period' (2019) 124 *The American Historical Review* 813.

[10] H Ebrahimnejad, *Medicine, Public Health and the Qajar State: Patterns of Medical Modernization in Nineteenth-Century Iran*, illustrated edn (Leiden, Brill, 2004); AA Afkhami, *A Modern Contagion: Imperialism and Public Health in Iran's Age of Cholera* 1st edn (Baltimore, Johns Hopkins University Press, 2019).

networks are treated as separate domains, and as constitutive parts in the birth of a modern nation state. As Prideux's vision makes clear, telegraphy was a crucial component of running quarantine networks in the region, not only because it enabled rapid communication, but also because it provided a blueprint for protecting and organising imperial space through enclaving. When telegraphy and health technologies have been linked in the existing literature, telegraphy is almost always understood as a one-dimensional disseminator and facilitator of central government health policies.[11] While these studies offer an important insight into the role of telegraphy in circulating new ideas of nation and hygiene, the telegraph is stripped of its material and spatial contribution to quarantine stations and discussed only as a dematerialised medium for communication. In contrast, this chapter treats quarantine and telegraph stations as interconnected material and spatial technologies of boundary making.

To explore this relationship, the chapter has been divided into three sections. The first section analyses the overlaps between telegraphy, quarantine and mobility networks from the creation of the IETD in 1862 to the arrival of steamship lines and the subsequent spread of contagious diseases. This section offers an insight into the foregrounding of enclaves and entanglements and argues that the spatiality and materiality of quarantine stations became both objects of governance and locations for resistance. The next section looks at practices of enclaving and the reality of entanglement at Faw (Fao) telegraph station on the Anglo-Ottoman frontier in modern-day southern Iraq. It focuses on an outbreak of cholera within the shared telegraph station in 1889 and contextualises the struggle between the Ottomans and British over quarantine sites and regulations in the Gulf. This section highlights the important link between material, spatial and discursive attempts of enclaving by policy makers and telegraph clerks in the station. It argues that the telegraph was not only an important technology for tracking diseases, but a crucial material space whose boundaries were produced through anxieties around racial and microbial contagion. The next section focuses on British quarantine stations across southern Iran. Opening with the station at Bushehr, the section outlines confrontation between a German shipping agent and British quarantine authorities as an example of the contested nature of British quarantine jurisdiction. The section demonstrates how human and non-human actants challenged quarantine, how race and class were utilised as taxonomies for division and the utilisation of the material and spatial organisation of quarantine stations as forms of boundary making. The chapter concludes by looking at the transition from enclaving to entanglements in the 1920s, arguing that this transformation was due to local political changes as much as a changing etiological consensus.

[11] F Kashani-Sabet, '"City of the Dead": The Frontier Polemics of Quarantines in the Ottoman Empire and Iran' (1998) 18 *Comparative Studies of South Asia, Africa and the Middle East* 51; F Kashani-Sabet, 'Hallmarks of Humanism: Hygiene and Love of Homeland in Qajar Iran' (2000) 105 *The American Historical Review* 1171; Cyrus Schayegh, *Who Is Knowledgeable Is Strong: Science, Class, and the Formation of Modern Iranian Society, 1900–1950* (Berkeley, University of California Press, 2009).

Telegraphs, Steamships and Quarantine Sites: Circulations and Sedimentations

The IETD was created in 1862 as a department of the Government of Bombay and transferred to the Government of India in 1871. The Department and network were divided into two sections run by the respective Directors of the Persian Gulf Section (PGS) with its headquarters in Karachi and the Persian Section (PS) with its headquarters in Tehran. They were overseen from London by the Director-in-Chief who, in turn, answered to the Secretary of State for India. The PGS consisted of both landlines and sea cables, connecting its eastern terminus in Karachi with its western one at Faw (Fao), linking the telegraph networks of the Ottoman and British empires (see Figure 1.1). The PS line connected Bushehr (Bushire) in the south to Tehran in the north. Although the telegraph had been primarily built for inter-imperial communication between India and London, the IETD took advantage of its coastal stations in the PGS by distributing shipping news and granting local merchants the ability to converse rapidly across the network.[12] Rather than introducing completely novel practices of news consumption and communication in ports, the telegraph network supplemented and sped up existing commercial networks. By binding ports and markets physically and commercially through the materials of cables and wires, the PGS helped to solidify and expand Britain's economic dominance of Gulf commerce.[13] The opening of the Suez Canal in 1869 and improved shipping technologies also enhanced new commercial opportunities, as travel time between Asia and Europe was cut. In turn, these technological and infrastructural changes transformed the region's ecology as a rising number of farmers switched production to cash crops like opium to engage in an increasingly accessible global market.[14] Between 1873 and 1878 trade nearly doubled between India and Iran, and between Iran and London trade trebled.[15] By 1873 the GoI acknowledged the region's increasing importance by transferring the administration of the Persian Gulf region from Bombay to the Viceroy in Calcutta and deploying Royal Navy gunboats on the island of Qeshm in the strait of Hormuz. As the telegraph network became operational, steamship lines and post offices soon followed, either directly supplementing telegraph stations or tapping into new markets.[16]

[12] B Lew and B Cater, 'The Telegraph, Co-Ordination of Tramp Shipping, and Growth in World Trade, 1870–1910' (2006) 10 *European Review of Economic History* 147, 149–50.

[13] For the telegraph and global trade, see SM Müller and HJS Tworek, '"The Telegraph and the Bank": On the Interdependence of Global Communications and Capitalism, 1866–1914' (2015) 10 *Journal of Global History* 259.

[14] G Nashat, 'From Bazaar to Market: Foreign Trade and Economic Development in Nineteenth-century Iran' (1981) 14 *Iranian Studies* 53.

[15] F Ahmadi, 'Communication and the Consolidation of the British Position in the Persian Gulf, 1860s–1914' (2017) 10 *Journal of Persianate Studies* 78.

[16] The same year that the IETD completed its line, the Secretary of State proposed a line of steamers between Bombay and the Gulf. MQ Morton, 'The British India Line in the Arabian Gulf, 1862–1982' (2013) 5 *Liwa* 40.

Steamer lines facilitated the movement of people, information and goods in increasing numbers.[17]

Although steamer and telegraph networks facilitated and stimulated desired circulations, they also helped the spread of contagious diseases. Thickened infrastructural networks exacerbated this spread, which in turn diminished the circulations that these networks sought to promote. This relationship was most pronounced in the cyclical cholera epidemics of the nineteenth and early twentieth centuries.[18] Although its shift from an epidemic disease on the Gangetic delta to a global pandemic occurred before the proliferation of mobility and communication networks, cholera was only able to sustain and compound its devastating global reach because of new imperial networks. While cholera had first reached the Gulf via British troops travelling from India to the port of Bushehr in 1821, the disease did not reach its apex until the 1890s and early 1900s, coinciding with the zenith of global steamship and telegraph networks. Within this context, new commercial and infrastructural networks were understood by imperial powers as valuable arteries of wealth and power but also highways for disease. European powers acknowledged that while the spread of disease had to be slowed, it had to be done in a way that would not damage commercial traffic.[19]

After the imperial powers signed the General Berlin Act of 1885, the material and spatial form of quarantine and telegraph stations in southern Iran and the Gulf became increasingly important. While there is no direct evidence of the Act being invoked by quarantine or telegraph officials, the Act introduced the rules of 'effective occupation', which legitimated the acquisition of territory through material infrastructures that linked the frontier to the metropole, such as wires, poles and stations.[20] Yet the Act was terrestrially orientated with no provisions for the acquisition of coastal space. The ecological plasticity of shifting shorelines and the ambiguity around the acquisition of coastal space resulted in coastal quarantine and telegraph stations becoming points of friction and contestation.[21] Imperial and national powers engaged in this contestation, building quarantine and telegraph stations not only to combat disease and facilitate communication, but to stake a claim to contested space. 'Material power', defined by scholars Tony Bennett and Patrick Joyce, offers a means of understanding the role of materials in such contestations.[22] Material power accounts for the 'distinctive kinds of effectivity' material

[17] To get an idea of typical passenger capacity travelling on steamers, Morton cites that 'SS Chindwara, launched in 1879, carried 19 first-class and 1,104 deck-passengers': 'The British India Line' 49.

[18] Cholera is an infectious disease spread through faeces-contaminated water and food carrying the *Vibrio cholerae* bacteria. A person infected with the disease experiences sudden diarrhoea and stomach cramps. If untreated, the disease leads to rapid dehydration and death.

[19] V Huber, 'Pandemics and the Politics of Difference: Rewriting the History of Internationalism through Nineteenth-century Cholera' (2020) 15 *Journal of Global History* 394, 400.

[20] M Minawi, 'Telegraphs and Territoriality in Ottoman Africa and Arabia during the Age of High Imperialism' (2016) 18 *Journal of Balkan and Near Eastern Studies* 567, 575.

[21] On the difficulties of acquiring coastal and maritime space, see M Talbot, 'Maritoriality', in R Bavaj, K Lawson, and B Struck (eds) *Doing Spatial History* (Abingdon, Routledge, 2021).

[22] T Bennett and P Joyce (eds), *Material Powers: Cultural Studies, History and the Material Turn*, 1st edn (London, Routledge, 2010) 5.

objects and processes exert due to their position 'within specifically configured networks of relations that always include human and non-human actors'.[23] In this non-hierarchical understanding of power, attempts by imperial planners to instrumentalise the materials of quarantine and telegraph stations always faced resistance from human and non-human actors. Microbes, alluvial floods and coastal tides pushed against and interacted with the materials that made up quarantine and telegraph stations, configuring and transforming them in the process and vice-versa. From this Foucauldian perspective, walls and fences of enclaves are important because of their relationship to other materials and processes inside and outside the station. Viewing material power this way helps us understand the web of relations formed around quarantine and telegraph stations and the multidirectional dispersal of power.

Lacking the financial resources to run quarantine sites across its southern shores, the Iranian administration entered into an opaque agreement with Britain, handing over sanitary control of its southern ports in 1864, the same year the IETD network became operational.[24] While initial measures introduced by the British centred on the port of Bushehr, the vague agreement set the scene for a more expansive intervention by offering a foothold into Iranian health policies and, by extension, border control.[25] From here, the British would assert a growing influence in Iran's domestic sanitary policies and promote use of the quarantine network to advance its regional interests. Despite growing British control, other bodies were created to administer policy and combat contagious diseases. A domestic Iranian Sanitary Council was established in response to a cholera outbreak in 1867–1868. A decade later, the Board of Health in Tehran was created.[26] These bodies consisted of a mix of Iranian and European members. Dr Barker, medical officer of the IETD, sat on the Board of Health in Tehran as one of the British representatives, connecting the GoI's health policy with telegraph infrastructure directly and influencing domestic sanitary arrangements.

Although eager to control health infrastructure, the GoI was against the creation of the Sanitary Council and remained averse to international bodies interfering in southern Iran and the Gulf. The GoI feared that these bodies would be utilised by Iran, the Ottomans and other imperial rivals to disrupt British-dominated trade. A trenchant British distrust of these bodies fed into, and was compounded by, a

[23] Bennett and Joyce, *Material Powers*, 5.

[24] The agreement over sanitary control in the Persian Gulf is cited by Sir Percy Cox who claimed that no official 'documentary agreement' was signed. It is likely that the Iranian state agreed to this to cut expenditure and counterbalance Russian influence in Iran. Copy of letter from Sir P Cox to Sir W Townley, Bushire, 22 January 1913. No 16. Enclosure in No 1. Persian Gulf quarantine service (1913) British Library IOR/L/PS/11/47, P 908/1913.

[25] British influence in southern Iran was formalised in 1907 in the Anglo-Russian Convention that granted Britain a sphere of influence in the south. See H Lyman Stebbins, *British Imperialism in Qajar Iran: Consuls, Agents and Influence in the Middle East* (London, IB Tauris, 2016).

[26] Informal health councils had existed before, but in 1868 the councils were solidified into a semi-official majles-e hefz al-Sehheh (Sanitary Council). Note that the Sanitary Council and wider health policies were connected to police administration and practices. Ebrahimnejad (n 10) 46–47.

wider etiological debate between contagionists and anti-contagionists. The British adopted an anti-contagionist perspective, arguing well into the 1890s that cholera was a miasmic disease, originating outside India in what they considered the unsanitary communities and environments of Central Asia and Arabia. Reluctance to identify India as the widely agreed point of origin of cholera, and to combat its spread through the creation of internationally run stations was underpinned by wider commercial interests in the Indian Ocean.[27] External measures by the Istanbul Board of Health to set up quarantine stations at Hormuz and Basra were seen by the British as inflicting 'an amount of loss' in commerce 'totally disproportionate to the degree of the danger it is intended to guard against.'[28]

Most delegates of the Vienna Sanitary Conference in 1874 agreed that land quarantines were largely ineffectual and instead stressed maritime quarantines and ship inspections outside of Europe. Building on its 1864 informal agreement of control over quarantine at its Gulf ports, the Iranian administration issued an appeal for British assistance in maintaining quarantine by sea as plague spread throughout the region in 1876. In response, the GoI sent a steamer to enforce maritime quarantine at Bushehr, initiating the maritime and the coastal, rather than the terrestrial, as the field for managing and contesting infectious diseases in southern Iran and the Gulf. While Britain had been granted an informal jurisdiction over quarantine in Bushehr and its waters, it was not until the arrival of the 1896 Bombay bubonic plague that Britain obtained permission from the Iranian state to establish a more substantial network of quarantine stations in southern Iran. The Political Resident in the Persian Gulf initially refused the offer of utilising the British navy in quarantine operations across Iran's southern coast. Ultimately, he accepted with the understanding that quarantine in British hands would mean minimal damage to British trade. Quarantine of five days was established at Khorramshahr and Bushehr, and seven days at ports closer to India.[29] Permission was granted for the creation of stations in Bandar Abbas, Lengeh and Khorramshahr and doctors were sent by the GoI to run the facilities. The IETD telegraph network, in operation since the 1860s, meant that there was an established and experienced pool of staff to draw upon. Medical staff often moved between the IETD and the quarantine services: one example was the assistant surgeon in charge of the telegraph dispensary at Faw, who was appointed quarantine officer at Bandar Abbas.[30] The cadre

[27] Krista Maglen has termed this approach the 'English system'. See K Maglen, *The English System: Quarantine, Immigration and the Making of a Port Sanitary Zone* 1st edn (Manchester, Manchester University Press, 2014). From this perspective, quarantine and telegraph networks were part of broader human and non-human networks, linked to local ecologies and labour. 'Memorandum on Sanitary Measures in the Persian Gulf since 1894' in File 2908/1907 Pt 2–3 'Persian Gulf: Quarantine' 1907–11. British Library IOR/L/PS/10/124.

[28] Confidential Report by Dr Theodore Thomson on the Sanitary Requirements of certain places in or near the Persian Gulf, &c. July 1906. National Archive, Kew. Foreign Office (FO) 368/37 – Persia. Code 134 Files 352-2073.

[29] Afkhami (n 10) 121.

[30] Letter from Eustace Edward Gunter to Raynor Childe Barker, Karachi, 1 May 1916, No 1055. File 657 'I Medical matters 11 Aug 1915–30 Dec 1925' British Library IOR/L/PWD/7/1539.

of new Medical Officers employed by the GoI were 'invariably attached directly or indirectly to a local British Consulate or Telegraph station' and were 'always connected with or actually in charge of the Consular or Telegraph Dispensary'.[31] Existing expertise on the ground from the telegraph network aided the operation of the quarantine network.

By 1906–07 new equipment such as disinfectors were purchased, while two more stations were opened in Jask and Bahrein. A Chief Medical Officer, overseeing the entire operation, was also appointed at Bushehr. In the pursuit of 'knowing' this newly networked sanitary space and turning it into an object of governance, the GoI had to produce southern Iran and the Gulf through practices of surveying.[32] In 1906 surveyors were sent to inspect the state of existing quarantine stations and possible locations for new stations. The ports were praised by an inspector for their shallow approaches, forcing ships to anchor far from port, thus minimising contact between ships and the port.[33] Shallow approaches were seen as natural barriers, separating ships from the 'generally filthy' towns and streets where it was believed diseases would thrive.[34] The station at Bandar Abbas was criticised as 'deficient' because of its proximity to a 'native village' and lack of enclosure 'by any wall or fence'.[35] This preference for distance in tackling contagious diseases reflected contemporary notions of disease prevention as being most efficiently tackled through separation. Such notions were informed by colonial views of unhygienic 'native' spaces and an obfuscation of the actual origin of most contagious epidemics emanating from British India. The survey also created parameters for choosing locations and constructing quarantine stations. Accessibility, 'general healthiness' and a station's 'central position' were articulated as the key organising principles for deciding where stations should be built.[36] The survey constructed local space as unhygienic and presented the imperial enclave, removed from urban population centres, as the solution. A quarantine station had already been established at Bushehr on an island three miles from its port. Bandar Abbas and Lengah quarantine stations had been built three and two miles from their ports respectively. This form of spatial isolation was mirrored in PGS telegraph stations. In Jask, for example, the 'telegraph town' and the old town were separated by a wire fence and Sepoy patrols (see Figure 1.6). The 1906 survey helped to officiate the enclaving of quarantine stations as policy. However, the practice of enclaving was

[31] Letter from Chief Quarantine Medical Officer Persian Gulf to the Director League of Nations Health Bureau Singapore, Bushehr, 21 January 1927. File 3122/1921 Pt 1 'Persia: Quarantine arrangements', British Library IOR/L/PS/10/1006/1.

[32] On how surveys and similar technologies were utilised by the British for producing space, see J Hevia, *The Imperial Security State: British Colonial Knowledge and Empire-Building in Asia* (Cambridge, Cambridge University Press, 2012).

[33] Dr Theodore Thomson 'Confidential Report on the Sanitary Requirements of certain places in or near the Persian Gulf, &c', 12 July 1906. FO 368/37.

[34] Thomson, 'Confidential Report' (n 33).

[35] Thomson (n 33) 'Appendix 2 The Persian ports of Jashk, Bunder Abbas, Linga, Bushire and Mohammerah', 17. FO 368/37.

[36] Enclosure 2 in No 1. 'Note on a site for a proposed Quarantine Station in the Persian Gulf, with special reference to facilities for obtaining a water-supply'. FO 368/37.

much older, going back to the construction of telegraph stations where, as we shall see in the next section, it was adopted under a combination of etiological and racial anxieties of contagion.

Despite a desire to enclave away from 'insalubrious' local communities and environments, continued operation and maintenance of these stations relied on local peoples and resources. Assistant quarantine workers called Guardians were employed to assist British Quarantine Medical Officers and the Chief Quarantine Medical Officer. Boatmen, cleaners, cooks, water carriers, caretakers, clerks and other 'menials' were hired to ensure continued operation of both networks. Contrary to a hermetic enclave, the operation, maintenance and expansion of quarantine and telegraph networks depended on local labour.

The quarantine network was produced as a sedimented infrastructure. It built upon existing mobility and communication networks, with quarantine stations mirroring the location of telegraph stations and ports-of-call. The thickening of networks inadvertently led to an increase of infectious diseases and hindered the very connections the network sought to promote. The IETD telegraph network was important to the quarantine network as a pioneering imperial infrastructure in southern Iran and the Gulf, presenting a blueprint and a medium for creating and operating an imperial enclave. The telegraph facilitated the integration of quarantine stations and other nodes of British influence into a single communication system, while also offering a material blueprint for demarking space and

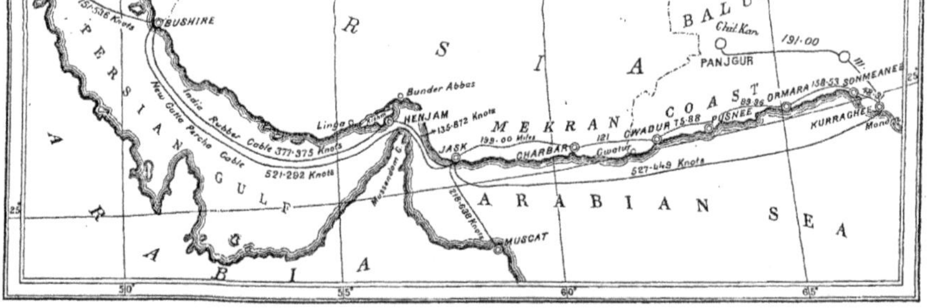

NOTE.—Gwatur is the boundary between the Khanate of Kalát and Persian Baluchistan as settled by the Seistan Boundary Commission.

Figure 1.1 Indo-European Telegraphs-Persian Gulf Section (1907) British Library IOR/V/13/272[37]

[37] F Ahmadi, 'Linking India with Britain: The Persian Gulf Cables, 1864–1907' (PhD diss, University of Exeter, 2003) 226.

creating enclaves. Attempts were made by the British to utilise the material power of quarantine and telegraph stations by constructing enclaves. However, efforts were continually frustrated by unintended consequences, as materials, objects and people formed their own connections – such as microbes to their human hosts – and contested the material formation of stations. To understand this process on the ground, I will now turn to Faw telegraph station.

Disease, Race and Space at Faw Telegraph Station

Al-Faw peninsula (Fao) is located on the western bank of the Shatt-al-Arab near the mouth of the river in modern-day Iraq. Its alluvial terrain during the late nineteenth and early twentieth centuries was liable to flood during south-easterly winds that frequently pushed tides inland, turning the banks and land leading to the telegraph station into soft greasy mud.[38] Opened in 1865, the idiosyncratic arrangements at the shared Anglo-Ottoman telegraph station were formed under the conditions of the Anglo-Ottoman Telegraph Convention. The Convention envisioned signallers sharing office and living space, 'with the view to combined operations' of a common service.[39] Article 4 of the Convention stated that British and Ottoman equipment was to be placed in 'close proximity to each other', and clerks were to exchange messages on their receipt from their respective lines for transfer 'through a window'.[40]

However, soon after the station was opened, British and Ottoman employees separated into distinct spaces within the station as a practical solution to an increase in Ottoman staff. A second bungalow was built for the British and a new joint office was constructed in the centre of the station between the two bungalows. The joint office was divided by a partition wall and a half door for the exchange of messages. The British were given the new bungalow as living space but did not have the right of ownership over the structure or the site.[41] Shortly after the creation of a separate British bungalow, mud walls and wire fencing were erected between the two 'compounds'. The British enclave was enclosed by cable fencing, a frequently flooded creek and a sloping sea wall made of mud (see Figure 1.2). Despite efforts to protect the bungalow, regular flooding meant that the wooden piles gradually degraded. By 1876 the superintendent of Faw wrote to the IETD informing them that the 26 wood piles supporting the building were 'in a very bad condition'.[42] By 1903, a British engineer noted that the 40-year-old wooden

[38] P Stewart, 'Report by Lieut Col P Stewart on Laying Down the Submarine Cable between Bushire and Fao' British Library IOR (V/27/762/1 report no 1) 8.

[39] JA Saldanha, 'Précis on Commerce and Communication in the Persian Gulf, 1801–1905' (1906) British Library IOR (V/27/762/1 précis 75).

[40] Saldanha, 'Précis on Commerce and Communication in the Persian Gulf, 1801–1905'.

[41] Saldanha (n 39).

[42] Letter from Ffinch to Robertson, Karachi, 5 February 1888. No 145. British Library IOR/L/PWD/7/691.

building was in terrible condition and had become a 'fever trap' during floods. While the Convention was clear that the British did not have ownership of the buildings in the enclave, the Anglo-Ottoman Telegraph Convention lacked clarity over whether the British had the right to build and repair the buildings they occupied. Throughout the 1880s the Ottomans continually denied the British this right as the Sultan's military advisers had persuaded him 'that the Telegraph office structures are intended for a hostile military purpose'.[43] As a result, the height, width and type of materials used became politically sensitive. Stone was resisted as a material of repair because of its physical and symbolic durability.[44] While mud walls and wire fencing were seen as materials to protect British space by demarking its enclave with clear spatial boundaries, the entry of flood water into the compound literally and figuratively muddied this process, entangling the enclave with external ecological processes.

While daily operations of exchanging messages meant that interactions with Ottoman staff were inescapable, the separation of space became seen as a political and sanitary necessity. In April 1888 during a visit to the station, the Vice Consul in Basra, PJC Robertson, reported that the Ottomans had suggested that the garden within the nominal British enclave be used for camping Ottoman soldiers. Robertson protested that such use of space would render the British 'bungalows so public as to be uninhabitable by the English staff and their families'.[45] Lord Cross, the Secretary of State for India, suggested that a cordon of at least 15 to 20 metres be made between Ottoman troops and the British station to mitigate visual and physical contamination.[46] Viewing 'the habits of Turkish soldiers and Arab villagers' in Faw, the Director of the PGS explained, was 'such that to overlook them is as unpleasant as to be overlooked by them'.[47] Like its 'natives', local ecology was understood as unhygienic and hostile to the integrity of the British enclave. The Director of the IETD explained that the 'so-called "meadows" marked on maps of Faw are like "the mudbanks of a river like the Ganges" and "[t]he creek is like a tidal 'khal' off the Hooghly"; while beyond the boundary wall, the entire ground is like … [a] jheel [lagoon]'. The 'Turks' and their soldiers who were stationed outside the walls of the telegraph station 'have no better manners than dogs' and their compound 'no cleaner than outskirts of a Bengali village'.[48] Such discourse not only reveals the colonial Indian origins of the Department, the attitudes of staff

[43] Letter from White to Tweedie, Istanbul, 7 October 1889. British Library IOR/L/PWD/7/691.

[44] For example, the Vali of Basra continually denied the building of stone walls, see copy of translated letter from the Vali of Basra to the Consul of Basra, 7 Dec 1890. No 735. British Library IOR/L/PWD/7/691.

[45] Letter from Robertson to Consul General Baghdad, 24 April 1888, No 182. British Library IOR/L/PWD/7/691.

[46] Letter from Godley to Pauncefote, London, 16 May 1888. British Library IOR/L/PWD/7/691.

[47] Letter from Ffinch to Director General, Karachi, 29 May 1888. No 702. British Library IOR/L/PWD/7/691.

[48] Letter from Mallock to the Secretary of the PWD, India, 22 April 1889, British Library IOR/L/PWD/7/691.

to 'native' space and communities and the racial hierarchical ordering of shared space, but it also demonstrates the way sanitary and racial concerns were intertwined. This convergence aided in the ordering of space into a legible imperial Indian frame that could be understood and demarcated. The Shatt-al-Arab became the Hooghly and the Ottoman camp a Bengali village. Complicated ecological and social entanglements in Faw resulted in officials drawing on familiar colonial Indian frames to understand and define the British enclave.

Like the British, the Ottomans were also attempting to secure frontier space at Faw through built infrastructures. In 1872 they established proto-quarantine sites at Faw and Basra. The sites were part of a larger emerging network along the Ottoman-Qajar border to monitor and control Arab traders in the south and Shi'i pilgrims crossing from the Gulf and Iran into Ottoman Iraq.[49] While ostensibly created to stop disease entering the Ottoman Empire, the medical space at Faw was also used to monitor and obstruct British mobility. The IETD, which relied on mobility between British India, southern Iran and the Ottoman Empire for its continued operations and maintenance, continually complained of lengthy delays and obstruction at Basra quarantine station.[50] In early 1892, the Ottoman government called for its quarantine site at Faw to be internationally recognised. Both Russian and British members on the Istanbul Board of Health opposed the measures and it was dropped. However, two years later, at the Cholera Conference in Paris, the Ottomans proposed the construction of a large sanitary centre with an official quarantine station at Faw. Again, Britain opposed the proposal arguing that its creation would be at the expense of British shipping, causing increased cost and delays.[51] While the Ottoman proposal for Faw was denied, Ottoman delegates managed to secure a five-day quarantine imposed on all Indian vessels. By the 1903 Paris Sanitary Conference, the British Delegation were under instruction that an official station in Faw should not be permitted 'under any circumstance'.[52] Ottoman demands were driven by the political desire to control British access into Iraq, and also directed by environmental concerns.[53] The materiality and spatiality of telegraph and quarantine stations, such as where they were placed and the types of materials used to demark their boundaries, were mobilised by both the British and Ottomans to secure and monitor space at Faw. While the British sought to enclave through discourses of separation and the material demarcation of microspace inside

[49] Sabri Ateş, *Ottoman-Iranian Borderlands: Making a Boundary, 1843–1914* (Cambridge, Cambridge University Press, 2013).

[50] For example, see letter from Ffinch to Director General, Karachi, 30 May 1888. No 713. British Library IOR/L/PWD/7/691.

[51] *Gazetteer of the Persian Gulf*. Vol I. Historical. Part II. JG Lorimer (1915) 2527–28. British Library IOR/L/PS/20/C91/2.

[52] Memorandum on Sanitary Measures in the Persian Gulf since 1894, File 2908/1907 Pt 2–3 'Persian Gulf: Quarantine' 1907–11. British Library IOR/L/PS/10/124.

[53] For information on how the Ottomans viewed disease and environment in Iraq see IA Bolaños, 'The Ottomans during the Global Crises of Cholera and Plague: The View from Iraq and the Gulf' (2019) 51 *International Journal of Middle East Studies* 603.

the telegraph station, the Ottomans attempted to monitor and prohibit British movement into Iraq through quarantine stations. The arrival of cholera at the station, like the flood waters, saw a convergence of anxieties around contagion and enclaving as complex non-human processes confused attempts at neat boundary making.

The most serious outbreak of cholera in Faw occurred in the summer of 1889 as the disease entered the region via a steamer travelling from Bombay to Bahrein, and quickly spread to the Ottoman garrison in Basra and then the city.[54] Despite the lack of quarantine facilities, the location of the disease was identified through the sharing of information by IETD clerks at Faw who remained in continuous communication with India. The flow of information followed the hierarchical pattern of command within the IETD with clerks sending telegrams to the Director of the PGS in Karachi, who then forwarded the information to the Director-General in Simla.[55] By late August, clerks reported that almost all Europeans had departed the region and Basra and Faw were in 'a perfect panic'.[56] On 20 August the disease reached the station, claiming an unnamed Indian servant and an Ottoman preventative officer.[57] The arrival of cholera prompted the IETD clerk-in-charge, Mr Hawkins, along with two other clerks, to send a telegram to the Director-General asking to be 'speedily relieve[d] … from these cholera-stricken parts'. Hawkins cited the general vulnerability of health amongst clerks in Faw due to 'enduring excessive heat of last two summers' and rhetorically questioned the importance of the station by asking if it 'is such as to justify risking staff lives and consequently those dependent upon them'. Unfortunately for Hawkins and his colleagues, Faw station was deemed important enough for the IETD Director to claim that the station could not close 'until the Turks remove their own telegraph staff' as this would violate the agreement signed between the two powers.[58] While a steamer was sent to evacuate the women and children to vacant rooms in Jask station, the male workers were obliged to continue working the line.[59] By the end of the month, however, the IETD's apothecary at Faw managed to save two infected patients from cholera.[60] A few days later, the clerks at Faw reported that there had been only one case of cholera and the patient was recovering.[61] Although cholera at Faw passed with few casualties to staff, health concerns vocalised by the clerks reflected a wider general fear of the poor sanitary conditions of the station and a concern over the porous boundaries of the British enclave. Panic arose with the realisation that the staff

[54] Afkhami (n 10) 77.

[55] For example, see letter from Ffinch to Mallock, Karachi, 20 August 1889. British Library IOR/L/PWD/7/691.

[56] Ffinch to Mallock, Karachi, 22 August 1889. British Library IOR/L/PWD/7/691.

[57] Ffinch to Mallock, Karachi, 20 August 1889. British Library IOR/L/PWD/7/691.

[58] Mallock to Ffinch, Simla, 26 August 1889. British Library IOR/L/PWD/7/691.

[59] Ffinch to Mallock, Karachi, 22 August 1889. British Library IOR/L/PWD/7/691.

[60] Ffinch to Mallock, Karachi, 23 August 1889. British Library IOR/L/PWD/7/691.

[61] Ffinch to Mallock, Karachi, 28 August 1889. British Library IOR/L/PWD/7/691.

and station were not safely enclaved but deeply entangled with local ecologies, communities and spaces. From this perspective, the clerks' fear of contagion was reflective not only of health concerns, but a wider anxiety around the permeability of the enclave.

The materials of quarantine and telegraph stations were utilised by both British and Ottoman officials to secure space at Faw. However, such attempts failed or resulted in unintended consequences. British walls, wire fencing and discourses of separation did not keep out flood water, foreign bodies and cholera. Ottoman attempts at monitoring and obstructing British movement through the establishment of official quarantine stations were only partially successful with a station established in Basra, but not Faw. The telegraph station was utilised as a material and spatial technology of boundary making, demonstrating the multiplicities of infrastructural space in imperial contexts. Moreover, Faw shows us that, even on a micro-level, resistance, both human and non-human, was wrapped up in efforts of boundary making. To understand how similar contestations and entanglements with human and non-humans unfolded across GoI quarantine stations, I will now turn to the creation and contestation of these stations in southern Iran.

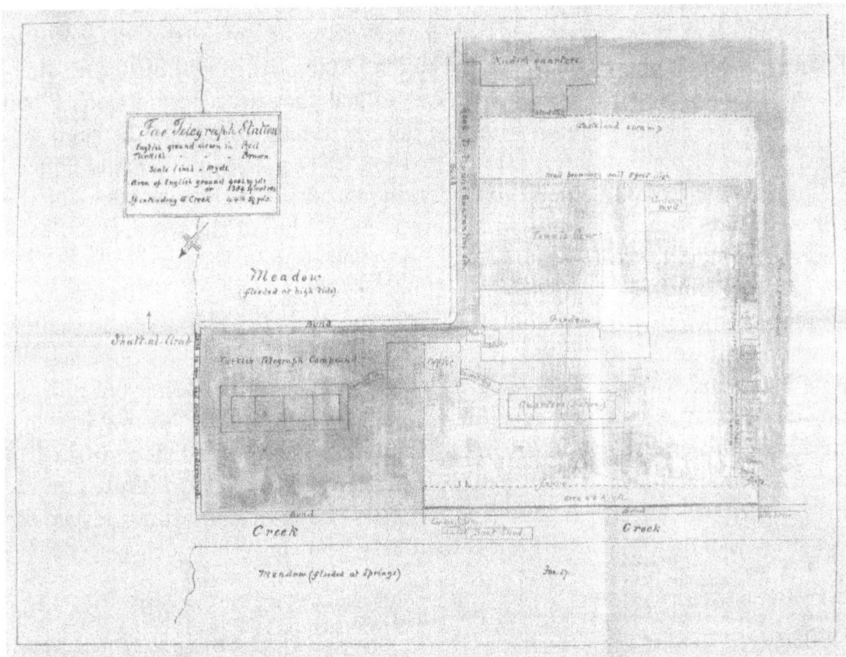

Figure 1.2 Plan of the telegraph station at Faw, 1891 © British Library Board IOR/L/PWD/7/691. (The British compound is outlined from the mud boundary wall at the top of the map and the fence to the bottom and divided with the 'Turkish Telegraph Compound' from the office.)

Quarantine and Contestation

In 1908, Mr Krumpeter, agent of the commercial Hamburg-Amerikanische Packetfahrt-Actien-Gesellschaft (Hamburg-America Shipping Line, HAPAG), boarded the *SS Galicia* near the port of Bushehr. Dr Williams, the British Chief Quarantine Medical Officer, seized the opportunity to confront and reprimand Krumpeter for boarding the ship before it had been inspected. Two days after the incident Williams wrote to the German Consul to complain that Krumpeter's actions were 'in opposition to the quarantine rules of the port' and that if repeated he would 'report the matter to Teheran' and 'take such local measures as the case might require'.[62] The incident prompted the German Ambassador, Count Albert Graf von Quadt-Wykradt-Isny (henceforth referred to as Quadt), to write to the Tehran Sanitary Council and lodge a complaint against the British. He explained that the HAPAG steamer *Galicia* had run aground a few nautical miles from the entrance to the port of Bushehr. Krumpeter, as a senior agent for the company, had boarded the ship 'to see if it was necessary to send boats to unload part of the cargo'. Within a few hours of Krumpeter boarding, the Count explained, the boat was floating again without damage or assistance. Quadt complained that the German Consul in Bushehr had been ignorant of any quarantine rules for the port and demanded to know 'when, and on behalf of which Administration, these rules had been issued, and how a copy could be obtained'.[63] Perceptively, Quadt identified the opaque legal and spatial difficulties of administering quarantine in a contested coastal space. He argued that because the *Galicia* had been beached several leagues from the port, it remained outside the supposed jurisdiction of the port administered by the Chief Quarantine Medical Officer. Krumpeter, Quadt explained, 'could hardly wait for the doctor's visit, for the simple reason that the doctor would not come on board the steamer until the latter arrived' in the port's waters.[64]

Quadt's point raised awkward questions over the boundaries of British quarantine jurisdiction. The shifting sandbanks, shoals and coastline in the shallow approach to Bushehr meant that British quarantine jurisdiction was quite literally liquid, moving in accordance with changing tides. Understanding the difficulties raised by Quadt's comments, the British Minister, Charles Murray Marling, 'declined to discuss this point as to the facts' and instead wrote that he wished 'to bring about smoother relations between the German Consul at Bushire and the British Medical Officer'.[65] By dodging the issue, Marling tacitly acknowledged the opaqueness of British quarantine jurisdiction in Bushehr. While such spaces could

[62] Translated copy of letter from Count Albert Graf von Quadt-Wykradt-Isny to Lokman-ul-Mamalek, 14 August 1908. Enclosure 1 No 1. British Library IOR/L/PS/10/124.

[63] von Quadt-Wykradt-Isny to Lokman-ul-Mamalek (n 62).

[64] von Quadt-Wykradt-Isny to Lokman-ul-Mamalek (n 62).

[65] Letter from Marling to Sir Edward Grey, Qolhak, 20 August 1908, No 227 British Library IOR/L/PS/10/124.

be protected from interference under the cover of vague boundaries and jurisdictions, they were also subject to challenges for the same reason.

Far from an isolated case of Anglo-German rivalry, the incident unfolded against the context of wider German challenges to British hegemony across southern Iran and the Gulf.[66] In 1906, HAPAG began a service of steamers in the region as a direct competitor to the British India Steam Navigation Company.[67] The targeting of Mr Krumpeter as a senior official in HAPAG was part of a larger coastal struggle between established British infrastructures and emerging German networks.[68] The GoI's quarantine regime at Bushehr was marshalled to protect British infrastructure and obstruct rival networks.

As with Faw, British quarantine space was structured around practices of racial and social boundary making[69] with the 'separation and segregation of individuals, or groups of individuals' as its primary taxonomy.[70] Separation based on class reflected a colonial notion that lower-class Muslim pilgrims were the primary vectors of a 'twin infection' of infectious diseases and dangerous pan-Islamism.[71] Telegraph stations were sometimes directly enrolled into the process of dividing quarantine. For example, at Jask, the telegraph station doubled as a quarantine station for 'Europeans' only. Even within the category of 'Europeans', third-class passengers at Jask had to undergo 'observation' inside the station, while first- and second-class passengers were subject to a lighter 'surveillance'. The stark racial division meant that even 'Persians of importance' on first-class tickets were not permitted to quarantine in the telegraph station and were instead placed in the fort.[72] As with Faw, the telegraph station at Jask was a protected European enclave and quarantine was used to uphold separation to stop racial and microbial contagion.

The conditions and materials of quarantine stations reflected the racial and class hierarchies used to organise space. At Jask, third-class 'non-Europeans' were expected to quarantine in a stone and mud structure of 'ruinous condition'

[66] For more information on the Krumpeter incidents see G Crouzet, 'Between Imperial Rivalries and Cooperation: Epidemic Diseases and Health Policies in the Arabo-Persian Gulf in the Long 19th Century' in J Vögele and H Umehara (eds), *Gateways of Disease: Public Health in European and Asian Port Cities at the Birth of the Modern World in the Late 19th and Early 20th century*, vol 7 (Göttingen, Cuvillier Verlag, 2015).

[67] Morton (n 16) 47.

[68] For other examples, see anxiety over German shipping and buoying activity in the Gulf and Shatt-al-Arab in Copy of a letter from His Excellency the Naval Commander in Chief to the Secretary to the Government of India, Marine Department, Bombay, 25 February 1911. No 38-1462-XO. File 252/1910 Pt 2 'Persian Gulf: lighting and buoying; buoyage of Shatt al-Arab'. British Library IOR/L/PS/10/169b.

[69] In 1899 the Iranian government had complained of the uneven use of quarantine by the British in Bushehr. British ships coming from India were rarely subjected to quarantine while 'non-Europeans', particularly Muslim pilgrims, were forced to complete quarantine in poor accommodation. Major PZ Cox to Marling, 17 October 1907, Shiraz, No 18. British Library IOR/L/PS/10/124.

[70] Enclosure K, Copy of letter from the Chief Quarantine Medical Officer in the Persian Gulf to the President of the Sanitary Council Tehran, Bushehr, 13 August 1925. No144. British Library IOR/L/PS/10/1006/1.

[71] William Roff, 'Sanitation and Security: The Imperial Powers and the Nineteenth Century Hajj' (1982) 6 *Arabian Studies* 143.

[72] The Persian Ports of Jashk, Bunder Abbas, Linga, Bushire, and Mohammerah. FO 368/37.

(see Figure 1.3) without a roof and sewage system.[73] At Bandar Abbas (see Figure 1.4), first- and second-class passengers stayed in stone buildings equipped with a kitchen, bathroom and latrine, while third-class 'non-European' passengers were expected to stay in reed huts made from date-sticks and matting.[74] At Bushehr there were 'three pucca buildings, a bungalow for 1st class passengers, one for second class passengers and a disinfector building' (see Figure 1.5). In all the stations there was no special accommodation for the sick and often not enough stocks of medicine or medical equipment. This disparity and lack of uniformity in the network was acknowledged as 'not consistent'. Instead, each Quarantine Medical Officer had the authority to issue orders for specific ports in times of epidemics.[75] Quarantine was not only unevenly applied to different peoples, but quarantine stations themselves were irregularly organised. Marking these disparities was the material organisation of the buildings. While accommodation for first-class 'Europeans' were made of stone, equipped with essential rooms and health technologies like disinfectors, third class 'non-Europeans' were designated buildings made of less durable materials and with few essentials.

Figure 1.3 Jask quarantine station from behind. Confidential Report by Dr Theodore Thomson on the Sanitary Requirements of certain places in or near the Persian Gulf, &c. 12 July 1906. FO 368/37

[73] Thomson (n 33).
[74] Thomson (n 33).
[75] Memorandum from the Residency Surgeon in the Persian Gulf to the Political Resident in the Persian Gulf, Bushehr, 18 August 1925. Enclosure A, No 146. British Library IOR/L/PS/10/1006/1.

Figure 1.4 Bandar Abbas quarantine station. Confidential Report by Dr Theodore Thomson on the Sanitary Requirements of certain places in or near the Persian Gulf, &c. 12 July 1906. FO 368/37

Figure 1.5 Bushehr quarantine station on the island of Abasak. The building in the foreground is the second-class block; the hut just beyond is the first-class block; and in the distance is the third-class hut of the disinfecting house. Confidential Report by Dr Theodore Thomson on the Sanitary Requirements of certain places in or near the Persian Gulf, &c. 12 July 1906. FO 368/37

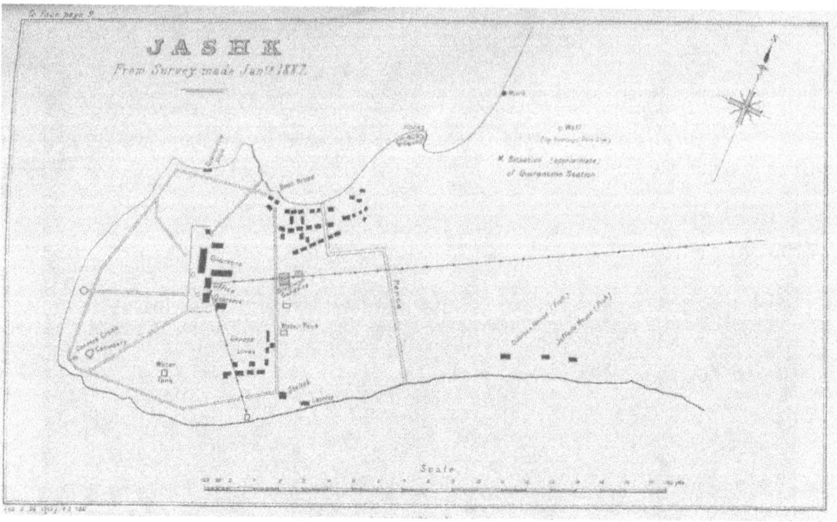

Figure 1.6 Map of Jask from survey made in January 1887. Confidential Report by Dr Theodore Thomson on the Sanitary Requirements of certain places in or near the Persian Gulf, &c 12 July 1906. FO 368/37

A prominent feature uniting these sites was their spatial organisation into enclaves. Bushehr, Bandar Abbas and Lingah quarantine stations were located two to three miles from the port and, in the case of Bushehr, on an island. Like Faw telegraph station, but for different reasons, these quarantine stations were spatially imagined and materially designed as enclaved sites, removed from local towns, peoples and ecologies. Their material and spatial organisation was structured around racial and class divisions as a means of boundary making. Despite these efforts, political and ecological entanglements from shifting sand banks and political actors challenged the smooth production of the British enclave.

Conclusion

Even though Captain Prideaux initiated enclaved infrastructure in 1876, as noted at the beginning of this chapter, the British began to embrace an entanglement of infrastructure by the mid-1920s. The GoI adopted a new etiological consensus, with the Indian Medical Department describing cholera in 1924 as a miasma-bacteria hybrid. Cholera was described by the Indian Medical Department as 'caused by a minute germ' found in water and contaminated food whilst also thriving 'when the atmosphere is strongly infected'.[76] Equally important to this

[76] Circular No 135. British Library IOR/L/PWD/7/1742.

shift were political calls by Iranian nationalists who sought to subsume the GoI's quarantine stations into the new apparatus of the Pahlavi state. Notwithstanding the receding of major epidemics like cholera in the 1920s, the British considered maintaining control of the quarantine network an essential prerequisite to protect British shipping.[77] As a result, British officials began to design new quarantine stations as imbedded or entangled in accessible urban centres. These quarantine sites served multiple purposes within a city, acting as hospitals with enough resources to deal with the sick whilst also providing space for quarantine duties.[78] Yet, despite attempts to entangle GoI quarantine stations into the urban fabric of Iran, the British were unable to stave off calls for the transfer of the network into Iranian hands. In 1928, the GoI agreed to hand over its quarantine facilities to the Iranian state because the concession could no longer be creditably maintained.[79] At the same time, the IETD network was being nationalised by the Iranian state. The British eventually transferred landlines to Iran in 1931 and cables and wireless infrastructure to the commercial Imperial and International Communications Company. Both telegraph and quarantine networks emerged in 1864 and were consolidated a decade later, reaching their zenith in the early 1900s; by 1931, they had been almost entirely subsumed into the Iranian state. British imperialism in southern Iran and the Gulf did not vanish with the loss of these networks. In fact, other infrastructures emerged as imperial priorities shifted. The construction and maintenance of airstrips and the infrastructure for the extraction of lucrative fossil fuels were built upon, sometimes quite literally, the footprint left by the IETD and the GoI's quarantine network.

In the wake of the COVID-19 pandemic, readers will undoubtedly draw connections between recent global attempts by modern nation states to control infrastructural networks and the British imperial activity of the nineteenth century examined in this chapter. While the historical contexts are vastly different, a similar predisposition to utilise a combination of quarantine and communication technologies reliant on material, spatial and discursive boundary making is striking. Interconnections produced through trade and communications are coupled with attempts to disconnect people and things, particularly in the context of contagions. While the British sought to encourage certain types of connections, they also desired the production and maintenance of enclaves to isolate themselves from others. This dynamic produced unequal and inequitable inter/dysconnections as race and class were utilised to determine desirable and undesirable connections. However, the conception of telegraph and quarantine stations enclaves would never, and could never, be fully realised. Instead, telegraph and quarantine stations became porous spaces that were susceptible

[77] Confidential letter from the Resident of the Persian Gulf and Consulate-General to Minister in Tehran, Bushire, 29 October 1927. No 121/378-S. British Library IOR/L/PS/10/1006/1.

[78] Resident of the Persian Gulf and Consulate-General to Minister in Tehran (n 77).

[79] Draft Paper Minutes, 21 July 1928. P3777. Pt 1 'Persia: Quarantine arrangements' File 3122/1921. British Library IOR/L/PS/10/1006/1.

to entanglements because they relied on local spaces and actants that resisted attempts of imperial boundary making.

The dynamic highlighted in this chapter around inter/dysconnectedness through quarantine and telegraph stations demonstrates the precarity of governing through contagion. The supposed advanced technological 'tools of empire', such as steamship and telegraph networks, were points of vulnerability as well as strength. Their very existence exacerbated undesirable connections and the spread of contagious diseases. The telegraph and quarantine station sought to mitigate these undesirable connections, but in the process became the location of contestations, as actants, through acts of resistance, confused and complicated British attempts of imperial boundary making.

2

Wastewater Surveillance in Colonial and Present-Day Hong Kong

Governing Through Contagion from Below

DHIRAJ NAINANI*

Introduction

In October 1894, 7,000 Chinese residents of the district of Taipingshan in the British colony of Hong Kong watched as their neighbourhood was razed to the ground.[1] At this point, six months had passed since the first case of bubonic plague had been detected in the district. The then-Governor of Hong Kong, Sir William Robinson, had decried the 'filthy habits'[2] of the Chinese labourers living there, and had attempted to quell the outbreak by quarantining it and conducting highly controversial house-to-house 'cleaning operations' – but to no avail. Faced with rising death rates, the authorities decided the only solution was that the neighbourhood be 'destroyed, as far as possible, by fire'.[3] More than a century later, on 23 January 2021, the Hong Kong government initiated its first 'compulsory restriction-testing declaration' during the COVID-19 pandemic by instituting an areawide lockdown of the Jordan district.[4] A few days prior to this, a public health official, Dr Raymond Ho, had come under fire for suggesting that members of the

*I would like to thank Assoc Prof Janelle Thompson and Prof Monamie Haines for their helpful comments. This research is supported by the National Research Foundation, Prime Minister's Office, Singapore, under its Campus for Research Excellence and Technological Expertise (CREATE) programme, Intra-CREATE Thematic Grant (Cities) grant NRF2019-THE001-0003a and the Singapore Centre for Environmental Life Sciences Engineering (SCELSE) from the Singapore Ministry of Education and National Research Foundation through an RCE award to SCELSE.

[1] R Peckham, 'Hong Kong Junk: Plague and the Economy of Chinese Things' (2016) 90(1) *Bulletin of the History of Medicine* 32, 33.

[2] Quoted in EG Pryor, 'The Great Plague of Hong Kong' (1975) 15 *Journal of the Royal Asiatic Society Hong Kong Branch* 61, 65.

[3] Quoted in: C Lynteris, 'A 'Suitable Soil': Plague's Urban Breeding Grounds at the Dawn of the Third Pandemic' (2017) 61 *Medical History* 343, 352.

[4] C Lau D Tsang, P Siuand and C Leung, '10,000 Residents in Hotspot Placed under Lockdown' *South China Morning Post* (Hong Kong, 23 January 2021).

South Asian ethnic minority community were 'culturally unable' to follow social-distancing rules.[5] Although authorities swiftly disagreed with these comments, numerous tabloid papers shared pictures and videos of unmasked South Asians on social media. The subsequent implementation of the lockdown in Jordan – home to many of Hong Kong's low-income South Asian population[6] – correlated with a rise in discrimination complaints by South Asian people afterwards, who claimed they had been negatively associated with the disease.[7]

As Lynette Chua and Gary Lee have suggested, the COVID-19 pandemic has highlighted how techniques like quarantines and lockdowns have long been utilised by states to 'govern through contagion'. As a response to Chua and Lee's invitation to further explore the non-human and spatial aspects of governing through contagion, this chapter explores the events in Taipingshan in 1894 and Jordan in 2021 to understand how the 1894 quarantine and 2021 lockdown functioned through the legal surveillance and control of space and those inhabiting it. This, in turn, reveals the inter/dysconnectedness between the state and vulnerable populations but in two diverse ways: whereas the quarantine only exacerbated the harsh techniques of everyday control used by the colonial government upon the Chinese labourers in 1894, the lockdown provided the Hong Kong government an opportunity to briefly reframe and redeploy existing strategies of legal governance towards low-income South Asian residents in 2021 in an unexpected manner.

In addition, flowing from the analyses of these two Hong Kong cases, this chapter also considers how non-human agency – specifically, sewage and sanitation infrastructure – plays a major role in the spatio-legal surveillance and governance of (and through) contagion. It explores how, as a technology of moralisation, sanitation infrastructure is transformed from a system *requiring* surveillance to one capable of *conducting* it. Moreover, while the *absence* of a sewage system in the colonial case of Taipingshan assisted in furthering a 'scientifically' racialised narrative that promotes a connection between 'filthy (Chinese) habits' and the black plague, the deployment of surveillance by the contemporary government 'from below' actually led to a disruption of racial logics that linked 'culturally ignorant (South Asian) habits' with COVID-19. As a result, surveilling from below allows for the securitisation of space and the governance of populations based on factors that are not explicitly linked to race.

As Chua and Lee write, governing through contagion is as much a spatial endeavour as it is a legal one. Vaccines, for example, 'possess the capacity to turn around public health governance, especially laws regulating border controls, travel and other movements across public and private spaces'.[8] Yet these complex spatio-legal

[5] T Yu and S Mahtani, 'Wave of Coronavirus Cases Brings a Tide of Racism in Hong Kong' *Washington Post* (Washington DC, 11 February 2021). Ho elaborated that: '[t]hey have many family gatherings and like to gather with fellow countrymen. They like to share food, smoke, drink alcohol and chat together … [t]hey also need to share sanitary facilities with neighbours if the living environment is crowded'.

[6] That is, people primarily from the countries of India, Pakistan, Sri Lanka and Nepal.

[7] Yu and Mahtani 'Wave of Coronavirus Cases Brings a Tide of Racism in Hong Kong' (n 5).

[8] JJG Lee and LJ Chua, 'Smallpox Vaccination and the Limits of Governing through Contagion in the Straits Settlements, 1868–1926' (forthcoming), 3. *Italics my own, and will remain as such throughout the chapter unless stated otherwise.*

arrangements are often enacted and emplaced via infrastructural means; for example, border control measures not only involve the material infrastructures of airports and runways but also a broader infrastructure of securitisation.[9] This also speaks to existing literature on the political and poetic significance of infrastructural systems, and how their complex functionality can carry an expressive weight.[10]

I look to the events in Taipingshan and Jordan as a means of understanding how the biopolitical formation of governing through contagion is expressed through the ordering and regulation of space, as well as the workings of sanitation infrastructure. Although the legal bodies, institutions, objects and buildings that inform quarantines and lockdowns demonstrate how the law regulates urban space, its users and a host of non-human actors through state power, it is the covert role that sanitation infrastructure plays that aesthetically symbolises and politically realises the surveillant and regulatory capabilities of the state, thereby allowing the governance of contagion from above *and* below.

This chapter is divided into three sections. In the first, I look to the events of 1894 – along with the broader historical context of colonial rule in Hong Kong – as a means of exploring how the state deployed the 'constant technology' of the law to govern during times of epidemiological crisis. I show how the distinct lack of a sanitation infrastructure in Taipingshan led to the surveillance – and eventually the legally mandated destruction – of its 'filthy' or 'contaminated' spaces. Next, I turn to the Jordan lockdown of 2021 to understand how the biopolitical logics and motivations of governing through contagion inform the present day. Here, state power is deemed capable of surveilling and regulating diseased space at a much larger scale and register than a century ago, temporarily erasing certain existing forms of biopolitical difference while drawing up new ones. Finally, I focus on the role that sanitation infrastructure played in 'governing from below' in the Jordan lockdown, in that it allowed for the temporary displacement of the racial logics that informed everyday urban space in Hong Kong by producing a population that needed to be made 'healthy'.

As I go on to demonstrate, both instances of governing through contagion involve the regulation of human bodies, the manipulation of (un)contaminated objects and the removal of unclean spaces. At the same time, however, the spatio-temporal disruptions created and caused by quarantined or locked-down space reveal a divergence in the rearticulation of difference between the state and vulnerable subjects, leading to either a furthering (in 1894) or displacement (in 2021) of dysconnectedness.

Law, Surveillance and the Burning of Taipingshan, 1894

In 1894 the bubonic plague was first detected in Hong Kong in the district of Taipingshan, home to hundreds of dilapidated and overfilled buildings that were

[9] M Tedeschi, 'The Body and the Law Across Borders During the COVID-19 Pandemic' (2020) 10 *Dialogues in Human Geography* 178.

[10] See, for example, B Larkin, 'The Politics and Poetics of Infrastructure' (2013) 42 *Annual Review of Anthropology* 327.

occupied by thousands of poor Chinese labourers.[11] Governor Robinson decided to act by quarantining the entire area and sending a regiment of British soldiers to conduct controversial house-to-house cleaning and disinfection operations throughout the district.[12] In doing so, he began the process of governing the district through contagion, which specifically entailed the thorough and unwanted *inspection of 'unhygienic' bodies*, the *cauterization of 'contaminated' objects* and eventually the *razing of 'unclean' space.*

As will be discussed, these processes and techniques of governance can also be seen as an extension of the carceralisation that low-income Chinese migrants faced in Hong Kong. Even before the outbreak of the plague, Chinese subjects – especially those seen as 'coolies' or informal labourers – were subject to harsh laws and social commentaries that curtailed their spatial behaviours, branded their association with certain non-human actors as unclean and created borders or divisions between 'Chinese' and 'European' districts. Robinson's move to further biopolitically regulate and govern the district therefore signified a *furthering of dysconnectedness and difference* between European and Chinese bodies and the sites they occupied.

Using Article 32 of the 1887 Public Health Ordinance,[13] Robinson – through the auspices of an institution known as the Sanitary Board, which had been established in 1883 to implement hygienic building reforms targeting the overcrowded *tong laus* or tenement buildings like those in Taipingshan[14] – authorised soldiers to conduct house-to-house hygiene inspections in the district. The Whitewash Brigade, as they were called, would visit houses with the aim of finding and isolating new patients, burying the dead and disinfecting contaminated areas.[15] Locals, however, were not only mistrustful of 'Western' methods of medicine but also found the intrusion of quarantine personnel into their homes an affront to their sociocultural beliefs. When rumours circulated that the soldiers had 'unfavourable designs on the women and children' of Taipingshan,[16] residents blockaded their homes and stoned the soldiers, while an anti-government poster campaign spread as far as neighbouring Canton. In response, Robinson asked for more soldiers and pressed on.[17]

These unwanted bodily inspections were also an extension of the existing racialised forms of penalisation that Chinese residents faced when inhabiting space. For example, a night-time curfew for the Chinese population had been formally in effect since the enactment of the 1844 Good Order and Clean Health Ordinance,[18] and Chinese subjects were required to carry both a lantern and a 'night pass' from their

[11] Pryor, 'The Great Plague' (n 2).
[12] Pryor (n 2).
[13] Public Health Ordinance (No 24 of 1887) (OHK).
[14] MMW Chan-Yeung, *A Medical History of Hong Kong: 1842–1941* (Hong Kong, The Chinese University of Hong Kong Press, 2018).
[15] Kyu-hwan Sihn, 'Reorganizing Hospital Space: The 1894 Plague Epidemic in Hong Kong and the Germ Theory' (2017) 26 *Korean Journal of Medical History* 59.
[16] Pryor, 'The Great Plague' (n 2), 75.
[17] Pryor (n 2), 75.
[18] Good Order and Clean Health Ordinance (1844) (OHK).

European employer if they were outside after 8pm.[19] Although it had begun as a measure to supposedly reduce 'forms of nocturnal crime',[20] no reason had ever been given as to why it only applied to the Chinese. Although the 1844 Ordinance only imposed a fine for any 'disorderly offences' occurring during the curfew, a controversial piece of legislation passed in 1857 – The Peace of the Colony Ordinance – allowed soldiers to shoot and kill any Chinese subject whom they suspected of 'being so abroad for an improper purpose',[21] although this was seldom carried out.[22]

The house-to-house inspections, therefore, extended the reach of impositions on the spatial practices of Chinese labourers from public space to private space, reaching into the very houses of the Chinese residents to determine whether their bodies and spaces met Western norms of 'good' hygiene (while ignoring any other sociocultural normative practices). At the same time, the act of surveilling and inspecting bodies extended the murky affinity between hygiene and criminality that the 1844 Ordinance enshrined, branding 'unhygienic' behaviours a public nuisance. Consequently, to be clean was to be innocent, but to be unhygienic also meant being criminalised. Therefore, as the colonial state *inspected bodies* and spaces, it also rendered them invisible by reducing them to merely unhygienic sites.

As part of their duties, the Whitewash Brigade, who lacked any form of medical experience, were also required to burn any so-called 'contaminated objects' that they found in the *tong laus* of Taipingshan. This involved confiscating the belongings of the residents, taking them out onto the street and burning them in massive bonfires.[23] In the process, Chinese labourers and their homes became further synonymous with disease, filth and squalor. Official reports describe 'the enormous amount of filth collected in the houses'[24] of Chinese subjects, likening them to 'hovels' or 'black holes'. Newspapers reported seeing thick plumes of smoke rising from burning piles of 'indescribable rubbish' which was merely the furniture, bedding, and personal property of the residents.[25]

The exhalations of disgust surrounding the non-human actors and objects with which Chinese labourers were associated were not new. There had, for instance, been urgent calls to regulate food hygiene in the colony since the 1860s under fervently held views that Chinese practices of food preparation were unhygienic, Chinese chefs were untrustworthy, and Chinese hawkers were potential transmitters of disease.[26] In response to this, the 1866 Order and Cleanliness

[19] C Munn, Anglo-China: Chinese People and British Rule in Hong Kong, 1841–1880 (Abingdon, Routledge, 2001), 285.
[20] Munn, *Anglo-China* (n 19), 131.
[21] Peace of the Colony Ordinance, No 2 of (1857) (OHK).
[22] Munn (n 19), 285.
[23] GA Bremner and DPY Lung, 'Spaces of Exclusion: The Significance of Cultural Identity in the Formation of European Residential Districts in British Hong Kong, 1877–1904' (2003) 21 *Environment and Planning D: Society and Space* 223.
[24] Peckham, 'Hong Kong Junk' (n 1), 44.
[25] Peckham (n 1), 44.
[26] R Peckham, 'Bad Meat: Food and the Medicine of Modern Hygiene in Colonial Hong Kong' in KCA Leung and ML Caldwell, *Moral Foods: The Construction of Nutrition and Health in Modern Asia* (Honolulu, University of Hawai'i Press, 2019).

Ordinance[27] banned Chinese residents from keeping livestock in their homes, and penalised the sale of 'tainted, noxious, adulterated or unwholesome'[28] food. It is undoubtable that these actions did prevent further public health crises and improved overall levels of hygiene. However, it was also clear that, within this, there was a racialised narrative of disgust towards Chinese residents; their bodies, along with the spaces and objects with which they were associated, required decontamination in order to protect Europeans.

Once again, the events in Taipingshan marked a notable escalation in terms of prior disciplinary practices used to regulate the hygiene practices of Chinese subjects. The burning of contaminated furniture and personal belongings may have stemmed from the (at the time not disproven) need to prevent plague bacteria from 'falling' into other homes and spreading disease through its 'miasmas', but the spectacle of the event as it was being reported 'back home' also characterised the bodies and belongings of the Chinese labourers as inherently contaminated. The medically untrained Whitewash Brigade simply burned what it thought fit, but, in so doing, it also *cauterised the 'contaminated' objects* that were connected to the bodies of Chinese labourers, all the while reducing their possessions to ash.

By September 1894, five months after the house-to-house operations had begun, 7,000 homes had been quarantined for inspection (hundreds of which had been sealed off) and thousands of people had died (with the number of Chinese deaths much higher than those of the Europeans).[29] The Sanitary Board set up a Housing Committee to chart the best possible means to prevent the occurrence of future outbreaks, but the Committee decided to focus almost exclusively on the 'problem' posed by Taipingshan. Despite the confirmed identification of the plague bacillus at this point and the corresponding indication that the origins of the plague were zoonotic in nature, the Committee decided that the disease was miasmic and was emanating from within the very earth of Taipingshan itself.[30]

Using medical evidence that would be later recanted and ignoring widespread debate in the press, the Committee decided to that the ideal solution to prevent future outbreaks would be 'demolish all buildings [in Taipingshan] by fire'.[31] The 1889 Crown Lands Resumption Ordinance[32] – which was legislated on the basis that the power of land resumption could lead to sanitary improvements without provoking much dissent – was used to promulgate the 1894 Taipingshan Resumption Ordinance.[33] Roughly 400 buildings comprising an area of ten acres of land in the Taipingshan district were subsequently destroyed.[34]

[27] Order and Cleanliness Ordinance, No 9 of (1867) (OHK).

[28] Order and Cleanliness (n 27), art 11.

[29] Pui-yin Ho, Making Hong Kong: A History of its Urban Development (Cheltenham, Edward Elgar, 2018).

[30] Lynteris, 'A 'Suitable Soil' (n 3).

[31] R Peckham and DM Pomfret (eds), *Imperial Contagions: Medicine, Hygiene, and Cultures of Planning in Asia* (Hong Kong, University of Hong Kong Press, 2013) 31.

[32] Crown Lands Resumption Ordinance, No 23 of (1889) (OHK).

[33] Taipingshan Resumption Ordinance, No 2 of (1894) (OHK).

[34] Chan-Yeung, *A Medical History* (n 14).

Although land resumption – a process by which the state can legally acquire private land in order to build and develop public projects such as roads or public housing – would go on to have a major role to play in Hong Kong's development as a colony, its initial use here led to substantial disagreement between the government and wealthy British and Chinese businessmen. The latter were property developers and owners who sought to combat the proposed resumption by suggesting that, rather than the buildings themselves, it was the poor habits of the Chinese labourers that had contributed to the propagation of the plague in the district; this could be rectified by modifying the buildings rather than destroying them outright. These voices eventually ran silent after the government offered compensation to all owners and developers who would be affected by the demolition.[35]

Although the colonial state's deployment of the law to *raze unclean space* in the Taipingshan district may have marked the first major land resumption in Hong Kong's colonial history, it was built upon a history of racialised zoning practices that strived to minimise the interaction between 'clean' Europeans and the 'unclean' Chinese through the innovative legislative enforcement of racially demarcated building standards. The introduction of the European District Reservation Ordinance in 1888,[36] for example, prohibited the building of 'Chinese tenements' within any 'European districts'; these were the hillier, more elevated parts of Hong Kong Island, chosen because the

> health and comfort of Europeans in a tropical climate demand conditions which are inconsistent with the neighbourhood of houses crowded with occupants and otherwise used after the manner customary with the Chinese inhabitants.[37]

The Ordinance labelled a Chinese tenement as 'any tenement of the type usually designed for habitation by Chinese other than domestic servants'[38] and decreed that a tenement could be considered lawful as long as it was built in a way that guaranteed each inhabitant at least 1,000 metres of cubic space. This ensured that *tong laus* – which were deliberately built by developers to cram as many labourers into poorly designed, ill-maintained and unventilated buildings – would never be built in certain parts of Hong Kong, and that Chinese space would always be associated with uncleanliness, thereby necessitating its removal.[39]

What is equally intriguing, however, is the reason as to why Taipingshan carried a longstanding reputation amongst the colonial authorities for being so unsanitary. Here I turn to the colonial engineer Sir Osbert Chadwick and his 'sanitary survey' of Hong Kong in 1881, which was undertaken at the request of the British government. Having visited Taipingshan as part of this endeavour, he

[35] CL Chu, 'Combating Nuisance: Sanitation, Regulation, and the Politics of Property in Colonial Hong Kong', in Peckham and Pomfret, *Imperial Contagions* (n 31).

[36] European Reservation District Ordinance, No 16 of 1888 (1888) (OHK).

[37] European Reservation District (Amendment) Ordinance (1888), No 26 of 1888 (OHK), Preamble.

[38] European Reservation District (n 36), Art 3.

[39] CL Chu, 'Between Typologies and Representation: The Tong Lau and the Discourse of the 'Chinese House' in Colonial Hong Kong', in M Rajagopalan and M Desai (eds), *Colonial Frames, Nationalist Histories: Imperial Legacies, Architecture, and Modernity* (Abingdon, Routledge, 2012).

proposed several recommendations regarding the design and construction of *tong laus* that made up the district, including the addition of open spaces and windows for ventilation.[40]

Chadwick also emphasised that it would be imperative to improve Taipingshan's water supply and sewage infrastructure; as rubbish constantly blocked drains and residents used contaminated wells for their water needs, the district was a 'hotbed for disease and a breeding ground of filth'.[41] Chadwick went on to declare that one could not label the Chinese as a 'hopelessly filthy race till they have been provided with reasonable means for cleanliness'.[42] However, the publication of his sanitary survey had already set in motion the process of categorising Taipingshan (and its peoples) as filthy, diseased and contaminated.

His proposed reforms, however, remained unpassed. By the time the plague hit Hong Kong in 1894, the bodies and spaces of Chinese labourers had long been associated with dirt, squalor and overcrowding, as medical experts opined that to the labourers, 'cleanliness … or anything approaching it, is an absolutely unknown art'.[43] As the district which housed the most labourers, Taipingshan in particular was deemed by Dr Philip Ayres, then Hong Kong's Colonial Surgeon, as a place whose very 'floors were reeking with filth'.[44]

Small wonder, then, that Ayres eventually used both Chadwick's survey and the distinct lack of any sanitation infrastructure in Taipingshan as evidentiary reasons to justify its fiery demolition. To him, it was clear that the plague came from the 'sewage which is soaking through the soil'[45] and was irrevocably intermingling with Chinese bodies and Chinese spaces. After agreeing with his recommendation, the Committee also vowed to 'cast away the contaminated topsoil and redevelop the area with better built houses, ample open space, and a more efficient drainage system'.[46] Unsurprisingly, no such plan ever materialised.

Chadwick's sanitary survey therefore contributed to how the state governed through contagion in Taipingshan – through its spatio-legal quarantining and demolition – by marking it as a thoroughly contaminated space. Noting the lack of the Western sanitation infrastructure in the district – and the corresponding 'enlightenment' and 'education' that Western advances in sanitation infrastructure represented – it cast labouring Chinese bodies, spaces and objects as the creators, incubators and carriers of bubonic plague. These were, in turn, intrinsically entangled with non-human bodies of sewage and were thus declared sites of 'the most fertile soil in the world'[47] for the plague, thereby marking them for eventual destruction.

[40] Chan-Yeung. *Medical History* (n 14).
[41] O Chadwick, Mr Chadwick's Reports on the Sanitary Condition of Hong Kong with Appendices and Plans (London, Colonial Office, 1882) 52.
[42] Chadwick, *Mr Chadwick's Reports* (n 41) 34.
[43] Lynteris (n 3), 350.
[44] Chan-Yeung (n 14), 131.
[45] Chan-Yeung (n 14), 131.
[46] Peckham and Pomfret (n 31), 31.
[47] Lynteris (n 3), 349.

Governing through contagion in Taipingshan in 1894, therefore, entailed the use of law to order spaces and bodies that not only furthered the dysconnectedness and existing differences between the colonial authorities and European and Chinese residents, but also exemplified the centralising force of legal technologies, such as militarised house-to-house operations or the various treaties that enabled racialised spatial division. What these legal technologies aimed to combat – and, by extension, heighten and entrench the dysconnectedness between Chinese subjects and European ones – was the distinct lack of sanitation infrastructure, thereby marking the district and its residents as contaminated, diseased and filthy.

Law, Surveillance and the 'Saving' of Jordan, 2021

In the early hours of 23 January 2021, over 1,000 workers from various governmental agencies set up barriers around the district of Jordan, home to most of the city's socioeconomically marginalised ethnic minority citizens and asylum-seekers (most of whom were South Asian).[48] Invoking Section 19B of the Prevention and Control of Diseases Regulation,[49] the authorities subsequently declared that 150 buildings in Jordan (housing almost 10,000 people) had been locked down under the city's first area-wide 'compulsory restriction-testing declaration'. In effect, this meant that the residents of Jordan would have to remain in their homes until the entire area had been inspected and tested by healthcare workers, which would eventually take two days.

Although subsequent media coverage highlighted the difficulties that South Asian residents faced during the lockdown, I argue that governing through contagion in Jordan differed to that utilised in Taipingshan in 1894.[50] Here, the technologies of law centred around equally 'fostering' the economic productivity of *all* life, including those belonging to marginalised populations (eg, ethnic minorities). To that end, governing through contagion in Jordan involved *inviting 'unhygienic' bodies* for screening, *the circulation of new regulatory objects* and the *'cleaning' of erased space.*

In responding (even if imperfectly) to the particular needs of South Asian residents, the regulation of spaces and bodies in Jordan signalled a displacement rather than a furthering of dysconnectedness. However, in so doing, it also revealed how South Asian residents, objects and spaces are often regulated by the state through a myriad array of disciplinary and biopolitical techniques that

[48] Government of the Hong Kong Special Administrative Region, 'Hong Kong Poverty Situation Report on Ethnic Minorities 2016'. Available at: www.statistics.gov.hk/pub/B9XX0004E2016XXXXE0100.pdf. See also, G Mathews, 'Asylum Seekers as Symbols of Hong Kong's Non-Chineseness' (2018) 3 *China Perspectives* 51. For the purposes of this chapter, the ethnic minority citizens that will be referred to will be those belonging to the South Asian diaspora (unless otherwise stated).

[49] Prevention and Control of Disease (Compulsory Testing for Certain Persons) Regulation, (2020) Cap 599J (HK).

[50] Yu and Mahtani (n 5).

operate *outside and beyond* the spatio-temporal confines of any lockdowns. The government's actions in Jordan therefore only temporarily reframed its relation to a vulnerable population.

Shortly after the lockdown began, it was reported that South Asian residents were facing difficulties in fully comprehending why they were being asked to leave their houses and be tested. Although the government had initiated the lockdown stealthily to prevent residents from leaving the area, it was only after the cordon had been secured that it came to light that not everyone could understand English, Cantonese or Mandarin. A team of translators was therefore promptly despatched to accompany the government workers as they visited various houses.[51] At times they would be forced to yell out their request politely but firmly in Hindi or Urdu in order to be heard through the closed doors of an apartment. There were no reported instances of noncompliance, but if nobody was home, leaflets in several languages would be left wedged beneath the front door.[52]

These respectful invitations for bodies to be screened, however, contrast with other kinds of inspections that South Asian residents face in the city. South Asian men, for example, are frequently targeted by the millions of stop-and-search operations that are conducted by the police in districts like Jordan.[53] The entire encounter may take mere minutes – police officers ask the men to produce their identification documents for checking, and then, once this is done, they are free to go – but South Asian men have stated that they feel unfairly targeted based on their skin colour. They have also expressed the opinion that they are less likely to be stopped when they appear to be better dressed, which suggests that socioeconomic conditions also play a role when being stopped.[54]

The contrast in these two sets of legal technologies highlights the difference in the power of the law and its regulatory effect on bodies and spaces. South Asian bodies are made highly visible in the stop-and-search operation thanks to the swift transformation of public space into a potentially carceral one, based on a rhetoric of keeping streets 'safe' or hygienically sound. The feeling of being seen in this instance differs from what occurs during the lockdown, where the act of *inviting the bodies* of South Asian residents to be screened involves an element of consent (or assent) to stepping in to a surveillant hygienic space that has not been explicitly demarcated based on any racialised logics.

The leaving of medical leaflets and pamphlets by the team of translators also represented another change in how the state governed South Asian bodies: the introduction of new regulatory objects. Until the Jordan lockdown, information

[51] Ng Kang-chung, 'Officers from Ethnic Minorities Break Down Language Barriers' *South China Morning Post* (Hong Kong, 24 January 2021).

[52] Ng Kang-chung 'Officers from Ethnic Minorities Break Down Language Barriers' (n 51).

[53] P Boehler, 'Ethnic Minorities Complain of Racial Profiling by Police' *South China Morning Post* (24 November 2013).

[54] E Ng, 'Asia's World City? Hong Kong Ethnic Minorities Feel Targeted by Police Stop and Search Actions' *Hong Kong Free Press* (8 Octber 2017). Available at: hongkongfp.com/2017/10/08/asias-world-city-hong-kong-ethnic-minorities-feel-targeted-police-stop-search-actions.

about the COVID-19 pandemic had primarily been made available in Hong Kong's official languages. The realisation that this would not be sufficient, however, led to an increase in medical circulars and documents that provided information in a variety of South and Southeast Asian languages as well.[55] The government also began to update their dedicated COVID-19 website to include information in more languages, and opened an information hotline for ethnic minority citizens.[56]

As per the Prevention and Control of Diseases Regulation, the government was also required to 'ensure that every restricted person found on the restricted premises is provided with any basic necessities (including goods and services)',[57] and handed out food and care packages to households within the district. Although the contents of the food packages were criticised by some for not meeting all dietary requirements,[58] what is of interest here is the introduction of an additional typology of regulatory and uncontaminated objects: for instance, cardboard cartons, Styrofoam boxes and cans of food.

On the other hand, challenges surrounding the procurement of food were acutely felt by (both South Asian and other) asylum-seekers well before the COVID-19 pandemic.[59] It was not until 2014 that the government agreed to minimally increase their meagre stipend and give them the ability to purchase their own groceries, rather than forcing them to collect pre-prepared packages of low-quality foods.[60] Moreover, the state's desire to provide linguistically diverse information on COVID-19 differed from studies that have found that South Asian patients in Hong Kong consistently lack readily available interpretation services, and face a paucity of linguistically helpful literature.[61]

The state, therefore, introduced a host of new material accessories, or *regulatory objects*, to enforce their strategy of containment. Governing through contagion relied on the state's ability to (re)make Jordan's bodies and spaces compliantly hygienic through the circulation of techno-legal non-human actors such as cans, telephones and pamphlets. Yet the spatio-temporal displacement of dysconnectedness bought on by the lockdown stands in stark relief to the quotidian ways in which marginalised bodies (such as those belonging to asylum-seekers) are left wanting for certain resources; these are not so much cauterised as they are left to wither away.

[55] Government of Hong Kong Special Administrative Region, 'Restrictions in Jordan Lifted' (25 January 2021). Available at: www.news.gov.hk/eng/2021/01/20210125/20210125_111513_562.html.

[56] Government of Hong Kong Special Administrative Region (n 55).

[57] Prevention and Control of Disease Regulation (n 49), s 19N.

[58] L Westbrook and C Leung, 'Lockdown Residents Slam Food Handouts' *South China Morning Post* (24 January 2021).

[59] K Magramo, 'Refugees in Hong Kong Struggle to Buy Supplies as Panic Buying over Lockdown Rumours Sweeps Food off Shelves' *South China Morning Post* (4 March 2022).

[60] F Veccho and C Beatson, 'Asylum Seekers Occupy Movement in Hong Kong' (2014) 56 *Race & Class* 96.

[61] N Vandan, J Yuen-Ha Wong, J Jung-Jae Lee, P Siu-Fai Yip, and D Yee-Tak Fong, 'Challenges of Healthcare Professionals in Providing Care to South Asian Ethnic Minority Patients in Hong Kong: A Qualitative Study' (2020) 28 *Health and Social Care in the Community* 591.

The locking down of Jordan also led to a renewed focus on its many apartment buildings that are old, decrepit and considered to be fire hazards.[62] Moreover, these buildings are filled with illegally subdivided units that are built in ways that can lead to disease or fires.[63] However, under Hong Kong law, neither subdivided flats nor three-nil buildings are classified as illegal structures. As the city lacks comprehensive anti-racial discrimination legislature concerning housing, many low-income ethnic minority city-dwellers have little choice but to live in such structures.[64]

In response to safety concerns regarding three-nil buildings that arose a year prior to the Jordan lockdown, the government announced that they would be sending teams of cleaners to known 'black spots' in order to clean them.[65] However, calls to amend the relevant legislation to make the government responsible for maintenance works in such buildings were rejected due to 'the scale of the works and associated costs as well as the impacts to individual building owners'.[66] Although members of the low-income South Asian community have tried to seek refuge from discriminatory rental practices in such spaces,[67] they have not been mentioned in any annual government policies concerning housing.[68]

Though not as strong in its envelopment of South Asian bodies as the invitation of inspections or the introduction of objects, the *cleaning of erased spaces* as a form of spatio-legal biopolitical governance still assisted ethnic minority residents who were living in hazardous and precarious conditions. Moreover, unlike in Taipingshan, there were no state-led racialised narratives that guided the selection of these spaces in particular; if anything, Dr Ho's solitary attempt may have motivated the government to pay closer attention to the needs of vulnerable subjects. Subsequent area-wide compulsory declarations that took place in other districts with high numbers of South Asian residents went largely unreported.

However, as has been demonstrated, these brief acts of cleaning did not help with the erasure of such spaces. Rather, instead of taking the opportunity to wholly transform these differentialising spaces that had been made briefly 'visible' by the removal of uncleanliness, the state seemed to subsume and further prolong their

[62] These apartment buildings are referred to as 'three-nil' buildings due to a lack of (a) owners' corporations, (b) residents' organisations or (c) property management companies, which help to ensure that properties comply with ordinances relating to hygiene, security, fire maintenance and other matters.

[63] J-P Cabestan and E Florence, 'Twenty Years After the Handover: Hong Kong's Political and Social Transformation and its Future Under China's rule' (2018) 3 *China Perspectives* 3.

[64] SKL Chan, 'Enclave Tenement Trap: A Case Study of Ethnic Minorities Residing in Private Rented Housing Sector in Hong Kong' (2018) 9 *Environment and Urbanization ASIA* 909.

[65] Government of Hong Kong Special Administrative Region, 'Old Building Cleaning Enhanced' (News.gov.hk 11 February 2021). Available at: www.news.gov.hk/eng/2021/02/20210211/20210211_221510_808.html.

[66] Government of Hong Kong Special Administrative Region, Press Release: 'Fire Safety of "Three-Nil" Buildings' (News.gov.hk, 2 December 2020). Available at: www.info.gov.hk/gia/general/202012/02/P2020120200541.htm.

[67] Ng Kang-chung, 'Members of Ethnic Minorities Shut Out', *South China Morning Post* (5 October 2020).

[68] R Chu Man-Kin, 'Hong Kong's Housing Crisis Discussion Must Home in on the Struggles of Ethnic Minority Residents', *South China Morning Post* (13 October 2021).

longstanding invisibility. At the same time, little was done to assist ethnic minorities in the shaping of such spaces, thereby erasing their particular histories with them. Any displacement of dysconnectedness was therefore temporary.

Sanitation Infrastructures and Governing Through Contagion from Below

One hundred and twenty-seven years after Chadwick completed his sanitary survey, the Hong Kong authorities tested for viral RNA fragments of the SARS-CoV-2 virus in sewage samples that had been collected from drains in the district of Jordan.[69] This process, known as wastewater surveillance, had been swiftly embraced by governments worldwide during the COVID-19 pandemic, due to its ability to easily and inexpensively detect the presence of SARS-CoV-2 in human waste well before the development of any possible symptoms.[70] It is, therefore, important to highlight the role that sanitation infrastructure played in governing through contagion from below.

The Jordan lockdown was notable in that it marked the first time that the Hong Kong authorities had used wastewater surveillance publicly as part of their strategy to govern contagion.[71] Wastewater surveillance was used alongside case data in order to trace and isolate a specific area as a potential cluster of COVID-19. The state, however, was subtle in highlighting how it used sanitation infrastructure as a means of spatio-legal regulation. It presented wastewater surveillance merely as part of a gazetted notice on a government website, which stated that 'the ratio of the sewage samples found in the buildings located in the "restricted area" being constantly tested positive was higher than that of … other areas'.[72] The notice also contained a plain map that used a red box to highlight the restricted area, marking a spatiotemporal enclosure that could prevent unhealthy bodies from exiting urban space.

What was also notable about the deployment of wastewater surveillance in Jordan is that it evinced the legacy of colonial-era infrastructural projects and the seeds of biopolitical regulation that were embedded within. The lockdown demonstrated the biopolitical power of modern sanitation infrastructure and its ability to regulate urban space and its users, albeit based upon public health

[69] Xiaoqing Xu et al, 'The First Case Study of Wastewater-based Epidemiology of COVID-19 in Hong Kong' (2021) 790 *Science of the Total Environment* 148000.
[70] JR Thompson et al, 'Making waves: Wastewater surveillance of SARS-CoV-2 for population-based health management' (2020) *Water Research* 184.
[71] Wastewater surveillance would continue to be deployed over the next two years – albeit in far less controversial scenarios – for demarcating other compulsory restriction-testing declarations or area-wide lockdowns.
[72] Government of Hong Kong Special Administrative Region, Press Release: 'Government Makes "Restriction-Testing Declaration" and Issues Compulsory Testing Notice in Respect of Specified "Restricted Area" in Jordan'. (23 January 2021). Available at: www.info.gov.hk/gia/general/202101/23/P2021012300107.htm.

objectives rather than racial logics. It briefly, yet brilliantly, rendered low-income and asylum-seeking South Asian bodies highly visible, temporarily 'un-othering' them in the process of demarcating the spatio-legal borders for a lockdown. This, in turn, temporarily displaced the dysconnectedness and diverse articulations of difference that they faced beyond its spatio-temporal barriers.

Yet the surveillance and regulation of bodies – through an act of bordering done from data collected within a subterranean infrastructural network – was completed in a highly invisible manner. Indeed, the only indication of its vast sprawling legal materiality below was a sentence in an online gazette, akin to a no-smoking sign marked in the corner of a room. The vast collection of non-human agencies that made this possible (ie, viruses being captured in sewage that was, in turn, captured by pipes) were invisible to human bodies above ground.

Though it might have resembled the biopolitical techniques employed by the state in Taipingshan in 1894, governing through contagion in the district of Jordan in 2021 was an act that spatio-temporally displaced existing articulations of difference and dysconnectedness that low-income South Asian citizens faced outside of the lockdown. Here, regulatory technologies that took the material forms of translators, cleaners, Styrofoam boxes and Urdu pamphlets suspended racial logics correlating disease with ethnicity. Instead, the state strived to ensure that even vulnerable subjects could be made 'healthy' and therefore economically productive – as long as they remained firmly connected to it.

This was also reflected in how the biopolitics of sanitation infrastructure in Hong Kong developed and expanded over time. In 1894, the absence of sanitation infrastructure was used by the state to produce morally 'ignorant' and 'uneducated' populations; over a century later, however, the state was able to deploy this same subterranean infrastructure to surveil and spatio-temporally displace racial logics and normalise bodies, objects and spaces from below.

Conclusion

Chua and Lee conclude one of their pieces on governing through contagion by reiterating how intrinsically it 'depends on webs of human and non-human relationships'.[73] As the events of Taipingshan and Jordan demonstrate, these webs are constantly expanding, withering, colliding and becoming messily entangled with other webs. Despite this, it remains clear that to govern through contagion is to implicate a host of human *and* non-human bodies, objects and spaces, whether they are used in the act of governance or are its very targets.

One way of tracing the spatial, material and normative effects of the techniques and institutions that form the state's ability to govern involves understanding how law, sanitation infrastructure and other technologies are used to reorder space

[73] Lee and Chua (n 8), 22.

and bodies during times of contagion. Whether it is inspecting bodies or inviting them to be screened, cauterising certain objects or circulating new ones or the razing or erasing of space, the state's ability to govern through contagion – through spatial strategies such as the quarantine or lockdown – is implanted with legal and normalising technologies that influence the inter/dysconnection of vulnerable bodies.

This, in turn, also reveals the latent yet powerful role that infrastructural systems and networks play in governing through contagion. Colonial imaginaries surrounding the enlightening power of sanitation infrastructure were sufficient to condemn entire districts that lacked them. Modern sanitation infrastructure, on the other hand, retains not just the biopolitical purpose of mapping and surveilling populations, but is now able to manipulate and demarcate space 'above ground', thereby governing from below. Although these demarcations allow for new forms of screening and regulating the population along non-racialised markers or narratives, the spatio-temporal conditions they create offer a temporary respite from the everyday challenges faced by vulnerable subjects.

3

Regulating Pandemic Wastes

Governing Through Contagion via Disciplining Modalities

LEE GODDEN*

Introduction

Waste may seem inert and relatively innocuous until it is aligned with contagion. Waste in a society may take many material forms such as discarded belongings, unconsumed food, dead animals, decaying matter and the fluids and matter shed from human bodies such as 'phlegm'. Most pertinently here, in the COVID-19 pandemic, there emerged a category of pandemic wastes that brought into combination several existing regulatory classifications of waste, but which distinguished them in a new way as highly contagious. When filtered through medical/health experts' lens, pandemic contagion derived both from the wastes issuing from infected human bodies and from contact with the pandemic virus itself. This view of contagion in its alignment to waste, which was adopted and disseminated by specialist health experts, generated a regulatory response to pandemic wastes that pivoted on the modalities of disciplining bodies. In this instance, bodily governance extended for example to medical instructions as to how bodily COVID-19 wastes were to be managed to limit contagion. The more specific medical modalities of disciplining bodies became aligned to the wider functioning of the removal of waste in societies in order to reduce potential sources of pandemic contamination. Waste workers became pivotal to containing contagion by necessarily connecting with infected wastes, but simultaneously by virtue of that activity were placed beyond the safe spaces occupied by those separated from the waste by their labour.

Waste occupies a liminal space as ubiquitous in societies, but according to Lefebvre it is simultaneously perceived as residue, as existing in a parallel process

* The author acknowledges the funding provided by the Australian Research Council Discovery Project DP190101373 that assisted in the writing of this chapter, and the research assistance provided by Melbourne Law School Research Service and Ms Arshya Kulkarni.

of removal, suspension and confinement from productive, healthy lived spaces.[1] Efforts to confine wastes can occur at many levels in a society from specialist medical practices to public health laws that require occupants to clean away wastes that might give rise to diseases from homes and other premises. There are heightened efforts to confine waste from lived and productive spaces in a society during a pandemic. Arguably, that is what occurred in the COVID-19 pandemic context. The medical, legal and regulatory practices prescribed for dealing with contaminated COVID-19 wastes evolved into a pervasive set of 'disciplining modalities' forming part of the wider suite of measures deployed in governing through contagion in the recent pandemic.[2]

The practices for regulating COVID-19 infected wastes in the recent pandemic were not limited to national administrative and executive government strategies of control over bodies, spaces and wastes to combat infection. The regulation by governments to control pandemic wastes (in association often with medical experts) also co-opted and augmented a range of existing health and waste management laws and policy settings that had been developed in international health and sustainability forums, as well as selected aspects of domestic environmental legislation. Waste and infection control protocols, at least initially, were largely sourced by governments from the World Health Organisation (WHO). Prototypes of such measures had been initiated by the WHO in earlier large-scale outbreaks of contagion, such as the Ebola crisis in Africa. These measures were extended and redefined in the COVID-19 pandemic as a disciplining practice operating within medical, quarantine and residential settings in many countries.[3]

The resonances of such pandemic governance with the post-enlightenment scientific emphasis on sustaining life through bodily technologies focused on the control of populations are evident. Yet, such disciplining modalities were compromised at various junctures in the pandemic by the intrinsic unconfinable materiality of contagious waste. Indeed, governing through contagion, even in pandemic times, is not always totalising in its reach. While the nation-state usually exercises great control over its resident population, it may not gain complete dominance over social life.[4] In this manner, the iterative web of human and non-human relationships reveals the entanglement of human and non-human subjectivity.[5]

[1] On the abstraction, production and separation of spaces, see generally, H Lefebvre, *The Production of Space* D Nicholson-Smith (tr) (Hoboken, Blackwell, 1991). For analysis of the legal implications of Lefebvre's work, see C Butler, *Henri Lefebvre: Spatial Politics, Everyday Life and the Right to the City* (Abingdon, Taylor & Francis, 2012).

[2] See generally, LJ Chua and JJG Lee, 'Governing through Contagion' in VV Ramraj (ed), *Covid-19 in Asia: Law and Policy Contexts* (Oxford, Oxford University Press, 2021). For pertinent definitions of governing through contagion, see the introductory chapter to this book.

[3] United Nations Environment Programme, 'Guidance on Policy and Legislation for Integrated Waste Management during a Pandemic' (UNEP Guidance Publication, 2022) ch 1. Available at: www.unep.org/resources/publication/guidance-policy-and-legislation-integrated-waste-management-during-pandemic.

[4] JJG Lee and LJ Chua, 'Smallpox Vaccination and the Limits of Governing through Contagion in the Straits Settlements, 1868–1926' (forthcoming) 3.

[5] M Davies, *EcoLaw: Legality, Life, and the Normativity of Nature* (Abingdon, Routledge, 2022) 63.

Thus, in the legal, regulatory and policy framings for COVID-19 waste regulation that were adapted in the pandemic, contagion assumed a subjectivity and agency that was co-dependent on human populations.[6] Conversely, the materiality of contagion, manifest in burgeoning pandemic wastes, threatened to undercut the social order that the regulatory practices and protocols were instituted to maintain. Accordingly, the acknowledgment of the material conditions implicit to the coalition of wastes (dirt, pollution), contagion and social and regulatory order invoke earlier framings of cultural protocols for the avoidance of defilement.[7]

The juxtaposition of the sacred and life-enhancing practices with waste and pollutants as substances corrupting body and nomos have been explored by anthropologists, such as Mary Douglas in her seminal work, *Purity and Danger*.[8] Accordingly, this chapter, in considering pandemic waste regulation, draws upon not only the theoretical framings of disciplining modalities as set out in the concept of 'governing through contagion' but also explores how the exponential growth in infectious and non-infectious wastes in COVID-19 exposed the material vulnerability of bodies and populations, and precipitated a flurry of practices designed to ensure 'purity'. Even so, the chapter highlights the extent to which human populations in pandemics risk being subsumed by contagion despite the extensive superstructure of laws and protocols designed to avert 'danger'. The movement to institute laws and medical protocols focused on the containment of bodily wastes mirrors the wider social and regulatory efforts to separate wastes and contagion from lived spaces to create pure bodies. Even so, we need to consider the body that is affected by contagious waste as both figural and material. Indeed, feminist theory has challenged the view of the passive body that is simply constructed and represented through technologies of disciplining.[9] Butler, for example, explores how linguistic constructions shape reality via our participation in 'everyday' speech acts. By alluding to, and reaffirming, the conventions and ideologies of our constituent social and material world, we enact and perpetuate that reality.[10]

During the COVID-19 pandemic much attention focused on the nature of nation-state emergency powers in instituting disciplining techniques to contain infection by curtailing bodily movement and interpersonal contact. The classic modalities of quarantine and containment as responses to contagion were intensified as lockdowns became normalised and rationalised by the ever-mounting pandemic infection statistics issuing from international and national health and

[6] Chua and Lee, 'Governing through Contagion' (n 2) 115.

[7] M Douglas, *Purity and Danger: An Analysis of Concepts of Pollution and Taboo* (Abingdon, Taylor & Francis, 2002) 7.

[8] Douglas, *Purity and Danger* (n 7).

[9] See, for example, E Grosz, *Space, Time and Perversion: Essays on the Politics of Body* (London, Routledge 1995); D Haraway, *Simian's, Cyborgs and Women: the Reinvention of Nature* (London, Routledge 1991).

[10] While Judith Butler's work has focused on the performance of sexual and gender dimensions of the material body, her scholarship has application here given the pandemic quest for the bodily enactment of the divisions between contagious and healthy bodies. J Butler, 'Performative Acts and Gender Constitution: An Essay in Phenomenology and Feminist Theory' in S-E Case (ed), *Performing Feminisms: Feminist Critical Theory and Theatre* (Baltimore, Johns Hopkins University Press, 1990) 207.

government officials. As contagion spread exponentially in populations, waste, once the barely noticed residue of the concentration of the nation-state on fostering 'life', began to assume its own significance as an extension of conjoined pandemic governance and bodily disciplining. In this manner, it replicates, 'a broader process ontology in which entities are emergent rather than stable, essential, or fixed. The normative process is built into life; there is no existence without it, and it is a process of inherent change and adaptation to circumstances'.[11] In effect, waste had previously been regulated as 'inert and passive' in order to ensure it could be separated out from lived, productive spaces. In the COVID-19 pandemic, however, contagious waste itself began to assume an (emergent) identity as a central (disciplining) aspect integral to 'life'. Waste assumed an indirect agency as the inherent 'other' to the healthy, contagion-free body and productive spaces.

Significantly, as part of the normalisation of the facilitation of life by reference to the disciplining modalities of waste, 'populations' in the COVID-19 pandemic became heavily reliant on the law and technologies of waste management and the 'willingness' of designated workers under those laws to carry out the tasks of managing contagious wastes so that others were enabled to avoid contagion.[12] Accordingly, the following sections explore how the law and regulatory technologies pertinent to health and waste management during COVID-19 varied across the boundary of lived and waste-infected spaces, and also within a skewed set of relationships between the state, the governed population and the subset of 'workers' dealing with contagion waste – what Chua and Lee have called dysconnectedness. The purity and productivity of 'confined' populations became co-dependent upon designated essential workers in healthcare and non-healthcare settings performing tasks such as waste removal during the pandemic. Accordingly, this chapter draws on a research survey of international law, protocols, guidances and national legislation and practices[13] that were generated or amended in the pandemic to illustrate how the convergence of environmental and health laws and waste management practices 'produce' both human and 'more than human entities', such as contagion, as the objects of regulatory controls. The exponential growth in infectious materials and bodily excrement generated as part of COVID-19 responses exposed the vulnerability of populations to being engulfed in their own contagious detritus, and heightened the urgency of waste management; the efficacy of which depended, in part, on the regulatory scope of what was designated as 'wastes'.

What is Waste as a Regulatory Object?

As a general regulatory term, 'waste' has variable meaning in international law and in conventional national legislative contexts.[14] Effectively, legislative definitions

[11] Davies, *EcoLaw* (n 5) 63.
[12] Chua and Lee, 'Governing through Contagion' (n 2) 115.
[13] United Nations Environment Programme (n 5).
[14] United Nations Environment Programme (n 5) 17–18.

of waste derive either from a natural environmental/pollution control stream of regulatory practices or from health and medical regulatory settings.[15] A significant point of crossover in defining wastes between these two regulatory fields is environmental health laws and policies.[16] There was a wide scope in how waste was construed as the regulatory object of pandemic laws, protocols and guidelines. It is possible, though, within broad parameters to recognise a distinctive set of COVID-19 pandemic wastes, especially under international regimes such as that of the WHO with its medico-scientific orientation. Typically, the basis for identifying 'pandemic waste' was a circular reference back to its potentially contagious COVID-19 qualities. Medical waste such as masks and gloves generated in treating COVID-19 patients is an obvious example. Even these types of waste under various regulations, however, were segregated according to how intensely the waste was in contact with infection. Other medical contexts include the high levels of 'e-waste' where in overwhelmed hospital settings, the medical equipment used to treat patients that was potentially contaminated was simply abandoned in the streets or in landfills. These discrete medical forms of pandemic waste existed along a spectrum with more conventional wastes such as plastic food covering materials, designed to reduce the infection generated in residential and commercial settings. The designation of a set of pandemic wastes, with explicit links to control of contagion, is part of a longer regulatory history of regulation designed to guard against contagion.

Historically, waste regulation in its efforts to confine contagion from productive, healthy spaces can be construed as integral to a colonial instrumentality.[17] The class and racial bias of laws designed to secure environmental health, especially in colonial settings, has been highlighted by Lee and Chua.[18] Wastes in such regulatory contexts expressly take on an association with contagion and infection; consequently, such associations rhetorically justify measures for the control and cleansing of spaces that normatively regulate and confine certain sectors of the populations.[19] Such laws exemplify Douglas' contention that '[p]ollution ideas work in the life of society at two levels, one largely instrumental, one expressive'.[20] 'Similarly, the ideal order of society is guarded by dangers which threaten transgressors'.[21] The normative signalling of the danger of contagion in many societies finds expression in rules and norms that proscribe certain forms of behaviour, such as coming into contact with those persons who collect waste or eating certain foods believed to cause contagion.[22]

[15] L Godden, 'The Nexus between Environment Law and Public Health Law in Australia' in I Freckelton and B Bennett (eds), *Handbook of Public Health Law* (Alexandria NSW, Federation Press, 2023) 438–56.

[16] B Pontin, 'The Constitutive Tension Between Public Health and Environmental Protection – An Historical Perspective' (2020) 32 *Journal of Environmental Law* 345, 346.

[17] Godden (n 15).

[18] Lee and Chua (n 4) 4–5. Also see Nainani (Chapter 2 of this volume).

[19] C Reynolds, 'Public Health Law in the New Century' (2003) 10 *Journal of Law and Medicine* 435, 436.

[20] Douglas (n 7) 7.

[21] Douglas (n 7) 3.

[22] Douglas (n 7) 5.

Waste regulation, and the associated law and technologies at play in COVID-19 settings, also exemplify an instrumental trend to normatively discipline populations to ensure longer term socio-economic productivity – a trope which began to challenge strict state-based lockdown measures as the pandemic ensued. The phenomenon of burgeoning pandemic wastes and the eventual failure of regulatory responses to implement a strategy of contagious waste containment also point to the proliferating waste crisis facing nations. It is a waste crisis borne of excessive consumption, constituting a problem that societies now face as the consequence of their vigorous promotion of the life of populations in the face of impending death. The mounting COVID-19 pandemic wastes that threatened to overwhelm populations thus reveal the failures of spatial containment strategies. The material manifestation of contagion expands beyond formal attempts to confine it by regulatory systems that deploy technical health modalities and the mantra of recycling of waste via 'circular economies'.[23] The laws and the normative technologies of infectious waste management that emerged internationally, and which had parallels in many jurisdictions in the COVID-19 pandemic, relied on technical modalities that were consistently undercut by the sheer virulence of the contagion. In this way, the contagion exhibited some of the characteristics of agency that are often aligned with the human subject.

Subjectivity and the Materiality of Contagion

Accordingly, before turning to discussion of the specific waste technologies of law and normative controls that recursively produce 'governing through contagion',[24] it is helpful to situate the COVID-19 contagion as the material expression of a transgressive non-human 'agent' that threatens the bodily integrity of human 'subjects'.[25] The view that COVID-19 contagion in concert with the practices designed to avoid bodily infection may shape human subjectivity references Foucault's iteration of law, subject and knowledge production as co-constitutive.[26] Contagion exists simultaneously as a perceivable risk, a knowledge of the danger of infection, as well as materialising as the danger of the COVID-19 disease itself. Recognising that contagion has agency, and that it exists in close symbiosis with infected humans, challenges the classic conception of the autonomous

[23] The circular economies model is promoted internationally as involving waste reduction, waste recycling and reuse so that waste can re-enter cycles of 'sustainable' industrial production. See, for example, M Negrete-Cardoso et al, 'Circular Economy Strategy and Waste Management: A Bibliometric Analysis in its Contribution to Sustainable Development, Toward a Post-COVID-19 Era' (2022) 29 *Environmental Science and Pollution Research* 61729.

[24] Chua and Lee, 'Governing through Contagion' (n 2) 115.

[25] M Davies, 'New Materialisms' in M Davies (ed), *Asking the Law Question*, 4th edn (Brisbane, Lawbook Co, 2017).

[26] On this point there is extensive scholarship. See, for example, G Wickham, 'Foucault and Law', in R Banaker and M Travers (eds), *An Introduction to Law and Social Theory*, 2nd edn (Oxford, Hart Publishing, 2013) 220.

human subject. Conventionally in law we regard 'the subject … as an independent entity who is both self-contained and self-controlled'.[27] Moreover, this discretely conceived a priori subject is 'an autonomous thinking unit who is in control of her or his destiny'.[28] Where contagion materially exists in symbiosis with the human subject, it challenges the very foundation of individual autonomy as an entity in precise control of one's destiny. It also blurs the distinction between the subject and object of law and regulatory power.

Indeed, challenges to the characterisation of subjectivity are long-standing. Over several decades such challenges have given rise to a reformulation of the (liberal) human subject that previously was regarded as clearly distinguishable from external objects. Building on this insight, the concept of biopower describes the emergence of varied mechanisms of power that cross this divide, and which are focused on sustaining life (individual bodies and populations). Such disciplining powers in spheres such as pandemic healthcare are to be distinguished from the conventional coercive methods of governance that exert agency primarily through the legal and political sphere of sovereign (government) power.[29] Thus, the mechanisms of biopower function in a discursive or constitutive manner to create blurred subjects of regulation. 'Law, in this relation, functions increasingly in a normalising capacity, while nonetheless retaining its connection to sovereignty.'[30] According to these views, the regulation of pandemic contagion is necessary as the very agency of the contagion challenges the discursive focus of modern societies on sustaining health and life. Thus, modern discourses of law and governance have less focus on punishment and are more attuned to a nation-state whose purposes are the promotion of life and health.[31] More generally, prominent postmodern scholars suggest that disciplining modalities, acting in concert with law, work to produce the moral, disciplined subject as the outcome of regulation.[32]

Even so, most legislation, such as public health and waste management laws, typically remain largely structured on the underlying premise that there IS a human subject and an external world which act upon each other, but each remains essentially distinct. By contrast, scholars adopting post-structuralism, query the fundamental idea of the stable and determinate system of bounded entities.[33]

[27] Davies, 'New Materialisms' (n 25) 375.

[28] Davies (n 25).

[29] Foucault's scholarship on the topic of the spaces in which disciplining powers are exercised is prolific: see, for example, M Foucault, *The History of Sexuality, Volume 1: An Introduction*, R Hurley (tr), (New York, Vintage Books, 1990); M Foucault, *Discipline and Punish: The Birth of the Prison*, A Sheridan (tr) (New York, Vintage Books, 1995). By analogy, the pandemic waste regulatory settings display many of the similar characteristics to those described in Foucault's historical studies of the emergence of disciplining powers over life in, for example, hospitals and prisons.

[30] T Mulqueen, 'Naturalising the Myth: Hart, Biopolitics, and the Body Corporate' (2017) 43 *Australian Feminist Law Journal* 251, 268.

[31] Mulqueen, 'Naturalising the Myth' (n 30) and, see for example, AJ Means, 'Foucault, Biopolitics, and the Critique of State Reason' (2022) 54 *Educational Philosophy and Theory* 1968.

[32] A Hunt, 'Modern Anxieties and Moral Regulation' in A Hunt (ed), *Governing Morals: A Social History of Moral Regulation* (Cambridge, Cambridge University Press, 2000) 213–20.

[33] H van Rijswijk and P Crofts, 'Introduction: Implicated Legal Subjects' (2018) 30 *Law & Literature* 1.

Through this lens, contagion unsettles any determinative construction of the subject-object. Rather, the dynamic tension between subject–waste object and the pandemic governance system itself produces an 'entity' to be regulated, such as the COVID-19 contagion. Thus, the pathological condition of contagion or infection in pandemic settings is discursively read against its opposition. It takes its meaning against the grain of life and productivity. Moreover, there are wider ramifications to the identification of contagion as having its own 'agency'. Such agency and co-dependence between the human and contagion radically alter the ontological boundaries of 'being in the lifeworld'.[34] In simple terms, we now all 'live with' COVID-19 contagion together with the regulations and waste management practices that are designed to control it.

Preserving Life and Jettisoning Waste

The emergent interdependencies of pandemic life have now become more apparent. In the early pandemic phases, though, the efforts of governments and public health professionals at confining contagion and managing contaminated waste during the COVID-19 pandemic signalled frantic efforts to normatively resurrect the material conditions of a free-standing, healthy subject. The regulations aimed at social distancing are one such example, while the prohibitions on discarding COVID-19 infected waste in public places and the required cleansing of public places by waste workers are another. Moreover, the implicit aims of many first-phase COVID-19 waste laws were to discipline healthy populations by creating clean spaces which were disassociated from those (people and spaces) which were marginalised as COVID-19 'infected'.[35] Many pandemic regulations that arose in hospital settings, such as the guidelines for waste disposal that required the separation and immediate incineration of waste materials contaminated by bodily fluids, operated under a similar rubric. In this manner, the identification, cleansing and removal of waste by regulations associated with the jettisoning of bodily infection became integral to the continuing process of seeking to disassociate the human subject from a non-human, transgressive contagious 'object'.

Ironically, the healthy subject and its extremis – the marginalised, confined COVID-19 contagious body – existed in the same regulatory space, a space that required, for example, COVID-19 patients to die in isolation from their families. Such regulation drew on the scientific system of knowledge that comprehends health and medicine and the associated techniques, practices and protocols as regulatory technologies that seek to 'preserve' life. Thus, the goal of much early pandemic waste law can be crystallised as seeking to put into effect the

[34] Davies (n 5) 64.

[35] For a parallel with HLA Hart's positivist law as normalising the autonomous individual, see, Mulqueen (n 30).

circumstances whereby regulations aligned to the attainment of a healthy individual could be easily instituted. An important precondition to pandemic waste regulations were the more general emergency powers declarations or declarations under public health emergency powers that created the regulatory 'space' for the waste laws. Such waste laws took effect due to the power relationships put into play by the government declarations of a pandemic status under law.

Integral to the inauguration of a pandemic status at a national level was the overarching declaration of a pandemic by the World Health Organisation (WHO) in early 2020.[36] The WHO recognises that emergencies may arise due to natural hazards (for example, biological, geophysical or hydrometeorological hazards) or human-induced hazards (for example, technological disasters, violence or social conflict, financial crises). 'Pandemics' form a particular type of emergency deriving from natural, biological hazards such as viruses or other pathogens.[37] A pandemic is 'an epidemic occurring worldwide, or over a very wide area, crossing international boundaries and usually affecting a large number of people'.[38] The WHO has played a pivotal role in disseminating the guidance, protocols and practices that constituted the regulatory technologies to combat COVID-19 contagion that found expression in many national laws and health protocols. To appreciate how the 'effect' of both pandemic contagion and its counterpoint of healthy life was produced, a brief overview of pertinent WHO instruments such as treaties and policies and associated international instruments is instructive.[39]

International Law and WHO Protocols

The WHO is the United Nations' organisation with global responsibility for the promotion of public health. It regularly issues guidances and directives on best-practice health techniques that include directives around best-practice waste management, especially in the health sector.[40] A large volume of guidances and technical briefs were issued during the COVID-19 pandemic to deal with

[36] On the role of the WHO and International regulation as binding upon consenting nation-states in pandemic settings, see S Breau and P Lolaksha Nagaveni, 'International Health Regulations and Compliance in Asia' in VV Ramraj (ed), *Covid-19 in Asia: Law and Policy Contexts* (Oxford, Oxford University Press, 2020) 192–93.

[37] See, for example, World Health Organization (WHO), *A Strategic Framework for Emergency Preparedness* (WHO 1 January 2017). Available at: www.who.int/publications/i/item/a-strategic-framework-for-emergency-preparedness.

[38] H Kelly, 'The Classical Definition of a Pandemic is not Elusive' (2011) 89 *Bulletin of the World Health Organization* 540.

[39] Ironically, global financial institutions were concerned about COVID-19 waste impacts. See, for example, Asian Development Bank, 'Managing Infectious Medical Waste during the COVID-19 Pandemic' (Asian Development Bank April 2020). Available at: www.adb.org/publications/managing-medical-waste-covid19.

[40] World Health Organization (WHO), *Safe Management of Wastes from Health-Care Activities* 2nd edn (WHO, 2014). Available at: www.euro.who.int/__data/assets/pdf_file/0012/268779/Safe-management-of-wastes-from-health-care-activities-Eng.pdf.

COVID-19 wastes.[41] Initial COVID-19 containment measures within many countries typically were instituted through the auspices of executive power (for example, regulations, orders, Decrees, Resolutions, policies or guidelines including health-related directives) under a declared state of emergency, public health emergency or existing legislation that allowed for such executive orders.[42] Often, the content of executive orders closely replicated the WHO's technical guidelines and protocols for infection controls and the handling, storage, transport and disposal of wastes.[43] International health experts, working in liaison with national health officers, formed an important conduit for the incorporation of international measures in the design of national COVID-19 legal and policy guidance. The development of specific COVID-19 waste legislation in countries was unusual. Typically, governments amended national laws rather than enacting new legislation.[44]

Rapid deployment of techniques for confining and reducing contagion, such as quarantines and lockdowns, as well as measures for safe handling of a wide variety of infected materials that had been developed internationally, were implemented relatively quickly within national settings. The adaptation of international health and waste paradigms and technical directives by national governments reflected the perceived need for immediate pandemic responses, given that the all-consuming pandemic emergency set in play the imperatives of limiting contagion.[45] In situations where there was limited pre-existing national legal and institutional infrastructure for health care and associated pandemic waste management, or where the legal and institutional structures were not effective, countries experienced substantial governance challenges.[46] The pandemic governance risks were assuaged as the pandemic proceeded with a more profound insistence by governments and health authorities on guidances, protocols and practices for limiting contagion and dealing with waste.

Clearly, there are discernible parallels between the pandemic waste responses and the disciplinary techniques of healthcare that exist within the interplay of

[41] World Health Organization (WHO) and United Nations Children's Fund (UNICEF), 'Interim Guidance: Water, Sanitation, Hygiene, and Waste Management for SARS-CoV-2, the Virus that Causes COVID-19' (WHO, 2020). Available at: www.who.int/publications/i/item/WHO-2019-nCoV-IPC-WASH-2020.4.

[42] See, for example, State of Health Emergency Law of 23 March 2020 (*Loi no. 2020-290*) (France); The World Bank, 'Environmental and Social Commitment Plan (ESCP) Kenya COVID-19 Health Emergency Response Project (P173820)' (World Bank, 23 March 2020). Available at: www.documents.worldbank.org/en/publication/documents-reports/documentdetail/885881624960934799/environmental-and-social-commitment-plan-escp-kenya-covid-19-health-emergency-response-project-p173820; Emerging State Environmental Technical Standard which establishes specifications for the management of sanitary waste and COVID-19 waste generated or handled in the State of Mexico (Official Gazette July 2020); Supreme Decree No 008-2020-SA Declaring a National Health Emergency (Peru).

[43] Ministerial Resolution No 099-2020-MINAM Recommendations for the management of solid waste during the Sanitary Emergency due to COVID-19 and the State of National Emergency (Peru).

[44] An exception was Papua New Guinea, see, *Emergency (General Provisions) (COVID 19) Act 2020* (PNG).

[45] See, for example, R Mondal and others, 'COVID 19 Pandemic and Biomedical Waste Management Practices in Healthcare System' (2022) 11 *Journal of Family Medicine and Primary Care* 439.

[46] The acute situation of Zambia where the government effectively failed to function for a period during the pandemic is instructive.

a complex set of the discursive and material practices and political controls of biopower.[47] Yet, a critical difference to the theories which give an emphasis to biopower as a form of discursive power[48] is what occurred in COVID-19 contexts. The structural responses to the COVID-19 pandemic relied closely on law and regulation in addition to more normative modalities – albeit the content of such regulation was typically heavily reliant on health and technical expertise. An expanded scope for legal/juridical modalities that seek to normalise behaviour was apparent in the experience of many nations which used extensive legal controls and executive powers when seeking to manage COVID-19 wastes. Alternatively, we might also consider how efforts to normalise pandemic-centric behaviours by nation-states in turn was shaped in part by the 'agency' of the COVID virus itself.

The efficacy of non-human agency in influencing human behaviours is now increasingly acknowledged. Recent scholarship also has explored the co-dependence of bodies and non-human species, as well as the relational, shared lifeworld that human and non-human entities occupy. Thus, humans, waste and COVID-19 contagion cross boundaries, given 'the boundary of a living thing is not just a meaningless limit, but is ontologically complex: permeable, relational, and given meanings by the self and by others'.[49] Ontological distinctions between plant and animal, and between life and non-life, increasingly are difficult to maintain. An analogy can be drawn between the boundary shifting that is occurring in the categorisation of human and plant life, and recognition of the ecological symbiosis of humans and plants, with the transmission of COVID-19 contagion and its symbiosis with the 'human'. Revised perspectives in the science of ecology and biology have explored how plants and organisms such as fungi and viruses co-exist in interdependent communities and create effects in their habitat, including the humans in that habitat. By extrapolation, such interdependencies challenge the normativity of the separation of contagion, dirt, waste and pollution as counterpoised against the presumed purity of human life. The turn to materiality, and the growing acceptance that material 'things' can be imbued with 'agency', provides a basis for re-examining the interconnected fates of humans and others, whilst still acknowledging the relevance of scientific and medical modalities of power over human life.

Pandemic Waste – A Disciplining Modality or a Socio-spatial Materiality?

New materialism in legal scholarship is diverse, but generally can be characterised as a focus on how space/time and place embeddedness shape the nature of

[47] See here the convergence of European political philosophies of Marxism, Foucault and Agamben around the normalisation of the biopolitical in modern societies, for discussion, see, for example, K Genel, 'The Question of Biopower: Foucault and Agamben' (2006) 18 *Rethinking Marxism* 43.
[48] M Foucault, *Power/Knowledge* (Brighton, Harvester Press, 1980) 93–102.
[49] Davies (n 5) 64.

subjectivity,[50] and how law, reciprocally, shapes 'social space'.[51] A greater focus on materiality undercuts the view that law and society are empirically distinct spheres. 'They are not. The law is a construct of human ingenuity; laws are material phenomena. Similarly, society is a fiction we sustain through hard work and mutual communication'.[52] Similarly, recent investigations of law's materiality explore how law is shaped by its embeddedness in co-relation with material substances. In a pandemic setting, such material substances can comprise the virus itself, the spaces and bodies it infects, as well as the contagious wastes – bodily human wastes such as blood and saliva, together with the infected materials and instruments that are deployed to contain infection, such as specialised healthcare waste storages and incinerators.[53] The acute material affectivity of such substances and technologies informs and shapes human behaviour alongside the directives found in pandemic laws and normative guidances about how to manage such 'wastes' within the social space of hospitals, healthcare facilities, hotel quarantine and even the residential homes of those persons who were in isolation.

The pandemic ushered in a raft of spatial control techniques central to governing through contagion. The intensification of practices aimed at cleansing these spaces,[54] together with the sheer volume of the laws and technical guidance giving precise directions around handling, storage and removal of contagious wastes[55] (and how to handle the proliferating non-infectious wastes such as plastic containers) highlighted careful attention to material bodily practices. The body and its material practices and rhythms in this manner were constrained and 'brought within the ambit of a model of privatised consumption … which prescribes certain bodily attitudes as acceptable or unacceptable while insisting on their non-ideological character'.[56]

Hence, the relationship between law and space in a pandemic is not confined to the function of law and regulation in dividing and bounding spaces of contagion and non-contagion. Instead, spatial technologies, in conjunction with pandemic modalities, shape 'life' (human and non-human) as it is experienced in pandemic settings. Law interacts with normative systems *and* material conditions to generate compliant subjects in spaces of contagion, arbitrating the struggles and conflicts which determine controls over space, together with the meanings attributed to

[50] For a discussion, see B Latour, *Reassembling the Social: An Introduction to Actor-Network-Theory* (Oxford, Oxford University Press 2005) 87–89.

[51] See S Keenan, *Subversive Property: Law and the Production of Spaces of Belonging* (Abingdon, Routledge, 2014) 27.

[52] S Silbey, 'After Legal Consciousness' (2005) 1 *Annual Review of Law and Social Sciences* 323, 327.

[53] M Tsukiji et al, *Waste Management during the COVID-19 Pandemic: From Response to Recovery* (United Nations Environment Programme 2020). Available at: wedocs.unep.org/bitstream/handle/20.500.11822/33416/WMC-19.pdf.

[54] See, for example, United Nations Children's Fund (UNICEF), 'COVID-19 Emergency Preparedness and Response: WASH and Infection Prevention and Control in Healthcare Facilities' (Guidance Note, UNICEF 23 March 2020). Available at: www.unicef.org/media/66386/file/WASH-COVID-19-infection-prevention-and-control-in-health-care-facilities-2020.pdf.

[55] K Kapoor et al.,'Strategy Guidance: Solid Waste Management Response to COVID-19' (*UN Habitat* May 2020). Available at: unhabitat.org/sites/default/files/2020/05/un-habitat_strategy_guidance_swm_reponse_to_covid19.pdf.

[56] Butler (n 1) 126.

spaces. Law and space are co-constitutive of contagion. Thus, COVID-19 waste is a spatially realised, material artefact of pandemic settings that governments came to regard as a crisis to be intensely regulated.

Pandemic Waste as Crisis

The United Nations Environment Programme at the height of the COVID-19 pandemic stated, '[a]dverse impacts on human and planetary health will come from many sources as the world deals with COVID-19'.[57] Problematic waste trends were identified as a spike in hazardous waste, including personal protective equipment, electronics and pharmaceuticals, as well as increased quantities of healthcare and other infectious wastes. In addition, the COVID-19 pandemic disrupted waste management chains and undermined environmental protection standards.[58] Disruptions in waste management logistics within countries, in turn, interrupted transboundary movements of waste, placing further pressure on in-country capacity to manage contaminated and hazardous waste. Visions of contaminated hospital waste in overflowing landfills and the delays in burying those people who died from COVID-19 became commonplace pandemic news items.

International environmental law, while comprising a number of regimes around pollution controls and measures to control transboundary harm,[59] appeared only tangentially relevant as it typically operates beyond the embedded materiality of such wastes. Moreover, the central organising paradigm of sustainable waste management – the circular economy – appeared in some ways to be subsumed by the sheer volumes and intense human health risks of pandemic waste. The circular economy ideal is widely promulgated within integrated waste management legislative programs across the world.[60] The circular economy regime seeks to replace the 'end-of-life' waste disposal concept with a process that is aimed at eliminating or minimising waste, and, where that is not possible, to adopting measures for the cyclic reusing, recycling and recovering of 'waste' materials in the production, distribution and consumption phases of the industrial and commercial sectors.[61] Applying a circular economy model to pandemic wastes at one level may seem odd, where for example minimising infectious wastes seems counterintuitive (for example, wastes are generated due to treatments), and recycling COVID-19

[57] United Nations Environment Programme, 'Working with the Environment to Protect People: COVID-19 Response' (Report, UNEP 14 May 2020) 2. Available at: wedocs.unep.org/bitstream/handle/20.500.11822/32218/UNEP_COVID.pdf?sequence=1&isAllowed=y.

[58] See generally, N Sommer and R Pointon, 'Emergency Powers and Economic Recovery: A Review of Planning and Environment Law Reforms in Response to COVID-19' (2020) 35 *Australian Environment Review* 66, 70.

[59] See, for example, The Basel Convention on Prevention of Transboundary Movements of Hazardous Wastes and their Disposal [1992] UNTS 57/509.

[60] Negrete-Cardoso et al (n 23).

[61] For a review of the model, see DA Kumar and others, 'COVID-19 Pandemic and Health Care Solid Waste Management Strategy – A Mini-Review' (2021) 778 *Science of the Total Environment* 146220.

waste appears somewhat bizarre. Yet the adoption of a circular economy model, which was developed in Europe to deal with the excessive consumption of material goods by seeking to recycle them back into productive use, operated in pandemic settings to render even contagious waste open to a return to the spaces of productivity. The alignment of a circular economy with pandemic waste in this manner points to both the circular economy model and its material manifestation in waste being enmeshed in the discursive spaces of postmodern global capitalism. Given this orientation to global capitalist production, the model is problematic for the pandemic situations that arose in countries which fell out of the net of capitalist logistic spheres – as occurred in developing nations struggling with the socio-economic burden of the pandemic. These nations could not afford the capital-intensive forms of waste management implicit to a circular economy paradigm. In these nations, waste simply could not be intensively managed and recycled. Where nations were struggling to supply basic pandemic infection controls such as gloves and masks, investment in the technical capacity to convert pandemic wastes to some form of productive reuse simply was not available.

The pandemic waste disruptions to the circular economy paradigms that ordered waste management regimes in the governing legislation of many nations occurred against the backdrop of structural changes in transboundary waste management and global recycling systems. Countries such as China were no longer prepared to accept hazardous and non-hazardous waste exported from 'developed' countries.[62] Global waste management has long reflected North/South divisions in terms of which nations are able to effectively enjoy environmental protections against excessive waste and pollution. Many countries in the Global South have limited capacity to achieve sustainable waste management outcomes.[63] These inequalities in resources and available expertise to put in place effective waste management within countries were exacerbated in the pandemic – further entrenching post-colonial economic patterns that emerged after the mid-twentieth century spate of decolonisation. Such constraints greatly hindered effective implementation of the international directives and guidance on COVID-19 wastes in these countries.

Pandemic Waste, Essential Workers and Dysconnectedness

Nonetheless, an impending pandemic waste crisis in 2020 saw a flurry of activity around national laws and regulations directed towards waste management,

[62] For a representative response in a country which did export much waste to China see, *Recycling and Waste Reduction Act 2020* (Australia, 2021) ch 2. Available at: www.faolex.fao.org/docs/pdf/aus213263.pdf.

[63] The limited progress of many nations in respect of Sustainable Development Goal 11 Waste is Instructive; see also D Cibrario, 'SDG 11: To Ensure Sustainable Waste Services, We Must Value Waste Workers and Make sure They are in Decent Jobs' (Public Services International). Available at: www.2030spotlight.org/en/book/1730/chapter/sdg-11-ensure-sustainable-waste-services-we-must-value-waste-workers-and-make.

circular economies and the regulation of waste workers. While pandemic waste in its materiality has 'agency', such materiality iterates with human norms and practices that govern the key function of waste workers in removing contagious wastes to create clean and productive spaces – for other people. There was a heightened risk that these workers, whose labour was 'legally' co-opted under various statutes and declarations in order to remove contagious waste from societies, were likely to die at work.[64]

In the early phase of the COVID-19 pandemic, in the regulatory measures instituted under national executive powers, typically, waste collection was designated as an 'essential service'.[65] In many countries, this regulatory strategy was aimed at ensuring waste collection services continued despite lockdowns and labour shortages. As 'COVID-19 pandemic-related restrictions, including full or partial lockdowns, … impacted an estimated five billion people globally',[66] it was necessary to secure continuity in waste service provision in order to prevent contagion risks – especially from healthcare wastes.[67] Many, but not all, countries developed stipulations for the occupational health and safety conditions for essential waste workers in relevant sectors, who were to be provided with appropriate personal protective equipment (PPE).[68] Some nations expanded occupational health and safety regulation to cover waste collection practices, and to governing conditions within work spaces (for example, ventilation requirements).[69]

While such conditions became normalised in conventional labour and industry pandemic settings, significant regulatory coverage gaps arose where 'essential service' designations did not include all waste workers. Such gaps occurred in countries with a large informal waste sector and/or workers in quasi-formal waste recycling services, or in countries without adequate access to PPE supplies or occupational training for workers. Such workers, while deemed necessary to undertake regulated activities of separating contagion from the wider society, often did not themselves gain legal protections for such activities. Waste workers excluded from legal protections, such as those working in casual employment or in the informal waste picking sector, thus occupied the status of 'naked life'. Whyte translates this

[64] For discussion of capitalist labour relations and work-related deaths, see D Whyte, 'Naked Labour: Putting Agamben to Work' (2009) 31 *Australian Feminist Law Journal* 57.

[65] European Commission, '*Waste Management in the Context of the Coronavirus Crisis*' *(Guidelines)* COM(14April2020).projects2014-2020.interregeurope.eu/smartwaste/news/news-article/8320/waste-management-in-the-context-of-covid-19-crisis/.

[66] C Hartmann, C Hegel and O Boampong, 'The Forgotten Essential Workers in the Circular Economy? Waste Picker Precarity and Resilience amidst the COVID-19 Pandemic' (2022) *Local Environment* 1.

[67] See, for example, Ministry of Ecology and Environment of the People's Republic of China, 'Management and Technical Guidelines for Emergency Disposal of Medical Waste Infected by the Novel Coronavirus Pneumonia Epidemic (Trial)' (29 January 2020).

[68] For Canada, there were national and provincial government regulations. See, for example, Canada Labour Code, RSC 1985, cL-2; Guidance on Essential Services and Functions in Canada During the COVID-19 Pandemic (ongoing); *Occupational Health and Safety Act, SA 2020, cO-2.2* (Canada).

[69] See, for example, the 2022 updates to the Occupational Health and Safety Act, SA 2020, cO-2.2 (Canada).

status of naked life, in occupational contexts defined by an absence of (protective) law, as 'naked labour'. These forms of labour are distinguished by the 'coercive preconditions and regulatory techniques upon which the labour process is based'.[70] Waste workers in the Global South are particularly exposed to being exploited in this manner. The lack of formal employment designations in the waste zones of the Global South in the pandemic greatly increased the vulnerability of informal workers.[71]

The particular vulnerability of informal waste workers highlights a more fundamental disjunction facing waste workers in the pandemic. Waste workers must interact with contagious pandemic wastes to prevent them from infecting others, so these workers are at once 'connected' to waste, but further dysconnected and marginalised by this very connection from the society that is protected. Moreover, the precarious existence of a large, informal labour force in the waste sector operating alongside or partially integrated with formalised labour arrangements has been exacerbated by neoliberal privatisation in the waste industry sector,[72] and by the infiltration of organised criminal activities. At the same time, public provision of waste services has contracted in scope in many countries, with private companies only partially filling that gap.[73] The repercussion has been the emergence of a less-tightly regulated sector and a weakening of worker rights.[74]

There are an estimated 15–20 million informal waste pickers worldwide – many of whom are women and children.[75] The power dynamics of the regulatory gap are acute, and the lack of regulation reinforces structural gender inequalities. Large groups of informal waste workers exist in Latin America, African countries, including South Africa, Ghana and Kenya, as well as India. In some countries, such as India, catch-up regulation requiring provision of PPE to these groups did occur. Mostly, this happened later in the COVID-19 pandemic as the gaps in the coverage of these vulnerable workers were revealed.[76] South Africa instituted minimum standards for waste picker protections.[77] Yet, the 'pejorative view of waste pickers and the continued belief that waste picking is a mere passing occurrence [that is] held by municipalities only serves to undermine efforts to ensure adequate legal protection for them'.[78] The exclusion of such worker protections is 'a social justice

[70] Whyte (n 64) 57.

[71] Hartmann, Hegel and Boampong (n 66) 2.

[72] A Ossom, 'Setting the Standard for Waste Pickers' Rights: The Impact of Constitutional Court Cases in Colombia' (2022) 2 *The Global Labour Rights Reporter* 21, 22.

[73] Hartmann, Hegel and Boampong (n 66) 13.

[74] Hartmann, Hegel and Boampong (n 66) 13, but see Ossom (n 72).

[75] L Fernandez, 'Who Really Cares About Our Earth? Neglecting Waste Pickers' Contributions, Promoting Huge Business Profits' (*Women in Informal Employment: Globalizing and Organizing (WIEGO)*, 2017). Available at: www.wiego.org/blog/who-really-cares-about-our-earth-neglecting-waste-pickers%E2%80%99-contributions-promoting-huge-business.

[76] See, for example, I Occupational Safety, Health and Working Conditions Code, no 37 of 2020 (India) which belatedly covered informal waste pickers.

[77] National Environmental Management: Waste Act 59 of 2008 (South Africa).

[78] L Koen and ES Fourie, 'Waste Pickers and the Law: Contradictory and Fragmented Regulation in Three Metropolitan Municipalities' (2022) *Development Southern Africa*.

issue that highlights an important weakness of the circular economy as it currently operates … waste pickers perform an essential service and yet are not designated "essential workers"'.[79]

Ironically, stronger urbanisation and public health initiatives in cities have centralised waste management operations in these spaces over time, progressively excluding less formalised waste operations and stigmatising informal waste workers.[80] Even so, centralised waste management services were under extreme pressure in the COVID-19 pandemic in most countries. Various civil sector reports have identified that many of the technical guidances and protective measures around contagious wastes promulgated by the WHO and national governments were, for the most part, only effectively implemented in the most well-resourced countries with expansive regulatory networks.[81] Thus, the objectives of the international WHO regime that promoted tightly-controlled health modalities for governing wastes and regulating waste workers simply could not be achieved in many countries.[82] Despite precise instructions issuing from myriad international organisations on how to handle contaminated wastes, how to separate contaminated wastes from other wastes, how to store them, transport and dispose of them and, for some wastes, how to recycle them, the objectives of governing contagion through waste regulation, healthcare technologies and circular economy principles often could not be achieved.[83] Further, the model of waste management that underpinned international guidances contained some questionable assumptions (for example, the uniform availability of high intensity incineration facilities for contagious waste disposal) that simply did not reflect the underfunded reality of the healthcare and waste systems in many countries. In this manner, the disciplinary modalities of health and containment of infection were confounded by the overwhelming volumes of waste that overflowed the normative division of safe and dangerous social spaces.

The gap between the waste modality proposed by law and regulation and the pervasive materiality of the COVID-19 virus was further compounded by a failure to appreciate the critical role of waste workers. This situation, as expected, especially affected waste pickers in economies of the Global South, and in the casual worker sector in other economies. Waste pickers remain a vital but often

[79] Koen and ES Fourie, 'Waste Pickers and the Law' (n 78).

[80] Hartmann, Hegel and Boampong (n 66) 3.

[81] For an example, see the expansive scope of EU law and regulation – and the resources and expertise required to institute such measures, Directive 2008/98/EC of the European Parliament and of the Council of 19 November 2008 on waste and repealing certain directives [2008] OJ L312/3 (Waste Framework Directive); Council Directive 1999/31/EC of 26 April 1999 on the landfill of waste [1999] OJ L182/1 (Landfill Directive); Commission, 'Waste management in the context of the coronavirus crisis' (n 68); Commission, 'Shipments of Waste in the EU in the Context of the Coronavirus Crisis' (Information Document) COM (30 March 2020); European Commission, 'Gender Equality' (European Commission), ec.europa.eu/info/policies/justice-and-fundamental-rights/gender-equality_en.

[82] M Tsukiji et al (n 53).

[83] C Márquez et al, 'Inclusion of Waste Pickers into Municipal Waste Management Systems: A Comparison Between Colombia and Brazil' (2021) 30 *Journal of Environment & Development* 395, 417.

unrecognised part of the 'circular economy' in low- and middle-income countries.[84] Waste pickers make a significant contribution to achieving the material conversion of waste to a productive economic resource, even under a strained neoliberal, circular economy paradigm. Despite such contribution to the global capitalist economy, informal waste workers were 'forgotten' or perhaps judged to be expendable when the regulatory frameworks setting out the requirements for dealing with occupational risks around COVID-19 were developed in many countries.[85] The regulatory aporia in the treatment of informal waste workers which exposed them to contagion emphasises the continuing transgressive threat of pandemic contagion as a non-human 'species' that is invested with agency. That agency, expressed via its presence and co-dependency on humans, as well as its particular materiality, shapes the contours of socio-legal spaces. In pandemic socio-legal spaces, the regulation of pandemic wastes functions as a locus to draw together law and regulation, COVID-19 contagion and the disparate experiences of waste workers and those safeguarded by them. It did so by instituting a regulatory compulsion toward adherence to disciplinary practices and protocols that were aligned with COVID-19 governance.

Conclusion

In terms of a governing power over life, as a final thought, let us return to the idea that, 'governing through contagion imbues human subjects, their non-human co-species, and technologies with agency, each having the capacity to transform their interconnected fates'. Such webs of interconnection construct a space-time pandemic 'bubble' through which different qualities and elements are constantly being associated into unities.[86] The different bubble elements comprise, inter alia, human subjects, non-human viral co-species, disciplining health and legal technologies and pandemic wastes that intersect in myriad ways, despite regulatory best efforts to keep them separate. Regulation, rather than forming the singular boundary between human and non-human 'life', is imbricated in defining the shifting boundaries of the bubble itself, and thereby the interconnected fates of each element. Accordingly, the space of human beings is not the only 'reality'[87] into which other elements are discursively inserted. Nonetheless, that 'reality' remains the predominant understanding of how law 'works on regulatory 'objects' to produce its effects. International 'soft' law and the regulatory technologies of health and waste management issued by the WHO and similar organisations are inserted into national 'pandemic bubbles' to construct an archaeology of pandemic knowledges promoting techniques for the disciplining of compliant, pandemic-aware

[84] Márquez et al., 'Inclusion of Waste Pickers' (n 83).
[85] Hartmann, Hegel and Boampong (n 66).
[86] For discussion see Davies (n 5) 65.
[87] Davies (n 5) 65.

moral subjects. Concurrently, COVID-19 contagion and pandemic wastes can accumulate indiscriminately, revealing the ad hoc character of the implementation of pandemic waste regulation within national settings. Further, while governing through contagion clearly imbues human subjects with agency, the pandemic modalities of law and regulation ascribe varying degrees of agency to human subjects at risk of pandemic contagion. That 'effect' of power is clearly influenced by the materiality and variable 'agency' of the subjects inhabiting the socio-legal spaces in which such modalities are deployed. The disjunction between those secured against contagion and those who are exposed reveals, perhaps, not so much a universalised, interconnected fate of populations that is produced as an effect of the pandemic contagion discourse, but rather a more inequitably distributed 'fate' (life or death/infected or not).

4

Instruction and Information, Images and Icons

*Governing Through Contagion, Social Regulation and Public Health**

SHARYN ROACH ANLEU AND GEORGE SARANTOULIAS

Introduction

The novel coronavirus (COVID-19)[1] pandemic has been described as a 'natural experiment',[2] perhaps reminiscent of ethnomethodology's breaching experiments that disrupt and expose shared background assumptions and expectations.[3] Since March 2020, the pandemic has made visible much taken-for-granted ordinary social interaction usually hidden by the busyness of daily activities and relationships.[4] Given the medico-scientific understandings of the virus transmission, its control is inextricably linked with control of individuals and their social interaction

* This work was supported by Flinders University CHASS (College of Humanities, Arts and Social Sciences) Research Themes Funding (Round 2) 2021. We deeply thank Jordan Tutton for excellent and detailed research assistance. We appreciate the comments and discussion at the workshop, *Governing through Contagion: Perspectives Across Time and Space*, National University of Singapore, 19–21 April 2022, and thank the organisers of that event.

[1] The first case of novel coronavirus (SARS-CoV-2), known as COVID-19, in Australia was confirmed in the state of Victoria on 25 January 2020. The patient had arrived from China six days earlier. On 11 March 2020, the World Health Organization (WHO) declared the outbreak of COVID-19 a pandemic. As of 21 July 2022, 9,019,965 cases of COVID-19 (including Delta and Omicron variants) have been recorded in Australia, including 11,032 deaths: Australian Government, 'Coronavirus (COVID-19) Case Numbers and Statistics'. Available at: www.health.gov.au/health-alerts/covid-19/case-numbers-and-statistics.

[2] JC Alexander and P Smith, 'COVID-19 and Symbolic Action: Global Pandemic as Code, Narrative, and Cultural Performance' (2020) 8 *American Journal of Cultural Sociology* 263.

[3] H Garfinkel, *Studies in Ethnomethodology* (New York, Free Press, 1984); S Stanley and others, 'Making Something out of Nothing: Breaching Everyday Life by Standing Still in a Public Place' (2020) 68 *The Sociological Review* 1250.

[4] R Connell, 'COVID-19/Sociology' (2020) 56 *Journal of Sociology* 745; A Young, 'The Limits of the City: Atmospheres of Lockdown' (2021) 61 *British Journal of Criminology* 985; A Young, 'Locked-down City' (2021) 17 *Crime, Media, Culture* 21.

and strategies that rely on 'prevention, containment, enforcement, and education'.[5] To manage and contain the spread of the virus and its variants, many governments implemented public health programmes entreating people to maintain social/physical distance, wear face masks, wash hands frequently while limiting physical mobility and mandating work and school from home. These responses generated a slew of new norms and rendered deviant/unacceptable behaviour that was previously normal, ordinary and anticipated: shaking hands, hugging, jostling in crowds, standing close in a queue.

A striking characteristic of the pandemic is the reliance on visual imagery to convey information, which can also communicate emotions, such as fear, concern and anxiety. Images of the virus (created by medical illustrators) as a small crimson red ball with multiple uniform tentacles with suction cups hurtling through time and space, of graphs and bar charts showing case numbers and vaccination rates, maps illustrating hotspots, photographs of hospitals and pictures of empty streetscapes serve 'to grasp the "essence", the "deep meaning" of the crisis through a particular scene or moment'.[6] These images are also implicated in governing by contagion.[7]

Responses to the pandemic generated new social norms regulating everyday, ordinary behaviour, the self, interaction and required social distancing.[8] By activating emergency powers,[9] governments implemented social control measures restricting individual mobility with bans on international travel, prohibiting movement across state borders, issuing 'lock down' or 'stay at home' orders and quarantine requirements and slowed interaction by limiting where people can go, the spaces they can occupy, where they can stand or sit and proscribing a range of activities and amenities.[10] The emergency responses depended on advice from

[5] LJ Chua and JJG Lee, 'Governing through Contagion' in Victor V Ramraj (ed), *Covid-19 in Asia: Law and Policy Contexts* (Oxford, Oxford University Press, 2021) 115.

[6] J Sonnevend, 'A Virus as an Icon: The 2020 Pandemic in Images' (2020) 8 *American Journal of Cultural Sociology* 451, 460. See also Young, 'The Limits of the City' (n 4); Young, 'Locked-down City' (n 4).

[7] These images are also examples of the non-human and non-living components of governing through contagion. See JJG Lee and L Chua, 45(3) 'Smallpox Vaccination and the Limits of Governing through Contagion in the Straits Settlements, 1868–1926' (2023) *Law & Policy* 331–52.

[8] At the outset governments referred to social distancing, a misnomer as the imperative is to remain physically apart and separate from other individuals to reduce contagion.

[9] Emergency powers are special powers given to the executive in circumstances of dire threat to a community often associated with war, terrorism or natural disaster. In Australia, there are no formal powers for the Commonwealth government to declare a state of national emergency, rather each state and territory has legislation setting out the conditions for these laws to be activated. See, for example, The *Emergency Management Act 2004* (SA) and the *COVID-19 Emergency Response Act 2020* (SA). Most of the restrictions, internal border closures and public health policy messaging were state/territory based (not Commonwealth) and thus varied among the Australian states and territories, sometimes causing confusion and frustration for the national government. More generally, see CA Heimer and C Davis, 'Good Law to Fight Bad Bugs: Legal Responses to Epidemics' (2022) 18 *Annual Review of Law and Social Science* 1.

[10] Chua and Lee 'Governing through Contagion' (n 5); M De Visser and P Straughan, 'Singapore: Technocracy and Transition' in VV Ramraj (ed), *Covid-19 in Asia* (Oxford, Oxford University Press, 2021); M Tedeschi, 'The Body and the Law across Borders during the COVID-19 Pandemic' (2020) 10 *Dialogues in Human Geography* 178.

public health and medical experts, medical-scientific evidence, and data modelling to directly inform new regulations, often displacing the role of parliament and its law-making power.[11] The prevailing biomedical view that the primary form of spreading COVID-19 is via aerosols shifted the public health focus to ventilation and masking, while the droplet-spread theory, earlier espoused, led to emphases on handwashing, frequent cleaning of surfaces[12] and the widespread use of the term 'deep cleaning' and the availability of hand sanitizer. Social distancing became 'a central tenet' of many governments' strategies to lower the risk of infection by reducing contact with infectious individuals. 'Social distancing is now becoming a new norm and part of everyday life.'[13] Another widely implemented measure to reduce the spread of COVID-19 is the use of face masks and the mandatory use of Personal Protective Equipment (PPE) in health and care settings.[14]

Chua and Lee term these strategies of control as 'governing through contagion'[15] which regulates subjects' behaviour, activities and actions, to effect certain goals or purposes, most explicitly to curtail the spread of disease. This chapter elaborates on two aspects of governing through contagion: (1) the proliferation of new social norms that deviantise previously non-problematic, even expected behaviour; and (2) the mechanisms for the communication of these new norms – as information and instructions – often in the form of simple images and icons in posters and signs that are widespread in public settings. It investigates the form and content of various signs, instructions and notices for their normative underpinnings, their advice and directives which attempt to modify and regulate diverse activities. We suggest that these signs are one thread in the complex fabric of 'governing through contagion' embedded in ordinary, everyday settings. We discuss several photographs of posters/signs located in publicly accessible places across Adelaide (South Australia) and Melbourne (Victoria) and their surrounding suburbs. These signs and posters anticipate that individuals will (be able *and* motivated to) interpret instructions correctly and have the capacity to align their behaviour with the directives and advice in a manner that enables social interaction in ordinary activities to continue with minimal disruption. The potential for disruption will vary. Ye notes that in a city such as Singapore 'where the lack of space and proximity has been a way of life, this enforcement of social distancing between people is a big shift in civic behaviour'.[16] Signs and posters conveying a raft of new norms are widespread

[11] S Moulds, 'Scrutinising COVID-19 Laws: An Early Glimpse into the Scrutiny Work of Federal Parliamentary Committees' (2020) 45 *Alternative Law Journal* 180.

[12] T Greenhalgh, M Ozbilgin and D Contandriopoulos, 'Orthodoxy, *Illusio*, and Playing the Scientific Game: A Bourdieusian Analysis of Infection Control Science in the COVID-19 Pandemic' (2021) *Wellcome Open Research* 6:126, doi: 10.12688/wellcomeopenres.16855.3.

[13] B Nerlich and R Jaspal, 'Social Representations of "Social Distancing" in Response to COVID-19 in the UK Media' (2021) 69 *Current Sociology* 566–567.

[14] M Thiel et al, 'COVID Lessons from the Global South – Face Masks Invading Tourist Beaches and Recommendations for the Outdoor Seasons' (2021) 786 *Science of The Total Environment* 147486, doi: 10.1016/j.scitotenv.2021.147486.

[15] Chua and Lee (n 5) 115; Lee and Chua (n 7).

[16] J Ye, 'Ordering Diversity: Co-Producing the Pandemic and the Migrant in Singapore during COVID-19' (2021) 53 *Antipode* 1895, 1905.

across cityscapes and beyond. They constitute visible components of the 'governing through contagion' inventory and rely on legal and medical-scientific authority as legitimacy, as well as appeals to the common good and collective wellbeing. We focus on the signs and instructions regarding mask wearing.

The following section briefly examines the concept of social control in socio-legal scholarship, and then discusses the mechanisms conveying new social norms that were part of the COVID-19 pandemic public health restrictions. The use of signs and posters mandating mask wearing were embedded in the interaction order – ordinary, everyday social life – and played a role in shaping the *social imaginaries*, that is, shared beliefs, expectations, values and practices that influence collective perceptions of reality. Next, the chapter addresses the research design and method that relied on publicly accessible signs and posters, as photographed by the two authors, which represents the data for discussion. The chapter then outlines the eight images chosen to identify and unravel the new social expectations and the ways that information and governance become intertwined. A key conclusion relates to the requirements – conditions and resources – that underpin governing through contagion.

Social Control and the COVID-19 Pandemic

There are multiple dimensions of social control in the context of COVID-19 pandemic restrictions. Regulations take many forms and are embedded in daily life, in news reports, social media, billboards, posters on doorways in public spaces, workplaces, social clubs and other organisations. While presented as information and data, these visual displays have regulatory force that can potentially result in emotions of anxiety, fear, frustration or anger when others do not comply with instructions. They can also result in changed behaviour and desires, both in the present and the future, which align with government requirements.

Although bearing the insignia of legal authority, some signs try to convey messages of civic responsibility or appeal to a sense of community. Taylor's concept of *social imaginaries* refers to 'the ways people imagine their social existence, how they fit together with others, how things go on between them and their fellows, the expectations that are normally met, and the deeper normative notions and images that underlie these expectations'.[17] Social imaginaries should be thought of as 'backgrounds', which allow social life to operate, rather than as theories or ideologies.[18] They are the implicit 'common understanding that makes possible common practices and a widely shared sense of legitimacy'[19] and should not be thought of as static entities or immobile structures separate from history.[20]

[17] C Taylor, *Modern Social Imaginaries* (Durham, NC, Duke University Press, 2004) 23.
[18] Taylor, *Modern Social Imaginaries* (n 17) 23–6.
[19] Taylor (n 17) 23.
[20] Taylor, 'Modern Social Imaginaries' (2002) 14 *Public Culture* 91, 106.

Rather, social imaginaries are 'schematised in the dense sphere of common practice' and transformed through a dialectic process.[21] The social imaginary as theoretical framework helps us understand 'normatively charged collective imaginaries as logically prior to the construction of normative principles'.[22]

This idea of 'backgrounds' resonates with Goffman's concept of the interaction order,[23] the taken-for-granted, unspoken, unconscious norms and understandings of social life that become visible when disrupted, often requiring renegotiation, repair or 'damage control'. Goffman observes that 'each participant enters a social situation carrying an already established biography of prior dealings with the other participants – or at least with participants of their kind; and enters also with a vast array of cultural assumptions presumed to be shared'.[24] The interaction order depends on 'shared cognitive presuppositions, if not normative ones, and self-sustained restraints'.[25] As a locus of intervention – the interaction order – has two dimensions – (i) the individual body – and things for individuals to do or desist from doing – and (ii) interaction with others. Masks are not just explicitly about individuals' hygiene but collective responsibility and the slowing of transmission. Precisely, the COVID-19 pandemic and the associated norms and rules disrupted shared understandings of bodily co-presence and face-to-face interaction.

This mode of governance anticipates subjects willing to stem contagion, if necessary, by compromising their own self-interest to advance collective wellbeing because they (come to) believe that doing so is the only right and moral stance for everyone. It is also essential for the orderliness of the interaction order. Being the socially responsible subject requires self-surveillance and self-discipline. The new demands or requests, made in governing through contagion, are similar in form to other contemporary modes of governance; they are familiar and often unnoticeable.[26]

The pandemic also demonstrated an uneasy relationship among political leaders, authority and governance. There have been significant challenges to governments and their leaders to create and maintain authority in this time of crisis: '*symbolic* power does not necessarily follow from legal-rational [constitutional] authority'.[27] For example, in South Australia, the visible leaders of the efforts to contain the pandemic were the Public Health Officer and the State Coordinator (commissioner of police), neither of whom are elected officials. In some jurisdictions tension emerged between the political/electoral authority of government leaders and the authority of public health officials and their recommendations.

[21] Taylor, 'Modern Social Imaginaries' (n 20) 106.

[22] M Steele, 'Social Imaginaries and the Theory of the Normative Utterance' (2017) 48 *Philosophy and Social Criticism* 1045, 1046.

[23] E Goffman, 'The Interaction Order' (1983) 48 *American Sociological Review* 1.

[24] Goffman, 'The Interaction Order' (n 23) 4.

[25] Goffman (n 23) 5.

[26] K Cardell, 'From Puritans to Fitbit: Self-Improvement, Self-Tracking, and How to Keep a Diary' in B Ben-Amos and D Ben-Amos (eds), *The Diary: The Epic of Everyday Life* (Bloomington, Indiana University Press, 2020).

[27] Alexander and Smith (n 2) 264 (emphasis in original).

(See Morgan for analysis of UK leaders' need for extra-rational power[28] and Chan for discussion of trust/distrust of government in Hong Kong during the pandemic.[29])

Governing Through Contagion and Communicating New Social Norms

Governance relies on information, instructions and directives to be communicated to subjects, or people, often accomplished through signs – for example, traffic signs, warnings, entry and exit notices, the circle with a diagonal slash to convey prohibition – as taken for granted, publicly visible forms of regulation which 'mark, scar, and deface public spaces'.[30] Official graffiti is a distinctive regulatory form and 'consists of a great profusion of regulatory signs, notices, symbols, and instructions that figure in everyday life … [and] power is exercised in daily routines and is manifested in everyday consciousness'.[31] Official graffiti invokes authority and legitimacy from multiple sources – governmental, legal, moral, medical – and entails 'reduction of rule pronouncement to a lexicon of familiar and interchangeable icons'.[32] 'Official graffiti constructs self-regulating behavior that invokes judgments about personal character and integrity.'[33] 'The everyday reality of official graffiti only works effectively to the extent that its objects routinely engage in self-governance.'[34]

Central to effective governing through contagion is the interaction order, the workings of which 'can easily be viewed as the consequences of systems of enabling conventions, in the sense of ground rules for a game, the provision of a traffic code or the rule of syntax of a language'.[35] New norms conveyed in signs and posters disrupt existing shared 'ground rules' replacing them with different (sometimes opposite) expectations and an array of injunctions, warnings and directions.

[28] M Morgan, 'Why Meaning-Making Matters: The Case of the UK Government's COVID-19 Response' (2020) 8 *American Journal of Cultural Sociology* 270.

[29] RKH Chan, 'Tackling COVID-19 Risk in Hong Kong: Examining Distrust, Compliance and Risk Management' (2021) 69 *Current Sociology* 547.

[30] J Hermer and A Hunt, 'Official Graffiti of the Everyday' (1996) 30 *Law & Society Review* 455, 456.

[31] Hermer and Hunt (n 30) 457, 459.

[32] Hermer and Hunt (n 30) 464.

[33] Hermer and Hunt (n 30) 473.

[34] Hermer and Hunt (n 30) 474–75. The extent to which the signs and norms communicated affect social interaction and individual behaviour is an empirical question. Questions about the effectiveness of such signage are beyond the scope of this chapter. Hermer and Hunt caution of the 'need to remind ourselves of just how trivial, petty, intrusive, and unsuccessful regulation so often is', 457. Nonetheless, Australian research suggests that perceived risk of legal enforcement and trust in authorities did not predict compliance with lockdown requirements, rather normative concerns and collective duty were more powerful determinants of lockdown decisions (K Murphy, H Williamson, E Sargeant and M McCarthy 'Why People Comply with COVID-19 Social Distancing Restrictions: Self-interest or Duty' (2020) 53 *Australian & New Zealand Journal of Criminology* 477).

[35] Goffman (n 23) 5.

Most poignantly, the face mask disrupts the interaction order which relies on facework as sources of vital information and emotion management. '[F]orms of face-to-face life are worn smooth by constant repetition on the part of participants who are heterogeneous in many ways and yet must quickly reach a working understanding.'[36] Reaching such a 'working understanding' relies significantly on face-to-face interaction – and facework – including smiles, frowns, and other facial expressions – to decipher appropriate behaviour and responses.[37]

This loops back to Chua and Lee's point that governing through contagion disrupts social connectedness and interaction via quarantine mandates, stay at home orders, work/school from home requirements, physical distancing and covering the face, or part of it: 'Masks and other protective gear obstruct visual, aural, olfactory, tactile, and linguistic intimacy'.[38] The coronavirus epidemic 'has restricted ordinary F2F interaction by mandating masks and social distancing, weakening the cues ordinarily used interaction rituals'.[39] 'Looking at the other person's facial expressions, bodily gestures, as well as hearing their tone of voice and its loudness or softness, communicates what specific emotions are being felt', in turn affecting social interaction and social life.[40] When announcing in parliament on 21 February 2022 the imminent reduction of mask wearing mandates, the then Premier of Queensland, Annastacia Palaszczuk stated: 'Mr Speaker smiles are back. We can put our masks away.' She also tweeted what some described as a 'cringeworthy video' in slow motion where she removed her mask to the tune of Frank Sinatra's song *When You're Smiling*.[41]

These new norms often conveyed through signs and instructions are now familiar across many social settings. In the first round of public health messaging the emphasis was on handwashing, frequent cleaning and maintaining social/physical distance among people in public settings: shops, markets, venues and public transport.[42] A second tranche of public health messaging provided instructions and requirements regarding mask wearing and checking in with QR (Quick Response) codes.

Mask wearing is not just explicitly about individual hygiene and protection but encourages, even mandates, collective responsibility to slow or restrict transmission of the virus and increase community health and safety. Indeed, the face

[36] Goffman (n 23) 9.

[37] E Goffman, 'On Face-Work' (1955) 18 *Psychiatry* 213; EA Heerey and TSE Gilder, 'The Subjective Value of a Smile Alters Social Behaviour' (2019) 14 *PLOS ONE* e0225284, doi: 10.1371/journal.pone.0225284.

[38] Chua and Lee (n 5) 127.

[39] R Collins, 'Social Distancing as a Critical Test of the Micro-Sociology of Solidarity' (2020) 8 *American Journal of Cultural Sociology* 477, 478.

[40] Collins, 'Social Distancing' (n 39) 482.

[41] S McPhee and F Barton, 'Annastacia Palaszczuk Is Roasted by Everyone for "Cringeworthy" Slow Motion Video Taking off Her Face Mask' (*Daily Mail Australia*, 3 February 2022). Available at: www.dailymail.co.uk/news/article-10540871/Annastacia-Palaszczuk-ROASTED-cringeworthy-slow-motion-video-taking-face-mask.html.

[42] S Roach Anleu and G Sarantoulias, 'Complex Data and Simple Instructions: Social Regulation during the Covid-19 Pandemic' (2023) 59 *Journal of Sociology* 733.

mask 'has become a significant object, positioned as one of the most important ways that people can protect themselves and others from infection with the novel coronavirus by acting as a barrier (however imperfect) between their breath and that of others'.[43] More than a medical, preventative device, the mask has been the focus of politics, symbolic and actual resistance, compliance and enforcement efforts.[44] There are also attempts to personalise the impersonal, depersonalising mask through use of different patterns on fabrics, release of masks by named fashion brands, even patterns and instructions for making one's own bespoke mask.[45] As Goffman observes, even in the most homogenising of environments, individuals tend to carve out space for variation and discrete identities.[46] In other contexts, or historical moments, mask wearing or covering the face is labelled highly deviant, a symbol of resistance, indicative of unfamiliar religious or cultural traditions, obscuring identifiability, associated with criminal activity or a source of frivolity, theatre and performance. As a form and symbol of resistance, the use of masks in protests has been met with severe penalties.[47] During the COVID-19 pandemic mandates against the use of masks were quickly reversed based on the medico-scientific recommendations on how to respond to the virus. An interesting phenomenon, which has emerged due to the event of the pandemic, is that the act of wearing a mask, its symbology, conveys two opposing narratives. On the one hand, the mask is seen as a sign of conformity. The act of wearing masks suggests 'belief in medical science and a desire to protect one's neighbor from contagion'.[48] On the other hand, the mask 'communicates oppression, government overreach, and a skepticism toward established scientific principles'.[49]

The plethora of new norms is often communicated though simple images and icons in posters and signs distributed across diverse environments and social settings.[50] Strategies of communication rely on the compression of complex information – medico-scientific findings, epidemiological modelling and public

[43] D Lupton and others, *The Face Mask in COVID Times: A Sociomaterial Analysis* (De Gruyter 2021) 2.

[44] Cf JR Gusfield, 'Moral Passage: The Symbolic Process in Public Designations of Deviance' (1967) 15 *Social Problems* 175. See also Lee and Chua (n 7).

[45] H Booth, J Cartner-Morley and S Hughes, '"Remember to Smile with Your Eyes": How to Stay Safe and Look Great in a Face Mask' *The Guardian* (18 July 2020). Available at: www.theguardian.com/lifeandstyle/2020/jul/18/remember-to-smile-with-your-eyes-how-to-stay-safe-and-look-great-in-a-face-mask.

[46] E Goffman, *Asylums: Essays on the Social Situation of Mental Patients and Other Inmates* (Albany, Anchor Books, 1961).

[47] Prior to COVID-19, several governments banned masks in protests and public spaces. In 2012, at the height of student protests 'the city of Montreal banned the wearing of masks at protests, enforceable at the discretion of the police with a fine of up to three thousand dollars'. Later, in the fall of 2012, the Canadian government passed a bill 'criminalizing mask wearing at protests, with a maximum penalty of ten years in prison'. JB Spiegel, 'Masked Protest in the Age of Austerity: State Violence, Anonymous Bodies, and Resistance "In the Red"' (2015) 41 *Critical Inquiry* 786, 786.

[48] JD Ike et al, 'Face Masks: Their History and the Values They Communicate' (2020) 25 *Journal of Health Communication* 990, 990.

[49] Ike et al, 'Face Masks' (n 48).

[50] S Marshall, 'Navigating COVID-19 Linguistic Landscapes in Vancouver's North Shore: Official Signs, Grassroots Literacy Artefacts, Monolingualism, and Discursive Convergence' (2021) 20(1) *International Journal of Multilingualism* 1–25.

health policies – into a few words and simple images.[51] Indeed, some of the signage does not contain much information at all. Rather, the instructions and directives imply or assume the reader has sufficient knowledge or understanding of COVID-19, its transmissibility, health consequences, mortality rates and danger to follow these rules without elaboration (or does not need that information to comply). Some of the messaging relies on text, others use signs and icons; at times the message is reduced to emojis. The images are not just pictures that provide public health information, as they are normative; they carry with them instructions for what to do (or not) and expectations that the viewer/reader will comply, even if that means modifying their behaviour, compromising immediate self-interest or doing things they would not ordinarily do or experience as inconvenient. The images, then, are components of governing through contagion.

Research Design and Method

To investigate the visible normative statements aiming to regulate individuals' behaviour and activities during the pandemic, we (the two co-authors) each photographed several different posters/signs located in publicly accessible places across Adelaide (South Australia) and Melbourne (Victoria) and their surrounding suburbs. The images were easy to capture unobtrusively and did not require permission or access.[52] The research relies on image-based methodology and the photographic images are the data.[53] We then collected the photographs together, exchanged with each other the photographs each had taken and discussed which images to examine closely as vehicles for analysing the communication of social norms. We agreed on eight, and then in parallel we sought to disentangle the norms and assumptions about social interaction within each image, making notes that set out our reflections and interpretations. We discussed our observations and perceptions via e-mail and through the exchange of several drafts of this chapter.

While the two-dimensional photographs (reproduced here) are the research data, the analysis relies on the three-dimensional signs and posters. The posters and signs are objects 'which are culturally marked as being a certain kind of thing'[54] and have biographies embedded in social contexts so that 'social interactions involving people and objects create meaning' and, in this context, social regulation.[55]

[51] Roach Anleu and Sarantoulias 'Complex Data and Simple Instructions' (n 42).

[52] For an earlier, parallel study we sought guidance from the Flinders University Social and Behavioural Sciences Ethics Committee which advised there was no need for ethical approval or photo release, given the images do not include people (27 August 2020). Each of the images are in the public domain and photographs were taken by the two co-authors.

[53] S Pink, *Doing Visual Ethnography* (Thousand Oaks, CA, SAGE Publications, 2021).

[54] I Kopytoff, 'The Cultural Biography of Things: Commoditization as Process' in A Appadurai (ed), *The Social Life of Things: Commodities in Cultural Perspective* (Cambridge, Cambridge University Press, 1986) 64.

[55] C Gosden and Y Marshall, 'The Cultural Biography of Objects' (1999) 31 *World Archaeology* 169, 169; DL Brien, 'Object Biography and Its Potential in Creative Writing' (2020) 17 *New Writing* 377;

As objects, the posters and signs 'become invested with meaning through the social interactions they are caught up in'.[56] Thus, images or signs are data: 'sources of concrete visual information about the abstract concepts and processes which are central to organizing everyday social life'.[57] They are part of a governing/regulatory framework that seeks to influence individual human activities and collective behaviour.

The relevance of the objects depends on human audiences, who interpret the information and potentially modify their behaviour and subsequent social interaction. Signs and posters anticipate that individuals will (be able to) interpret the instructions contained therein, and then have the capacity and motivation to modify their activities to enable the interaction order to continue without disruption. In addition, we rely on our own observations regarding the placement of signs and the people interacting in the various locations.[58]

Posters and Signs/Signage Regulating Individual Behaviour and Social Interaction

The first image (Figure 4.1) is of a flyer located in the window of a building that is an entrance to a large Sunday morning fresh food market in an inner-city suburb. The design relies on eye-catching yellow as the dominant colour and, as it is placed next to the door, it is visible to all who enter. It is in the form of an A4-size flyer which has been downloaded and printed from the South Australian government website. It is not a bespoke flyer but a generic one that is used in various settings and can easily be attached to different surfaces and entrance ways. Those who pass through the doors are a heterogenous and transient public.

The sign relies on text and an image to convey the social norms. The first statement of the norm takes the form of a direction: MASKS ARE MANDATORY all in capital letters. This indicates that the wearing of a mask is not discretionary, not a personal choice, but a requirement, even statutorily required. Entering the building is tantamount to complying with the instruction, a contractual relationship. The language is direct with few syllables and can be read quickly by English-speaking adults and school-age children. Interestingly, the flyer gives no information on how to wear the mask properly, or on whether there are situations when it can be removed, for example when sitting down and eating. Nor does it indicate whether everyone, including children and babies, are mandated to wear a mask.

J Joy, 'Reinvigorating Object Biography: Reproducing the Drama of Object Lives' (2009) 41 *World Archaeology* 540.

[56] Gosden and Marshall 'The Cultural Biography of Objects' (n 55) 170.

[57] M Emmison, P Smith and M Mayall, *Researching the Visual* (Thousand Oaks, CA, SAGE Publications 2012) 62; see also De Visser and Straughan (n 10); Marshall (n 50); LJ Moran, 'Judicial Pictures as Legal Life-Writing Data and a Research Method' (2015) 42 *Journal of Law and Society* 74.

[58] Cf Collins (n 39).

Figure 4.1 Masks are Mandatory I
(Photograph by Sharyn Roach Anleu: 29 August 2021)

The image of the mask is the simple, widely available, single-use surgical face mask, that can be purchased in bulk. There are no instructions about proper disposal after use. The discarded disposable mask has become a ubiquitous feature polluting natural and built landscapes, beaches and oceans.[59] Perhaps to soften the injunction, the next line more civilly entreats the reader to 'please wear a mask

[59] Thiel et al (n 14); see also Godden (ch 3, this volume).

before entering' in sentence case lettering. Using 'please' acknowledges the reader and their emotions and perhaps their potential resistance to an autocratic directive. This is framed as a request rather than an injunction.

The flyer relies on two types of legitimacy: legal/governmental and medical, though allusions to both are peripheral to the dominant message. At the bottom of the flyer is the ensign of the South Australian government, which clearly pitches this as a state-wide issue, but not necessarily a national one. Other Australian states and territories have different rules about mask wearing. This also affirms the state's dominant role in governing through contagion. The flyer anticipates deviance, such as non-compliance, and indicates at the bottom that exemptions apply, providing details of the state health department as the place for more information. The poster gives no indication of what the exemptions are or to whom they might apply. By directing the reader to the webpage of SA Health, the anticipated exemptions are health/medical related. This suggests a technique of neutralisation; there are valid justifications for non-compliance, including an appeal to the detrimental health consequences of wearing a mask on the part of the non-compliant.[60]

What is especially notable is the missing information. There is no mention of the coronavirus or COVID-19. The flyer makes no connection between mask wearing and reducing the transmission of the virus; it does caution the reader they are about to enter a crowded space. There is no mention of the other activities associated with reducing contagion: social/physical distancing, washing hands, staying away if feeling unwell. There is no mention of the collective importance of mask wearing, no appeal to community responsibility, that is individual action is essential to wider collective benefit. The message is short and sharp, attention catching, without much more. The flyer makes assumptions about those entering the market and seeing the sign: perhaps they already have sufficient knowledge about COVID-19, the health risks of the disease, its contagiousness and their own moral responsibility to the community. Alternatively, the flyer may assume that market participants do not agree with the medical advice on mask wearing or would not wear a mask without requirement. The flyer does not mention sanctions for non-compliance, even though mask wearing is mandated. Enforcement comes in several forms: self-discipline, other shoppers or stall owners reminding people to wear their masks and official volunteers inside the market, who have undertaken the formal COVID-19 Marshal Training and wear specially labelled fluoro vests, asking people to wear masks, or wear them properly, and providing a free mask to those without.

Figure 4.2 is an elaboration of Figure 4.1. It continues with the first injunction but does several things that Figure 4.1 does not. It reinforces the command by providing more details: 'all people must wear a mask', anticipating no exception. Nonetheless, there is an implicit theoretical exception when not in the 'physical presence of other persons'. However, 'physical presence' is not defined. So, it is not clear whether this is the usual 1.5 metre distance rule.

[60] GM Sykes and D Matza, 'Techniques of Neutralization: A Theory of Delinquency' (1957) 22 *American Sociological Review* 664.

Figure 4.2 Masks are Mandatory II
(Photograph by Sharyn Roach Anleu: 7 September 2021. Entrance to a swimming pool)

The flyer then provides a mix of official graffiti, including the familiar circle with the diagonal slash, and text to elaborate proper mask wearing and disposal. These are designed as a series of six steps. These steps provide hygiene information – washing hands, not touching the mask – as well as technical advice about mask fitting – it is to completely cover the lower face and not hang around the neck or sit under the nose. The six points are informational and normative. It is deviant not to wear the mask properly. It states explicitly that single-use masks are rubbish and not recyclable, and responsible disposal means placing it in a rubbish bin.

Again, the acknowledgement of the authority source is peripheral and there is no mention of COVID-19 or the enforcement of these rules. There is no explanation of why people 'must wear a mask'. Perhaps as these are the second tranche of posters and signs relating to the pandemic, it is assumed that everyone will already know and understand the reasoning and comply without anything further, especially as coronavirus-specific rules and regulations that disrupt social interaction are no longer new. Anyone who has been in a public setting will recognise that very few if anyone complies exactly with these instructions. Collins noted in the US context that 'effective, or not, wearing masks now became a social marker of joining the effort against the epidemic, along with keeping 6 feet away from other people'.[61]

Compared with injunctions to remain physically apart, wash hands frequently, cover coughs and adopt general hygiene practices, mask wearing is more intrusive, and requires more effort: acquiring a mask, having it ready, remembering to bring it and wearing it properly. Mandatory mask use is a blatant incursion into daily social life and disrupts personal face-to-face interaction. The simple, declaratory wording in these flyers suggests they anticipate non-compliance or resistance to mask wearing.[62] Highlighting the word 'mandatory' conveys a strong instruction and legal requirement regardless of individuals' instrumental or moral/normative motivations. The word mandatory might also imply enforcement by agents of social control; however, most of the signs rely on self-enforcement or peer-enforcement by others in the same setting, including employees.

Figure 4.3 provides an image of a movable sign at the front of a daily fruit and vegetable market which also includes small cafes and restaurants. The mask wearing instruction is almost an add on to the main instruction – the check in procedure. The sign provides a large QR (Quick Response) code, essential for contact tracing, one of the pillars of the COVID-19 public health response, then sets out the four steps for checking in. It immediately reassures the viewer/reader that checking in 'is quick and easy', thus anticipating questions such as: How long will this take? Can I do this without assistance? Or conclusions such as: I don't have time to do this; I'm not doing this because it is too complicated. The poster underscores the technological response to COVID-19 – the reliance on smart phones and QR codes: 'Technology underwrites much of the pandemic management framework.'[63] What it does not refer to is the capacity of the QR codes to amass very large quantities of data about individuals' movements and whereabouts. The poster includes a reminder and reiteration of the injunctions that have been part of the COVID-19 response since the outset – and frequent

[61] Collins (n 39) 483.
[62] Lee and Chua (n 7).
[63] Ye (n 16) 1905.

Figure 4.3 COVID-19-Safe Check In
(Photograph by Sharyn Roach Anleu: 30 July 2021. Entrance to a city food market)

in the first tranche of public health signs and posters – to stay away if unwell, maintain physical social distancing and regularly clean hands.

The poster emphasises following the directions, which are outlined in a series of steps, and that is explicitly stated in the part that deals with masks: 'Please ensure you are wearing a mask as per the SA Government directions …'. Here

Figure 4.4 How to Wear a Face Mask
(Photograph by George Sarantoulias: 31 December 2021. A Greek Orthodox Church)

there is neither appeal to the collective; nor to the health and wellbeing of others, nor to the market community.[64]

It was relatively unusual to see signs that provide details on correct mask wearing. The sign in Figure 4.4, as with many others, has been downloaded from a state government website rather than being a bespoke set of instructions. At the outset

[64] Roach Anleu and Sarantoulias (n 42).

the poster indicates: 'There are two types of face masks you can use: cloth masks and surgical masks. Cloth masks are made of washable fabric and can be re-used.' The implication here is that disposable surgical masks are not multi-use and cannot be re-used.

The poster explains carefully what is required when fitting a face mask and underscores the importance of washing hands and touching the mask with clean hands, thus implying that to not do so lowers the mask's effectiveness. The poster appeals to the importance of individual behaviour in protecting the health of the community and the collective benefit: 'Wearing a face mask protects you and your community by providing an additional physical barrier to coronavirus (COVID-19).' The level of detail and information in this poster is in sharp contrast to that in Figure 4.1. Perhaps this is because the poster sought to stem the incidence of non-compliance by providing detailed mask wearing instructions. Often policies emerge after a problem has been identified, so the detailed instructions are a response to (anticipated) non-compliance, such as failure to wear masks or improper mask wearing. The poster provides further specification: 'Do not allow your mask to hang around your neck.' It seems that more information, or reiteration of information previously circulated, is an antidote to improper mask wearing. It is noteworthy that this poster, while generic, is in a Greek Orthodox Church. There are instances of religious communities disregarding the laws and regulations because of their beliefs (for example, Christ Embassy Sydney held a church service in violation of New South Wales public health orders and participants were issued with fines). This could also be an instance of policing diversity or targeting particular ethnic communities as potentially non-compliant.[65]

The image in Figure 4.5 was taken in front of a suburban aquatics and health club. Several aspects of this sign are ripe for analysis. First, the physical form of the sign and the way in which it has been displayed is of interest. The sign is metallic and is mounted on two metal posts suggesting that it was installed with the understanding that it will be there for an indefinite time period – such as a permanent installation. Second, at the top left-hand corner of the sign there are bold letters – a combination of lower and upper case – stating: 'Let's work together TO STAY SAFE', and on the right top hand corner there is the insignia of the City of Monash, the legal authority which legitimises the instructions conveyed. The message 'Let's work together …' is an indication of an appeal to the sense of community, an anticipation of bodily co-presence in a fragile interaction order and a restatement of social imaginaries as an antidote to individual self-interest. The message is completed by the upper-case script – '… TO STAY SAFE' – which emphasises the reason why the sense of community and collaboration are requested. Third, the sign is not about mask wearing explicitly; it is about the importance of maintaining physical distance from other people. At the centre of the sign, it states: 'Social

[65] Ye (n 16).

Figure 4.5 Let's work together to stay safe
(Photograph by George Sarantoulias: 18 December 2021. A suburban aquatics and health club)

distancing is critical. Stay 1.5 metres apart at all times. **If you're closer than the length of the sign you're too close.'**

The sign is large and made in such a way that the 1.5 metres between the two characters is explicit. The measurements have already been featured in the sign and the information has become even more simple for those reading it.

Even though the sign is not solely about mask-wearing, the two characters are wearing masks. This is done in a way that the viewer makes the connection that mask wearing is already something that they would be expected to do, mask wearing is now a given; it does not have to be explicitly stated; it is part of the social imaginary.

Figure 4.6 Stop sign
(Photograph by George Sarantoulias: 2 January 2022. Minimarket in a coastal town)

The image in Figure 4.6 was taken in a small coastal town, a popular destination for holidaymakers. The local shop sells provisions typically found at a supermarket and alcohol. The collage of signs is at the front entrance and it feels overwhelming when one confronts it. There is, simply put, a lot going on. Even though the installation of the signs is indicative of a feeling of anxiety or panic on the part of the individual who displayed it, there are several points of specific interest. The owners have used a STOP sign which is usually used at intersections on roads. The STOP sign, over the years, has solidified as one of the most common examples of official graffiti and, significantly, it is a sign which, if not followed, could result in dire consequences, including car accidents and fatalities. On top of the STOP sign there is an official Victorian government QR code for patrons to 'check in'. The same QR code print out is featured in three different locations, but they all cannot be used at the same time because that would violate the physical distancing rule of 1.5 metres. Under the STOP sign a piece of paper states:

> 'WE KNOW YOU ARE ON HOLIDAY
>
> BUT
>
> IF OUR STAFF GET COVID WE WILL CLOSE
>
> AND YOU'LL HAVE NO LOCAL SHOP
>
> **PLEASE WEAR A MASK**
>
> HAPPY NEW YEAR'

Some research suggests that individuals on holiday are in a mental space in which they are more likely to take risks and engage in inappropriate and non-conforming behaviours than they would ordinarily.[66] Perhaps, underlying the message is an expectation that patrons will desist and it seeks to appeal to their rationality and self-interest. Instead of the message asking patrons to realise that conforming to the rules is essential for the wellbeing of the community, it invokes the disadvantage and inconvenience for individuals if the local shop is shut down. The primary emphasis is not the health risks of COVID-19 for the employees or the patrons, but the inconvenience that could result and detract from the holiday experience.

The object represented in Figure 4.7 differs in form from the others discussed above. It is a small (five centimetres in diameter) button that can easily be pinned to clothing. It anticipates the enforcement of the requirement to wear masks in an instance when a person is not wearing one.[67]

[66] N Uriely, Y Ram and A Malach-Pines, 'Psychoanalytic Sociology of Deviant Tourist Behavior' (2011) 38 *Annals of Tourism Research* 1051.

[67] The Department of Health Services (Victoria) website stated: 'You do not need a medical certificate stating that you have a lawful reason for not wearing a face mask. If you have a lawful reason for not wearing a face mask, you do not need to apply for an exemption or permit. If you are stopped by police in a setting where face masks are mandatory, they will ask you to confirm the lawful reason you are not

Figure 4.7 Face mask exempt sign/button
(Photograph by George Sarantoulias: 30 December 2021. A Greek Orthodox Church)

wearing a face mask.' It provided a card stating: 'I am exempt from wearing a face covering for a valid reason' which can be downloaded, printed, and carried in a wallet, or even worn as a badge. However, it does not intimate what constitutes 'a valid reason'. Available at: www.dhhs.vic.gov.au/sites/default/files/documents/202009/I-am-exempt-face-covering-Wallet-Cards-A4-PRINT-covid-19-pdf.pdf. Another government website provided minute detail of the exemptions for not wearing a face mask: Victorian Government, 'Face Masks' (14 July 2022). Available at: www.coronavirus.vic.gov.au/face-masks.

It anticipates that the non-mask wearer will be called to account, that is to provide an explanation for their apparent deviance.[68]

Frequently providing accounts for apparent deviance could be very disruptive to the interaction order and frustrating for the person so called to account. The badge provides the explanation for the absence of a mask; they are 'medically exempt'. It expresses a legitimate reason for non-compliance, a medical reason; a powerful technique that neutralises the appearance of deviance.[69] It is repeated: 'medically exempt' appears three times and 'exempt' appears four times, out of a total of nine words!

A second noteworthy observation is that the badge is worn; the signage has moved to the body. As it is small and relies on others being able to easily read the explanation, there must be a limit on the amount of text or number of images displayed. The badge does not display the insignia of the Australian government or any other reference to legitimate authority.

The image in Figure 4.8 is taken inside a suburban Greek Orthodox Church and depicts a woman wearing a mask correctly. The writing on the sign states: 'Thank You! For wearing your mask **over your nose and mouth** before entering.' The instruction is not couched as a directive or a requirement – but as appreciation for wearing the mask properly. Nonetheless, the statement is normative; it reinforces the proper way of wearing the mask to cover the nose and mouth, thus rendering deviant other deployments of the mask, such as only over the mouth, hanging off one ear, hanging around the neck, being carried and not worn before entering.

This sign does not have the insignia of a government or other legal authority. It is, however, in a space of religious worship and, as such, associated with the authority and symbolic power of the parish priest and the Greek Orthodox Archdiocese of Australia. In a place of worship like an Orthodox Christian Church the space is comprised of unique practices and behaviours, among these include bowing to and kissing the icons of Christ and the various saints depicted. In the context of the transmission of COVID-19, these religious practices are redefined as high risk of virus transmission, unhygienic and thus must be curbed. Aesthetically, this photograph is very interesting as it depicts a juxtaposition of icons. The all-male religious icons contrast with the mask-wearing female image.

[68] TL Orbuch, 'People's Accounts Count: The Sociology of Accounts' (1997) 23 *Annual Review of Sociology* 455.

[69] Sykes and Matza (n 60).

Figure 4.8 Thank you …. In the church
(Photograph by George Sarantoulias: 30 December 2021. A (second) Greek Orthodox Church)

Conclusion: Governing Contagion Through Images and Icons

This chapter analyses signs regarding mask wearing and notices a shift in signs and posters away from appeals to the collective, and shared benefit, and toward directives regarding mask wearing. Instructions showing how to wear masks have resulted from the incorrect wearing of masks. At the start of the pandemic, we did not encounter many signs of this nature as mask wearing was not mandatory in Australia, except in health care and high-risk settings, such as nursing homes and aged-care centres. Our earlier research found a strong emphasis in the signs and posters on community benefit from complying with the introduced public health regulations.[70]

Many governments around the world instituted new laws and policies to curb the transmission of COVID-19 that aimed to regulate behaviours, practices and normative expectations through the legitimacy of their legal authority and symbolic power. Predominantly, the new rules have been conveyed through signs and images which bear the insignias of government authorities (for example, Figures 4.1, 4.2, 4.3, 4.4, 4.6). The legitimacy and symbolic power that emanate from the signs are due to the authority which communicates the message. These signs are embedded in the interaction order where individuals interact face to face and body to body with varying levels of shared assumptions. There are, however, signs that communicate the new rules without relying on the symbolic and legitimising power of government insignias (for example, Figures 4.7 and 4.8). Such signs can still be effective, but their effectiveness rests on other sources of legitimacy: Figure 4.6 is a collage of signs and, while it includes mention of the state in the bottom corners, its overall tone is to appeal to holidaymakers' self-interest to comply and wear a mask so that the shop can remain open, rather than because of government requirement or community benefit in stemming contagion. Figure 4.8 is located in a space – a church – already laden with normative restrictions. It might be assumed that as the congregation is relatively homogeneous and attuned to compliance with church rules, detailed justifications for mask wearing are unnecessary. In other situations, the diversity of participants and their discrete expectations might mean that stronger language or more detailed instructions is required to explicate the new normative order. This suggests that interaction orders, and social situations, are replete with normative instructions and shared assumptions of appropriate face to face and bodily interaction.

Governing through contagion requires certain conditions and resources, including mechanisms for communicating its rules and regulations. Central to the amalgam of new norms that emerged during the COVID-19 pandemic is the way information and instructions are communicated, often in the form of simple images and icons in posters and signs that compress complex information widespread in public settings where face-to-face social interaction occurs. These

[70] Roach Anleu and Sarantoulias (n 42).

posters and signs vary in terms of their reliance on law or legal language to enhance compliance. Use of the word 'mandatory' implies legally required, suggesting likely enforcement. Instructions regarding mask wearing can also be combined with other COVID-19 requirements such as using QR codes to check in and general hygiene reminders. Signs also vary in terms of appeal to collective wellbeing or self-interest. Often, the instructions and directives imply or assume that the reader has sufficient knowledge, information and understanding of COVID-19, its transmissibility, health consequences, mortality rates and danger that little information about the virus is conveyed. The signs and posters also rely on assumed shared social imaginaries, or understandings and perceptions of reality which form collective beliefs, values, and practices. Social imaginaries are both the needle and thread which form the social fabric of social interaction; they concurrently shape and are shaped by events such as the COVID-19 pandemic, thus forming a part of governing through contagion.

PART II

Inter/Dysconnectedness of Governing Through Contagion

5

Intimacy, Queer Men and the Law on HIV Risk Disclosure in Singapore

Governing Through Contagion at the Margins

DARYL WJ YANG, DANIEL WS HO AND RAYNER KJ TAN*

Introduction

> When I was first diagnosed, I actually wanted to be on medication, just to be like everyone else. As the years passed by, I would take my medication and see the doctor every six months. I thought eventually I'll be normal, like everyone else.

After Faris – a 31-year-old gay man – tested positive for the human immunodeficiency virus (HIV) in 2016, he tried to comfort himself with the fact that HIV could be managed as a chronic illness as long as he adhered to the antiretroviral therapy (ART) regimen. However, when he subsequently found out about the heavy criminal penalties that he might be subject to under Section 23 of Singapore's Infectious Diseases Act (IDA), he realised that the law would not treat him on an equal basis as others. 'When I came to know about this law, it made me feel very small and very vulnerable', Faris said.

Section 23(1) imposes a legal obligation on persons who know they have HIV to disclose the 'risk of contracting HIV' to their sexual partners before engaging in any sexual activity. Failure to do so may result in an imprisonment term of up to 10 years or a fine of up to $50,000.[1] Prior to a 2019 High Court decision, which adopted a literal interpretation of the statutory language,[2] people living with HIV were advised by public health officials that they were required only to disclose their HIV-positive status to their sexual partners. However, the judge affirmed the lower court's decision that 'merely disclosing one's HIV-positive status is not sufficient;

* The authors wish to note that their personal views and research are not affiliated to any organisations with which they are associated. The names of all research participants have been pseudonymised.

[1] Infectious Diseases Act (Cap. 137, Rev 2003), Section 23(1).

[2] *GCP v Public Prosecutor* [2019] SGHC 153 ('*GCP v PP*').

instead, there is a duty to ensure that the other party understands and appreciates the risk that HIV is transmissible through sexual intercourse'.[3]

Section 23(2) imposes a similar obligation on persons who do not know that they have HIV but who have 'reason to believe' that they have HIV or have been exposed to a 'significant risk of contracting' HIV/AIDS.[4] Other than communicating the 'risk of contracting' HIV/AIDS to their sexual partners, this group may also discharge their legal obligation under Section 23(2) by either (i) getting tested for HIV to confirm that they are not HIV-positive or (ii) take 'reasonable precautions' to ensure that they do not expose that other person to the risk of contracting HIV/AIDS.[5] Since this provision was enacted in 2008, there are no reported judgments involving Section 23(2) though prosecutions have been reported in the media.[6]

Although HIV non-disclosure laws exist in other jurisdictions,[7] Section 23 is unique in two respects. First, a person living with HIV must not only disclose their HIV-positive status but also communicate the 'risk of transmission'.[8] Second, while most HIV-specific legislations elsewhere apply only to those living with HIV, Section 23(2) requires those who may not have HIV but have 'reason to believe' that they are at 'significant risk of contracting' HIV to also take steps to ensure that they do not infect their sexual partners. As we demonstrate, Section 23 has furthered the marginalisation of persons who tested positive for HIV and even those who have not. In this regard, some, including the HIV/AIDS non-governmental organisation Action for AIDS, have advocated for its repeal.[9]

Globally, the gay, bisexual and other men who have sex with men (GBMSM) population has been disproportionately affected by the HIV epidemic.[10] This is the case in Singapore as well although the number of new HIV diagnoses among

[3] *GCP v Public Prosecutor* (n 2) at [30] and [35].

[4] IDA (n 1), Section 23(2).

[5] IDA (n 1), Section 23(2).

[6] Infectious Diseases (Amendment) Act (No 10 of 2008). See, for example, L Tang, '3.5 Years' Jail for Man Who Dodged HIV Tests, Although 6 Partners Tested Positive' *TODAY* (5 September 2019). Available at: www.todayonline.com/singapore/35-years-jail-man-who-dodged-hiv-tests-while-having-sex-men-some-whom-contracted-hivom-him.

[7] HIV Justice Network and The Global Network of People Living with HIV, 'Advancing HIV Justice 3: Growing the Global Movement against HIV Criminalisation' (2019). Available at: www.hivjustice.net/wp-content/uploads/2016/05/AHJ2.final2_.10May2016.pdf.

[8] *GCP v PP* (n 2) [35]–[38].

[9] RKW Chan and S Banerjee, 'Forum: Review Infectious Diseases Act after HIV-Positive Man Charged' *The Straits Times* (Singapore, 9 June 2022). Available at: www.straitstimes.com/opinion/forum/forum-review-infectious-diseases-act-after-hiv-positive-man-charged; D Ho, RKJ Tan and D Yang, 'Do HIV Non-Disclosure Laws in Singapore Still Make Sense Today?' (*Rice Media*, 28 September 2021). Available at: www.ricemedia.co/hiv-non-disclosure-laws-in-singapore; RKJ Tan, D Lye and R Chan, 'HIV Laws out of Touch with Scientific Evidence and Should Be Amended' *TODAY* (10 July 2019). Available at: www.todayonline.com/voices/hiv-laws-out-touch-scientific-evidence-and-should-be-amended; D Yang, 'Evaluating the Criminalisation of HIV/AIDS: Non-Disclosure Laws in Singapore' (2018) 36 *Singapore Law Review* 136.

[10] C Beyrer et al, 'Global Epidemiology of HIV Infection in Men Who Have Sex with Men' (2012) 380 *The Lancet* 367.

GBMSM has been falling since 2011.[11] In 2021, GBMSM made up 62 per cent of all incident cases of sexually transmitted HIV infections in Singapore, with those aged 15 to 39 making up 48.4 per cent of cases among GBMSM.[12] Indeed, during the 2008 parliamentary debates, the Minister for Health suggested that men who have sex with men would fall within the category of those at 'significant risk' of contracting HIV.[13] Yet, the impact of Section 23 of the IDA on the lives of GBMSM in Singapore has not been examined.

This chapter attends to this knowledge gap by examining how governing through contagion operates not only on the ground but also, specifically, at the margins. While some empirical studies have found that criminalisation has an insignificant impact on the sexual behaviour of individuals,[14] absent from the current debate is the perspective of those whose lives and relationships are directly affected by these laws. In this regard, some scholars have applied Foucault's concept of governmentality to theorise the criminalisation of HIV.[15] However, existing empirical research on HIV-specific criminal law have largely been confined to the North American context, where the legal and sociocultural marginality of GBMSM and persons living with HIV differ significantly from Singapore.

This chapter offers the first empirical study on the legal regulation of HIV risk disclosure in Singapore and how GBMSM conceive of and negotiate these laws in their everyday lives.[16] Based on a qualitative study with GBMSM, including those living with HIV, we put the concept of 'governing through contagion' in dialogue with existing scholarship on the governmentality of HIV risk to examine how individuals subject to criminalisation respond to and resist against the law.[17] In particular, we examine how governing through contagion operates at the margins via the tacit means of what we describe as the law's 'strategic ambiguity' and demonstrate the implications of using criminal law as a public health measure to combat the spread of HIV. We also call attention to the role of law in governing through contagion by attending to how those at the margins of law conceive of and resist the legal (and non-legal) modes of control of the most

[11] F van Griensven et al, 'The Continuing HIV Epidemic among Men Who Have Sex with Men and Transgender Women in the ASEAN Region: Implications for HIV Policy and Service Programming' (2021) 18 *Sexual Health* 21.

[12] Ministry of Health, 'Update on the HIV/AIDS Situation in Singapore 2021 (June 2022)' (*Ministry of Health*, 1 July 2022). Available at: www.moh.gov.sg/resources-statistics/infectious-disease-statistics/hiv-stats/update-on-the-hiv-aids-situation-in-singapore-2021-(june-2022).

[13] Singapore Parliamentary Debates, Official Reports (22 April 2008) vol 84 at cols 2703–2704.

[14] D Harsono et al, 'Criminalization of HIV Exposure: A Review of Empirical Studies in the United States' (2017) 21 *AIDS and Behavior* 27.

[15] RM McKie et al, 'A Theoretical Examination Using Governmentality to Understand Gay Men's Risk and Sexual Behaviours' (2019) 28 *The Canadian Journal of Human Sexuality* 343; JC Rangel and BD Adam, 'Everyday Moral Reasoning in the Governmentality of HIV Risk' (2014) 36 *Sociology of Health & Illness* 60.

[16] Rangel and Adam (n 15).

[17] Lynette J Chua and Jack Jin Gary Lee, 'Governing through Contagion' in Victor V Ramraj (ed), *Covid-19 in Asia* (Oxford, Oxford University Press 2021).

intimate parts of their lives – their sexual relationships and interactions – under the IDA. Echoing the editors' caution that such resistance performs complicitly with governing through contagion, our findings reveal how the dysconnectedness of the law is reproduced by GBMSM themselves through a cascading chain of othering.

Research Methodology

We conducted semi-structured in-depth interviews with men who have sex with men in Singapore between December 2021 to March 2022.[18] To be eligible for the study, participants had to be 21 to 64 years old, self-identify as GBMSM and be willing to be recorded for the purposes of the interviews. A total of 17 participants were recruited. Interview topics included participants' definitions of risk in general and in the context of HIV knowledge of the IDA, perceptions and attitudes towards the IDA, as well as the role of novel HIV prevention paradigms (for example, treatment as prevention or 'undetectable=untransmittable' or U=U) in shaping perceptions of risk as well as responsibilities within sexual partnerships.

Each interview lasted an hour on average and took place online through teleconferencing video software. As per institutional review board guidelines, participants were told not to turn on their video feed to ensure that their identities were protected. Participants were provided with an SGD50.00 (approximately USD35.00) shopping voucher as reimbursement for their time. All three study team members also served as interviewers and had previous experience in conducting in-depth interviews for the purposes of qualitative research. Given the sensitive nature of the questions asked and the lack of opportunities to build rapport through in-person or on-camera interactions, interviewers reflexively discussed the interview guide prior to the commencement of interviews and sought several ways to build rapport with participants. These included sharing about their own identities salient to this study with participants and starting from questions that were less sensitive.

Audio recordings were transcribed verbatim, and uploaded onto a qualitative data analysis management software, Dedoose. We undertook reflexive thematic analysis methods to develop themes in this study, which included six phases of (i) data familiarisation, (ii) initial code generation, (iii) generating initial themes, (iv) theme review, (v) theme defining and naming and (vi) report production.[19] All three authors engaged in the analytic process.

[18] The protocol for this study was approved by the National University of Singapore Institutional Review Board (Reference: NUS-IRB-2021-648).

[19] V Braun and V Clarke, 'Reflecting on Reflexive Thematic Analysis' (2019) 11 *Qualitative Research in Sport, Exercise and Health* 589.

Legislating Intimacy: The History and Development of Section 23

We take as a starting point the theme of the centralisation and effectiveness of law in social control. As Chua and Lee noted, Singapore is characterised by 'highly centralised state infrastructures with the potential to achieve totalisation'.[20] Because Section 23 attempts to regulate one of the most intimate and private aspects of one's life, its enforcement might appear to be challenging at first glance. However, we find that Singaporean authorities have carried out prosecution when individuals voluntarily report potential violations to the police.[21] Section 23 of the IDA was introduced in 1992 to address the 'risk that some of those who are already HIV-infected will continue to be irresponsible in their behaviour'.[22] According to the then Health Minister, it was necessary to 'strengthen the existing legislation to deter such irresponsible and dangerous behaviour'.[23] In 2008, Section 23 was amended to introduce Section 23(2) and increase the maximum criminal penalties fivefold. The legislative intent behind Section 23(2) was to 'shift greater responsibility to individuals whose sexual behaviour … puts their spouses and partners at risk of contracting HIV/AIDS'.[24] These amendments were purportedly aimed at protecting 'the innocent wives of men who visit prostitutes … [who are] totally unaware that their husbands had gone to different places, had fun and then passed on the HIV to them'.[25]

Notably, Section 23(2) differs from Section 23(1) in that it allows those at 'significant risk' of contracting HIV to discharge their legal obligation in three ways. First, like people living with HIV, they may disclose the risk of contracting HIV to their sexual partners and obtain their informed consent prior to engaging in sexual activity. Second, they may take a serological test to confirm that they are not HIV-positive before engaging in sexual activity. Finally, they may take 'reasonable precautions' to ensure that they do not expose that other person to the risk of contracting HIV. During the parliamentary debate on the 2008 amendments, the then Health Minister explained that what amounts to reasonable precautions is based on 'the current state of medical science' and referred specifically to the 'correct and consistent use of condoms each time a person has sex'.[26]

That same year marked the first prosecution under Section 23, involving a 43-year-old man who had engaged in oral sex with a 16-year-old male teenager in a shopping mall toilet.[27] The accused was arrested after the teenager sought help from

[20] Chua and Lee (n 17) 118.

[21] Other prosecutions arose from contract tracing, where public health officials would identify past sexual partners of a patient who has been diagnosed with HIV to inform them that they may have been exposed to HIV. In some instances, the contact tracing process may reveal that one of the past sexual partners is on the HIV registry and may have transmitted the virus to the patient. See, for example, *GCP v PP*, which we examine in the next section.

[22] Singapore Parliamentary Debates, Official Reports (27 February 1992) vol 59 at col 447.

[23] Singapore Parliamentary Debates (n 22).

[24] Singapore Parliamentary Debates, Official Reports (22 April 2008) vol 84 at col 2670.

[25] Singapore Parliamentary Debates (n 24) at col 2702.

[26] Singapore Parliamentary Debates (n 24) at col 2703.

[27] *Public Prosecutor v Chan Mun Chiong* [2008] SGDC 189 ('*Chan Mun Chiong*').

a security officer because the accused was stalking him around the mall after the sexual encounter. Though the risk of transmission was low since the accused was the receptive partner in the sexual act and did not transmit the virus to the other person, the prosecution urged the court to pass a severe sentence to 'uphold and give effect to the imperatives of public health and morality which the accused so blatantly breached'.[28]

The media also plays a role in giving life to Section 23 by reporting on prosecutions under this law which reinforces the fear of and stigma against HIV as well as the logic of HIV criminalisation.[29] However, while the state-funded media reports on prosecutions under Section 23 against both GBMSM and heterosexual offenders alike,[30] there have only been three other reported Section 23 judgments all of which involved men who have sex with men.

In *Public Prosecutor v GBY*,[31] the accused reported himself to the police after he ended a relationship with his partner to whom he did not disclose his HIV-positive status. It is not clear from the judgment why the accused decided to report himself, although it might be possible that his partner had threatened to do so if he did not; the accused's self-reporting was also taken into account in sentencing as a mitigating factor.[32] In *Public Prosecutor v GEO*,[33] the accused was investigated after two of his sexual partners lodged police reports against him for engaging in sexual activity with them without disclosing his HIV-positive status.[34] Finally, *GCP v PP*, the case mentioned in our introduction, arose because the accused's sexual partner had contracted HIV and the accused was identified via contact tracing conducted by a public health officer from the Ministry of Health.[35]

Moralisation at the Margins Through Strategic Ambiguity

Although enforcement of Section 23 has taken place through formal prosecutions, as we discussed above, we find that the effects of the provision operate not so much through explicit or direct modes of control but through 'strategic ambiguity'.[36]

[28] *Public Prosecutor v Chan Mun Chiong* (n 27) at [8].

[29] JM Kilty and K Bogosavljevic, 'Emotional Storytelling: Sensational Media and the Creation of the HIV Sexual Predator' (2019) 15 *Crime, Media, Culture* 279; DL Altheide, 'The News Media, the Problem Frame, and the Production of Fear' (1997) 38 *The Sociological Quarterly* 647.

[30] See, for example, S Alkhatib, 'Jail for HIV-Positive Man Who Had Unprotected Sex with Girl, 14, Multiple Times' *The Straits Times* (Singapore, 13 December 2021). Available at: www.straitstimes.com/singapore/courts-crime/jail-for-hiv-positive-man-who-had-unprotected-sex-with-girl-14-multiple-times; Tam Mei Tan, 'Man Jailed and Fined for Not Disclosing HIV Status to Prostitutes He Slept With' *The Straits Times* (Singapore, 26 July 2019). Available at: www.straitstimes.com/singapore/courts-crime/man-jailed-and-fined-for-not-disclosing-hiv-status-to-prostitutes-he-slept.

[31] [2017] SGDC 248.

[32] [2017] SGDC 24 at [22].

[33] [2022] SGDC 134 ('*PP v GEO*').

[34] [2022] SGDC at [8] and [10].

[35] *Public Prosecutor v GCP* [2018] SGDC 220 at [10].

[36] This should not be confused with the concept of 'strategic ambiguity' in political sociology, developed by Christian Fröhlich and Kerstin Jacobsson to describe the protest tactics of Russian citizens

That is, the public's lack of knowledge of Section 23 and the lack of clarity of how to comply with the provision place a moral burden on populations at the margins, in particular MSM. Chua and Lee have observed that moralisation is achieved by the state's 'deploy[ment of] technologies to discipline subjects, often chasing after and beating the recalcitrant into submission with the combination of law, surveillance, and medicalised equipment'.[37] Section 23 demonstrates how law can still achieve the GTC goal of moralisation, and thus social control, even when the technologies deployed are not overt or well-known.

The scope of one's legal duty under Section 23 is not the only ambiguity in respect of the criminalisation of HIV risk disclosure in Singapore; there is generally a lack of awareness about the law and who it even applies to. Despite the hefty criminal penalties that Section 23 of the IDA imposes on offenders, we found that most participants were unaware that the law in Singapore requires those living with HIV and those at 'significant risk of contracting HIV' to disclose the risk of contracting to their sexual partners before engaging in sexual activity. Even those living with HIV only had a vague conception of what the law requires of them, based on information that they were provided with by public health officials after they were diagnosed with HIV.

For those who are not living with HIV, their understanding of the law was largely confined to the idea that people living with HIV are required to disclose their status to their sexual partners. However, this was usually based on an intuition that it is wrong for people living with HIV to engage in sexual activity with another person without disclosing their status rather than actual knowledge of Section 23. For example, Amirul, a 25-year-old gay man who does not have HIV, thought that a person living with HIV's failure to disclose their HIV-positive status would constitute the offence of rape. Amirul's intuition is based on his exposure to such laws abroad through social media, and he had simply assumed that a similar law likely existed in Singapore:

> I think it's mostly like through Twitter, but I think that law was mostly for the US. I didn't see it in the Singapore context … When I saw that law in the US, I just assumed that we also have it … [but] I've never seen anything like this in Singapore or any [social media] page, you know, that has talked about this [law].

Similarly, though John, a 24-year-old gay man who does not have HIV, had actively tried to learn about the law, he was only aware of the Section 23(1) obligation imposed on those living with HIV and not Section 23(2) which applies to GBMSM not living with HIV like himself:

> I know [Section 23] exists. But when you're reading it off verbatim, then I'm like, okay, I'm quite surprised that my understanding is more the first part [i.e., Section 23(1)] … I didn't know about [Section 23(2)]. I was always operating under the impression that

to contest legal regulations against public assemblies. See C Fröhlich and K Jacobsson, 'Performing Resistance: Liminality, Infrapolitics, and Spatial Contestation in Contemporary Russia' (2019) 51 *Antipode* 1146.

[37] Chua and Lee (n 17) 123.

> people owe it to themselves for that matter to make sure that they get checked. Yeah, I didn't know about the second part.

As for whether the existence of Section 23 made those who do not have HIV feel safer, most were sceptical not only because of the lack of awareness of its existence but also because of the lack of education and knowledge about HIV and the risk associated with its transmission. As Peter, a 29-year-old gay man who does not have HIV, puts it:

> If you're talking about someone having to disclose their status, but the [other] person has no knowledge on what to make of that status, then I think that's not really communicating the risk … Because if you tell someone you are positive and untransmittable and he has no idea what that is, you know, he never learned about that – no one has ever told him. And the government has never bothered teaching people that, then I think that's not good for society. So, the government definitely has gaps to fill on their part.

In this regard, Mykhalovskiy has found that the ambiguity of the legal concept of 'significant risk' established in Canadian jurisprudence resulted in a range of interpretations among HIV counselling providers as to what sexual activity would pose a 'significant risk' of HIV transmission.[38] This sentiment that the law in and of itself is unhelpful was echoed by Leon, a 24-year-old bisexual man who does not have HIV, who described the law as 'unwieldly' because it 'presupposes that everyone has some kind of ability to understand the kind of risks that they themselves have been exposed to [and may be] a bit too charitable in assuming that people have the ability to handle risk communication'.

These findings reveal that, despite the legislature's enactment of Section 23, there is limited understanding among those who are subject to the law about their legal obligations. Yet, the lack of knowledge and awareness among GBMSM about Section 23 does not necessarily render it ineffective or irrelevant. Instead, the ambiguity of the law reinforces its moralising effect by placing the burden on those at the margins to work out the moral logic of Section 23 themselves.

For example, although he was unsure of the particular contours of Section 23, Amirul nonetheless thought that it was a necessary law to deter and punish the deviant subject, who is imagined to be immoral and irresponsible, from going around and infecting others with the virus:

> I think this particular law is very valid because it is a malicious act. Like you know, if you don't tell people that you have HIV, then you possibly want to have that risk of infecting them … I don't know if Singapore had this case before, but maybe in some other part of the world or maybe even here where maybe there have been people who intentionally, or like maliciously, wanted to infect other people with HIV for some reason. And I feel like [the law is necessary to] maybe to deter those kinds of people.

Similarly, Raj, a 30-year-old gay man not living with HIV, observed that the law characterises HIV as a 'weapon' that people may use to hurt others: '[The law]

[38] E Mykhalovskiy, 'The Problem of "Significant Risk": Exploring the Public Health Impact of Criminalizing HIV Non-Disclosure' (2011) 73 *Social Science & Medicine* 668.

poses a bit of stigma because it paints HIV in a very negative light … It's just painting HIV as like this weapon, or like a crime … [On one hand], it's doing a good job of deterring but at the same time also, it's not painting a very nice light for people living with HIV.' Nevertheless, Raj still thought that the law was necessary to 'prevent [people that intentionally infect others], or to hold people accountable for the actions if they intentionally do want to infect someone'.

Strategic ambiguity thus moralises through Othering. Had the specifics of Section 23 been abundantly clear to GBMSM, its unfairness and intrusiveness would have been obvious. Indeed, after Amirul learnt during the interview that Section 23 may also potentially apply to GBMSM not living with HIV like himself, he described the law as 'scary' and 'not fair' because most other GBMSM may still risk prosecution despite their lack of knowledge about the law:

> Obviously, this law would implicate a lot of people. But knowing that the community possibly doesn't know of the existence of the law, it's quite scary, because technically they can get fined and all that even though they'd be like, oh, I didn't know … Yeah. So, this law is scary … I mean, not everyone has the time to go to like [Singapore Statutes Online] to read all this. So especially if the younger people in the community, they don't know a lot of things. It's definitely not fair for them to basically just have laws that dictate their sexual life, people just want to have fun and have sex. It's a bit crazy just to think about like, oh, I have to know all this before I go and have sex.

Notably, the ambiguity of Section 23 is not a legislative oversight. For example, during the 2008 parliamentary debates, numerous Members of Parliament sought clarification as to who would be considered a person who 'has reason to believe that he has or has been exposed to a significant risk of contracting' HIV under the new Section 23(2). In response, the Minister of Health suggested that this was a 'straightforward' issue and offered an illustration:

> A man who has unprotected sex with prostitutes or with other men, or a man who has unprotected sex with multiple partners, or a man who shares injection needles with other drug addicts would clearly be aware of his activities and he should have reason to believe that he has been exposed to a significant risk of contracting HIV.[39]

When asked to include these illustrations in the legislation itself, the Minister said that this was unnecessary for two reasons: first, the examples 'will never be exhaustive' and second, because 'our public health education programmes will clearly emphasise what activities put a person at risk of contracting HIV/AIDS and the necessary precautions to be taken to reduce that risk'.[40] However, most participants, like Peter noted above, found the sexuality education they received in school to be severely inadequate and instead obtained their knowledge of HIV/AIDS from other GBMSM or organisations that serve the GBMSM community. What the state considers to be more or less risky may, therefore, diverge from what GBMSM themselves perceive. Indeed, as the next section demonstrates, strategic

[39] Singapore Parliamentary Debates (n 24) at col 2711.
[40] Singapore Parliamentary Debates (n 24) at col 2711.

ambiguity can exacerbate the dysconnectedness suffered by MSM, especially those living with HIV, because of the disparity between the law on the books and life on the ground.

Dysconnectedness as a Consequence of Governing Through Contagion

During the 2008 parliamentary debate on the amendments to the IDA, the Health Minister emphasised that the new Section 23(2) was enacted not to 'discriminate against or to criminalise HIV-infected patients', but to 'push them to act more responsibly and not to hide behind the ignorance of their HIV status'.[41] In his words, 'real situations on the ground' trumped theoretical considerations.[42] This section thus examines how the lived experiences of GBMSM, whose sexual behaviour are regulated by Section 23, magnify social divides and inequalities, in this case by perpetuating the stigma and shame associated with HIV.

While governing through contagion can connect individuals, it also 'practices differences to effect strategies of control';[43] these technologies can divide 'inequitably, unjustly, and cruelly'.[44] These effects of Section 23 as a legal technology of governing through contagion emerged from our interviews with participants living with HIV, who expressed the fear that the law may be *unfairly* employed against them – effectively discriminating against them despite their best efforts to abide by it. For example, Hafiz, a 33-year-old gay man living with HIV, shared the experiences of another individual living with HIV, whom he had befriended while he was incarcerated. The latter was reported for the offence despite believing that he had taken the appropriate measures to inform his sexual partner of his status:

> I think it's a bit unfair because, sometimes we abide to the rule, like informing the other person, but sometimes you might not know, the other person might backfire you and just like, 'Oh, you didn't tell'; you can't really protect yourself because you already engaged in the sexual interaction, so there's nothing to protect you, like no evidence to say that you had already declared. Like one of our inmates, he shared that he told the other person and a few days later he was reported to the authorities, and he felt it was really unfair.

George, a 26-year-old non-binary person who also identifies as gay and is not living with HIV, also noted how the heavy criminal penalties effectively mark those living with HIV who already are suffering because of their diagnosis and may also be disadvantaged in terms of employment opportunities as social outcasts

[41] Singapore Parliamentary Debates, (n 24) vol 84 at col 2713.
[42] Singapore Parliamentary Debates (n 24).
[43] Chua and Lee (n 17) 127.
[44] Chua and Lee (n 17) 127.

even though they should be supported as vulnerable members of the community instead:

> There's a sense of othering that comes with that heavy of a sentence. It's almost like the law is branding the HIV positive person as a person that does not belong within a society because it almost seems like the law is trying to put you down rather than help you up. I think it's very strange. It's very inhumane, if implemented in that way …. so that's this thing that concerns me: if somebody who is of a low socio-economic status and you somehow contract HIV, you don't even have friends who are lawyers who are able to interpret this for you, how likely are you to be used by the law as an example or as somebody who just can't afford to be HIV-positive, and then have all these things thrown at you?

Dysconnectedness also impacts those living with HIV in terms of how they view their own condition, often to the detriment of their self-esteem and other functional domains of their lives, such as their romantic and sexual relationships. For example, because of the legal requirement to disclose his HIV-positive status, Faris highlighted how '(he was) in a very vulnerable position' after he was diagnosed: 'It's kind of like, for the past six, five years, it affect(ed) my self-esteem. So, whenever I start chatting up with someone, it is always on my mind: is this person, you know, will he be okay, with me being HIV positive?' Those living with HIV may end up suffering an alienation from self and others as a result of the dysconnectedness perpetuated by the law.

This self-stigma was echoed by participants who did not have HIV, when considering how a possible HIV diagnosis may impact their lives. Beyond the direct effect of the law on their sexual relationships, John highlighted how a positive-HIV diagnosis might impact his social relationships and his psychological well-being, resonating with research that suggests the association between HIV-stigma and psychological wellbeing:[45]

> So, I think I'll become very panicky and start to withdraw myself from society. Especially, because I think I wouldn't be ready to take it and accept it yet. Also, I think for a few months, I probably would just isolate myself from the community I'm in … I probably wouldn't actively go and search for [sexual] encounters and all that already. Because I know that I'm putting myself and others at risk as well. I don't want to put myself in trouble. Because going back to that legislation, if you know you are infected and you go on to end up infecting other people, you're guilty of [a] crime. I think generally my disposition will become a lot poorer than it is, I will become isolated, more like a hermit, not wanting to interact with people.

Beyond the inequitable impact of governing through contagion, the internalisation of responsibility and blame also features in the ways that GBMSM think about sexual risk and informed consent as compared to how lawmakers had conceived

[45] JR MacLean and K Wetherall, 'The Association between HIV-Stigma and Depressive Symptoms among People Living with HIV/AIDS: A Systematic Review of Studies Conducted in South Africa' (2021) 287 *Journal of Affective Disorders* 125.

of and legislated those issues under the IDA. While Section 23 was intended to provide participants with HIV an avenue to seek retributive or restorative justice against the person from whom they had contracted the virus, none expressed an interest in doing so. Therefore, a gap lies between the law's construction of those who contract HIV as victims at the time of their diagnosis and how those living with HIV conceive of their own experiences.

For example, Faris explained that he did not think about using the law to go after the person from whom he believes he had contracted HIV because he felt responsible for his own sexual health. According to this logic of individualised responsibility,[46] it did not matter whether the other person had disclosed their HIV-positive status to him because he should have taken the precautions whether or not he knew that they had HIV:

> [Taking revenge] didn't actually come to my mind at all. I feel that the sexual encounter was with my consent, and his consent. I didn't have that thought of blaming him because he didn't disclose his status or, you know, for passing me HIV. That didn't actually come to my head … It doesn't make any difference because, I should probably take charge of my own sexual health and I don't really question if the other person is positive … I feel that I should take charge of my sexual health, regardless of whether the other person is HIV positive or negative. So, for example, if I were to engage in unprotected sex, I should get myself tested and to be on PreP, and just [use] condom.

This reconceptualisation of personal responsibility challenges what McKie et al have described as the neoliberal redistribution of responsibility where the person living with HIV is responsible for informing their sexual partner of their HIV-positive status.[47] According to Weait, this also challenges traditional notions of criminal responsibility because, whether or not a person living with HIV has disclosed their status, 'if a person agrees to participate in the kind of sex which carries the risk of HIV infection and is infected, we must question whether it is right to attribute sole responsibility to and punish the person who transmits the virus, when that would not have happened but for the other person's willingness to accept that risk'.[48]

This line of reasoning was articulated by 44-year-old Trevor, to whom the current law, which embodies this neoliberal logic, fails to consider the individual responsibility of the sexual partner who does not have HIV:

> Don't you think you're supposed to be responsible for taking that risk as well? Even though the other person is not telling you? Don't you know that you're supposed to know the person better before going for one night stand or at least have protected sex. I mean, it's a two-sided thing, but then you're putting the blame on the person who is HIV-positive but the negative person, don't you have responsibility at all? But … our Singapore law actually makes it that the positive person is at fault for transmitting. It's a responsibility to be shared by both parties.

[46] Rangel and Adam (n 15) 63.

[47] McKie et al (n 15) 347.

[48] Matthew Weait, 'Taking the Blame: Criminal Law, Social Responsibility and the Sexual Transmission of HIV' (2001) 23 *Journal of Social Welfare and Family Law* 441.

In addition, Trevor had practical and strategic reasons for why Section 23 has little significance after he was diagnosed. First, he was unsure of who he had acquired HIV from and suspected that he may have contracted HIV while he was overseas. Second, as a member of the gay community, he believes that a criminal prosecution under Section 23 would simply result in unnecessary negative publicity: 'When there is anything that happens, or when there's any news that goes around HIV, the first thing that is going to lead with is gays, and the next thing you see is gays are supposed to be burned in hell. So, you're already facing all those issues and then you still get those negative remarks. It is actually very demoralising.'

Finally, though Kelvin, a 32-year-old gay man living with HIV, had thought about using the law against whoever had transmitted HIV to him, that thought was 'fleeting' because he was more concerned about who he might have transmitted the virus to:

> At the point of diagnosis, I was more worried about who I might have infected and needed to contact trace than who infected me. So that thought of, like justice or revenge against the person who, who infected me was not as strong as the possible guilt, not possible, but the guilt of who might be positive [because of me].

Another dimension of dysconnectedness derives from the incongruence between the law's conception of risk and responsibility and public health policy that encourages *personal* responsibility in testing as well as messaging around HIV prevention and management (for example, U=U). For example, Peter highlighted how the law reinforces ongoing stigma surrounding HIV, which could in turn dissuade at-risk individuals from getting tested:

> Oh, yeah, I think [the increase in penalties in the 2008 revision to the law) can … make the stigma even worse, because, you know, there's this … extra section just for HIV positive people, so some people might maybe rather, they'd rather not know? Like to be in the [HIV] registry? Who knows what kind of surveillance or this kind of thing? I think it's only natural that people become paranoid because of the different laws being targeted at HIV-positive people. You know, they'd rather be ignorant about their status.

Similarly, some participants raised concerns about how the law does not reflect current medical research around the prevention and management of HIV. For example, Raj highlighted how the law needs to catch up with the scientific consensus that undetectable viral loads are untransmittable (U=U) in serodiscordant sexual relationships:

> I feel like there should be clauses in place where [Section 23(1)] says that the person has taken significant effort or is undetectable as part of the viral load so they will not be susceptible to being prosecuted. And in the end, the person won't be prosecuted because there's no chance of them transmitting HIV. That's why I feel like it [should be] inside [the IDA], because if a person is undetectable, they won't get prosecuted … I think it doesn't take a lot of effort to get HIV, but it takes a lot of effort to keep it at bay. That's something that should be recognised. That's missing from this Infectious Disease Act. That essentially, it hasn't caught up with the science … like, hello, things have changed.

This was likewise echoed in Faris' personal experience with his colleagues and potential sexual partners, highlighting how the law may undermine messaging about medical advances in HIV management and prevention that could destigmatise the disease:

> Even in my job, or in my personal capacity, I've been trying to tell people I'm U=U and undetectable … but there's this stupid law that says that I have to explain the risks. So, it kind of contradicts, and when people try to believe that you know about U=U, but there's this law. So, it makes them very doubtful [about] this scientific evidence of U=U.

Rearticulation of Difference as Resistance and Complicity: Cascading Constructions of the Law's Deviant Subject

While the law lays out several conditions for individuals to communicate the risks of contracting HIV to their sexual partners, our findings demonstrate how GBMSM creatively find ways to avoid compliance with these measures: because participants 'lack the means and know-how', they may 'blithely ignore the measures', or even 'wilfully resist' these laws.[49] Yet, in resisting the applicability of the law to themselves, participants discussed a complex chain of agency that constitutes governing through contagion, and reproduce its logic in relation to imagined Others. In effect, governing through contagion produces a cascading construction of the deviant subject who must be restrained by the law, reproducing marginalisation among different groups of GBMSM based on their HIV status, rendering those who resist complicit in the law's cruelty.

First, participants refused compliance with governing through contagion by reasoning away the relevance of the law to their own lives as a form of 'wilful resistance'.[50] For instance, Leon did not think that the law was relevant to him because he did not engage in high-risk sexual activity and did not need the law's protection since he already takes the necessary precautions to protect himself:

> Because of the way that my sexual practices have played out, I don't think it's very relevant. because I don't think I engage in high-risk sexual behaviour. Unless you consider having multiple sexual partners high risk [but] that's a bit like … okay sure. To have sex with more than one person, I guess that's very high-risk. Better not to have sex at all right? But yeah, I mean other things like specific kinks and unprotected sex, those constitute high-risk behaviour. So, I don't engage in any of those, and most people who engage in sexual activity, we also don't partake in these kinds of things. So yeah, I don't think the law is relevant … I don't need the law to protect me because I protect myself.

[49] Chua and Lee (n 17) 130.
[50] Chua and Lee (n 17) 130.

George demonstrates similar reasoning in contextualising the regulatory role of the law in his own sexual behaviour and potential risk of acquiring HIV:

> In my current lifestyle, I will probably say no, because I'm in a monogamous relationship, and when we do have sex, we try to ensure that it's protected. So, in terms of risk, I think I'm considered by medical experts as a low-risk category. Yeah, because the law says 'who has been exposed to a significant risk of contracting HIV' right, so I feel like that doesn't apply to me.

This is consistent with prior research that found that risk perception of the same sexual behaviour can vary depending on the type of sexual and emotional relationship within which it occurs.[51] For Kyle – a 33-year-old gay person living with HIV – the state flattens the complexities of the risks surrounding public health concerns when it enshrines a particular notion of what is considered to be an unacceptable level of risk.[52] Instead, he conceives of risk as a relative and subjective concept that comprises different dimensions beyond the risk of contracting HIV:

> I think especially with COVID, I think about risk quite a bit also and thinking about how it's so hard to assess risk from only an objective level, right? Because subjectively, like realising that we'll have very different kinds of risk calculus, also, depending on and you see how those risk calculus shift at different points of the pandemic as well, right, like when, you know, is the risk of getting COVID? How does that weigh against the risk of my mental health or the risk of my economic suffering? Risk is such an artificial abstraction. And that doesn't mean that it's not meaningful and important. But I think there's so much thickness around risk, beyond a percentage or a number.

While many participants, such as Leon and George above, perform such resistance by rationalising their risks of contracting HIV in the context of the law, the avoidance of knowledge about one's HIV status can also serve as another means of resistance.[53] As John describes, one can avoid the marginalising effect of Section 23 by avoiding knowledge of one's HIV status:

> I suppose if people have very strong reason to suspect they are positive, and if they go do the test and find out that they're truly positive, then they are really subjected to [Section 23(1)], that you consciously inform people, and you make sure to take every attempt to not get [them] infected with HIV. But if one chooses to live in denial, then it's just telling himself that oh, you know, I'm fine. I'm just having the flu. And that he will always classify himself as not being fully aware, because he didn't make that effort to go and find out. So, he wouldn't be subjected to [Section 23(1)], because he is not a confirmed case. Because he did not take the test … because if you find out the result, and if it is positive, then you're subjected to a huge new set of responsibilities. Some people are not ready to accept the truth and they end up telling themselves they are fine.

[51] G Hart and M Boulton, 'Sexual Behaviour in Gay Men: Towards a Sociology of Risk' in P Aggleton, P Davies and G Hart (eds), *Aids* (London, Taylor & Francis 1995).

[52] Mykhalovskiy (n 38).

[53] MA Kesler et al, 'Prosecution of Non-Disclosure of HIV Status: Potential Impact on HIV Testing and Transmission among HIV-Negative Men Who Have Sex with Men' (2018) 13 *PLoS ONE* 1.

Similar attempts at resistance also emerged from participants' understandings of advancements in HIV science that have implications for HIV transmission risks. Participants largely cited the U=U campaign which draws on evidence that there is effectively no risk of the sexual transmission of HIV by individuals with an undetectable HIV viral load. Many participants, like Kelvin, felt that the law has not reflected such advancements:

> I think with time and research and understanding about U=U, I feel that the law in its current state is a bit generalised based on science, when the law was first enacted. So, if we truly believe in science, now with U=U, I am no different from any person who is not living with HIV. Why should I still be prosecuted if I was on treatment and totally undetectable? But I still, because of the law, have to risk [disclosing my HIV-positive status]. So, in this case, that form of risk, of maybe losing a relationship, or losing potential sexual partner, because I'm ordered by the law to say this, although I am undetectable anymore.

Many interviewees living with HIV also believed that there was effectively no risk of them transmitting HIV given that they personally achieved viral suppression in their own treatment journeys. As a result, participants such as Faris found it perplexing that they still had to communicate the absence of transmission risk to others, at the risk of exposing themselves to stigma and discrimination:

> So, I find it quite stupid, because it doesn't make sense for someone like myself, who already have an undetectable viral load to, you know, explain the risk to the other person. Because there's already like a lot of stigma and discrimination surrounding people like me while living with HIV. So, if you were to say that there's risk but there's actually no risk, it kind of contradicts everything.

Indeed, in *GCP v PP*, the High Court held that an offender with an undetectable viral load would pose a low risk of transmission when determining the appropriate sentence but a person with an undetectable viral load would not be exempt from the strictures of Section 23.[54] Notably, in June 2022, a HIV-positive man was sentenced to an imprisonment of one year even though the court accepted that there was 'effectively no risk of HIV transmission' as he had an undetectable viral load at the time of the offence.[55] The court rejected the defence's argument that the accused did not disclose the risk of transmission because he knew that there was no risk of transmission at all; instead, the court observed that his failure to disclose had 'den[ied his sexual partner] of the freedom to choose whether to engage in sexual activity with the accused even though no viral load was detected'.[56]

Apart from rejecting the applicability of the law based on their own perceptions of personal risk, interviewees also demonstrated their resistance through the construction of the deviant 'Other' to whom the law should apply instead. Thus, in Faris' view, though the law should not apply to someone who already has an

[54] *GCP v PP* at [76].
[55] *PP v GEO* (n 33). The accused filed an appeal which was subsequently withdrawn.
[56] *PP v GEO* (n 33) at [20].

undetectable viral load like him, it should still apply to those who are not on treatment: 'There might be still like a number of [people living with HIV] who are not on treatment but the majority of us who are already on treatment, there's no reason for us to disclose our status when we are really on treatment and won't be able to pass it to the other person.'

Like Amirul, who considered Section 23 necessary to deter the malicious sexual deviant who was deliberately concealing his HIV-positive status so that he can transmit HIV to others, some interviewees drew on their understandings of risk to discuss how the law should not apply to them, but rather to others who are engaging in 'irresponsible' behaviour. As Kelvin puts it:

> I don't think a complete repeal [of the law should be made], but maybe just more nuanced and differentiated to be a bit more targeted … so I think you have to go back to the intention of the law. If the intention is to prevent transmission, which is understandable, then it could be scoped down even more narrow[ly] to target people who are not on treatment, people who are still transmissible and I think that will be a fairly just piece of legislation based on science. Because I think from a public health perspective, knowing that you are transmissible and going around … transmitting, because sometimes that's not your main intention. I don't want to go around to transmit. But I think knowing that you are transmissible and still engaging in possible acts that might transmit the virus is an irresponsible thing to do. And that is different from people who are responsible and go on treatment already and have it undetectable.

This construction of a deviant 'Other' illustrates how governing through contagion operates at the margins by rearticulating differences even within the GBMSM community, engendering new forms of dysconnectedness and marginalisation, rendering those who resist complicit in reproducing the logic and power of governing through contagion.

Conclusion

In developing the concept of 'governing through contagion' to describe the strategies of control that a state may employ in managing the spread of a contagion, Chua and Lee outlined three main themes: centralisation and technology of law, normalisation and technologies of moralisation and inter/dysconnectedness and the rearticulation of difference.[57] Our empirical study has engaged with each of these themes and offers three insights into how they manifest at the margins.

First, our findings emphasise the inescapability of law as the primary mechanism of governing through contagion as it is experienced and imagined by those living at the margins. This extends the insight as to how centralised state infrastructure may result in the totalisation of governing through contagion. In particular,

[57] Chua and Lee (n 17).

we highlight how totalisation is not necessarily achieved through explicit and overt methods of moralisation. Instead, when it comes to the taboo topic of sex and a sexually transmitted infection like HIV/AIDS, totalisation can be achieved through tacit understandings and practices that we coin strategic ambiguity. Specifically, in the case of Section 23, such strategic ambiguity manifests in the lack of public awareness of the law's existence and the vagueness of the language of the provision itself as to who is bound by it and what exactly it is one must do to comply with the law.

Second, just as Section 23 may operate as a technology of moralisation, it is not a one-way street. Instead, participants demonstrated creativity and thoughtfulness as they sought to protect their dignity and moral status as responsible members of society by reasoning away the applicability of the law to themselves. In so doing, they exercised their agency in articulating an alternative logic that challenges the state's marginalising discourse which paints all GBMSM and people living with HIV with the same brush. At the same time, try as GBMSM might, whether they are HIV-positive or not, they remain bound by the moralising logic of Section 23 as to what constitutes sufficient disclosure to obtain informed consent.

Finally, we offer a glimpse into what resistance at the margins of governing through contagion looks like as GBMSM 'stay with the dysconnectedness' not merely as objects to be governed through contagion but also active participants in the process.[58] Further, echoing Matsuda's call for legal scholars to 'look to the bottom',[59] our chapter calls attention to those at the margins of Singapore society and how they grapple with the dysconnectedness of governing through contagion as they strive to protect themselves and each other from the virus that threatens to desecrate their most intimate moments in life. In doing so, we uncovered not only *how* such resistance takes place but also *why*: in resisting against the marginalising effect of the law, GBMSM were motivated by a desire to maintain their dignity as respectable and responsible members of society.

In closing, we call on scholars and policymakers to pay greater attention to the role of law, particularly criminal law, as a tool in governing through contagion at the margins.[60] Inasmuch as governing through contagion may seem inevitable or necessary, our chapter suggests that the legal methods of control through which it operates should not be enacted or implemented without careful consideration.[61] In this regard, the Ministry of Health announced in December 2023 that it was re-examining Section 23's continued relevance as part of a broader review of the

[58] Chua and Lee (n 17) 130.

[59] M Matsuda, 'Looking to the Bottom: Critical Legal Studies and Reparations' (1987) 22 *Harvard Civil Rights-Civil Liberties Law Review* 323.

[60] See also A Klein, 'Criminal Law, Public Health, and Governance of HIV Exposure and Transmission' (2009) 13 *The International Journal of Human Rights* 251.

[61] JM Dwyer, 'Legislating AIDS Away: The Limited Role of Legal Persuasion in Minimizing the Spread of the Human Immunodeficiency Virus' (1993) 9 *Journal of Contemporary Health Law and Policy* 167.

IDA and would take into account the latest scientific evidence in evaluating the law's alignment with Singapore's public health policy goals. Especially when the contagion is one that disproportionately targets communities at the margins of society, it is incumbent on those implementing strategies of control not to inflict further harm and marginalisation against the vulnerable among us.

6

The Vagrancy Law Model

*Governing Through Social Contagion in the Anglo World, c. 1824–1932**

CHRISTOPHER ROBERTS

Introduction

This chapter aims to trace the nature and impact of what is termed the 'vagrancy law model' over the course of the century or so after passage of England's influential Vagrancy Act 1824. Despite relative lack of attention, this chapter suggests the vagrancy law model has been enormously influential. In the view of Christopher Tiedeman, a late nineteenth-century American police power theorist, such laws were essential because the vagrant was 'the chrysalis of every species of criminal'.[1] From our perspective, we might say such laws were essential because, more than any other measures, they enabled the authorities' criminal-making project.[2] The power of the vagrancy law model has been enhanced by how little noticed and hence how little challenged it has been, a lack of attention cultivated both by the tendency of such laws to be linked to minor penalties, often administered through summary and less-judicialised processes, as well as through the stigma and sense of degradation and contaminatory threat generated by the ideological developments considered herein.

Understanding the history of vagrancy law, this chapter suggests, is key to understanding various regimes that might be understood as different forms of governing through contagion. In the first place, it is worth noting that English vagrancy laws themselves initially emerged in the wake of the bubonic plague, as

* The research for this chapter was supported by Early Career Scheme Research Grant 24601320 from the Hong Kong Research Grants Council.

[1] C Tiedeman, *A Treatise on the Limitations of Police Power in the United States* (Charleston, Nabu Press, 1886) 117.

[2] For a classic study of the development of this project in nineteenth-century England, see M Wiener, *Reconstructing the Criminal: Culture, Law, and Policy in England, 1830–1914* (Cambridge, Cambridge University Press, 1990).

a means, according to the most common understandings, of attempting to redress the improved bargaining position the much smaller pool of surviving potential labourers gained in the wake of that catastrophe, by subjecting workers to punishment should they refrain from providing their labour in a compliant manner. While not focused on combatting a pandemic as such, vagrancy laws were directly targeted at the consequences, in terms of the ruling elites' loss of control, that might flow from and follow mass pandemic-related death and upheaval.

The connection between the vagrancy law model and the idea of governing through contagion runs deeper, however. As the remainder of this chapter will explore, vagrancy laws, as they evolved over time, came to combine several elements which, while not perhaps unusual, are under-explored in most legal scholarship. Vagrancy laws came to target several different sorts of loosely affiliated activity, and targeted those elements in support of a combination of aims, including most essentially the above mentioned aim of labour discipline as well as the broader aim of public order control. By rolling up and penalising numerous forms of activity together, in support of multiple aims, vagrancy laws came to play an important role in shaping popular images and ideas of the nature of social threats and of the character of the worst off in society. Along the way, they seamlessly combined the juridical, disciplinary and security modalities of power described by the governing through contagion model.[3]

While the precise combination of activities and ways of being vagrancy laws targeted is in some senses obscure, the attention of vagrancy laws can be broadly understood through reference to the idea of social contagion. All of the activities that vagrancy laws came to target – be it those broadly classifiable as linked to poverty, those classifiable as linked to immorality or those classifiable as linked to criminality – came to be understood, in the minds of the authorities and elites within society, as negative practices transferable from one individual to another by means of contagion. The fourth characteristic of vagrancy laws meanwhile – their tendency to target migrants – represented a natural extension of all of the above, as the logic of social contagion called for migration to be sharply limited, in order to prevent the above negative characteristics from spreading. The manner in which vagrancy laws directed their attention was remarkably flexible over time, moreover. While the poorest and most marginalised were always targeted, whether and how racial differentiation was introduced into the picture varied. In addition, the grounds upon which the poor were characterised – and accordingly, the policy responses that seemed most appropriate – differed over time and space: at times, their idleness was perceived as their most significant negative characteristic; at times, their moral depravity; at times, their potential to engage in violence, either individually or collectively; at times, their genetic inferiority.

These various tendencies of vagrancy law demonstrated other component aspects emphasised by the governing through contagion model as well. First, the

[3] See LJ Chua and JJG Lee, 'Governing through Contagion' in V Ramraj (ed), *COVID-19 in Asia: Law and Policy Contexts* (Oxford, Oxford University Press, 2021) 115.

expansion in the power of law vagrancy law advanced was almost always linked to the growing power of the central state, which enhanced its powers both geographically and in terms of the extent to which it could interfere in individual lives across the period considered. Second, vagrancy law was linked to technological developments, at least insofar as the expansion of both law and ideology in the period were themselves enabled by various forms of technology, insofar as the complex legal systems that developed could themselves be thought of as a sort of technology and of course with particular clarity in the context of the medical developments that enabled forced sterilisation to be utilised in the early twentieth century. Third, the vagrancy law model that developed in the period was centrally concerned with what Chua and Lee have termed *inter/dysconnectedness*, the delineation of particular lines of difference within populations and the development of particular modes of thinking about the populations so defined.

The vagrancy law model, and associated forms of public rhetoric and ideology, therefore, can readily be understood as forms of governing through contagion. At the same time, the prominence of such a non-directly pandemic-related form of 'contagion' governance raises certain questions in relation to the significance and impact of the more specifically health crisis-related form of contagion governance identified and explored by Chua and Lee.[4] Leaving difficult questions around origins aside, the simple fact is that vagrancy law has formed a consistent, fundamental part of legal systems all around the world for the past several centuries at the very least. Governing through social contagion, in short, has been and remains central to modern legal systems. The additional elements and wrinkles introduced in the context of health-related contagions, therefore, so eloquently and thoughtfully explored by Chua and Lee, may perhaps be understood as an additional layer of governance that can, in certain situations, come to sit on top of – and unfortunately, in many circumstances, augment the worst aspects of – governance through social contagion of the sort explored below.

This impact of vagrancy law is traced on two fronts in the following discussion. The next section discusses the Vagrancy Act 1824. As the section details, while the Act was not lengthy, it was remarkably internally diversified. In particular, this chapter suggests the Vagrancy Act 1824 had four different forms of repressive law within it: anti-poor law; anti-criminal law; anti-immorality law; and anti-migrant law. It was a seeder law in this sense, helping to advance all of the above regimes at a time when they were still relatively underdeveloped individually, before each area of law was ultimately able to develop more fully on its own.

Rather than diminishing its strength, this combination of aspects enhanced vagrancy law's effectiveness and public legitimacy, as the normative strength of all of the above perceived ills could be combined together to justify anti-vagrancy actions. The strength of vagrancy law measures in practice was enhanced and justified by various rhetorical and ideological frameworks that developed over the course of the century following the passage of the Vagrancy Act 1824, in close

[4] See Chua and Lee 'Governing through Contagion' (n 3).

connection to the operation of such laws. The relevant rhetorics and ideologies took many different forms; broadly speaking, however, they were all linked to the idea of 'social contagion'. The chapter next explores the relevant ideological and rhetorical developments. These developments in turn helped pave the way for even more dramatic developments within the vagrancy law tradition, one of which, forced sterilisation, is explored briefly in the final section.

The Vagrancy Law Model

As noted above, vagrancy laws in England are typically traced to the era of the bubonic plague, in the wake of which the government of Edward III passed the 1349 and 1351 Statutes of Labourers.[5] Rather than fading away after the worst years of the plague, however, the new approach to labour control those laws advanced remained an essential part of the law over the following centuries.[6] While a firmly established vagrancy law framework was already in place by the nineteenth century, therefore, that century nonetheless saw several important further developments. The 1810s were a period of serious unrest in England, leading to the deployment of a large army to the north of the country, the Peterloo massacre and the passage of several draconian laws.[7] The disturbances of the period were investigated by a series of Parliamentary inquiries conducted between 1815 and 1821.[8] One result of those inquiries was a call for more forceful vagrancy law. This led in turn to the passage of the Vagrancy Act 1824,[9] an incredibly influential act that provided a basic template for the further development and dissemination of vagrancy laws over the subsequent centuries, to such an extent that its impact may still be strongly felt in numerous jurisdictions around the world today.

The Vagrancy Act 1824 defies brief description, such was the range of the functions it fulfilled. For present purposes, the most interesting and significant characteristic of the law was the extent of the categories of action and ways of being which it subsumed under the heading of 'vagrancy'. While 'vagrants' were broken down into the categories of the 'idle and disorderly 'rogues and vagabonds' and

[5] See 23 Edw III (1349); 25 Edw III s 2 (1351). For more see L Poos, 'The Social Context of Statute of Labourers Enforcement' (1983) 1 *Law & History Review* 27; S Cohn, 'After the Black Death: Labour Legislation and Attitudes towards Labour in Late-Medieval Western Europe' (2007) 60 *Economic History Review* 457.

[6] For more, see C Roberts, 'Discretion and the Rule of Law: The Significance and Endurance of Vagrancy and Vagrancy-Type Laws in England, the British Empire and the British Colonial World' (2023) 33 *Duke Journal of Comparative & International Law* 181.

[7] For more, see S Palmer, *Police and Protest in England and Ireland 1780–1850* (Cambridge, Cambridge University Press, 1988) 168–88; R Poole, *Peterloo: The English Uprising* (Oxford, Oxford University Press 2019).

[8] See Committee on the State of Mendicity in the Metropolis, Report, House of Commons Paper No 473, Session 1814–15 (1815); Select Committee on the State of Mendicity in the Metropolis, Report, House of Commons Paper No 396, Session 1816 (1816); Select Committee on the Existing Laws Relating to Vagrants, Report, House of Commons Paper No 543, Session 1821 (1821); all cited in A McLeod, 'On the Origins of Consorting Laws' (2013) 37 *Melbourne University Law Review* 103, 109 n 37.

[9] 5 Geo IV c 83 (1824).

'incorrigible rogues' in the law itself, the implications and functions of the law can be understood more clearly through a more purposeful, analytical typology.[10] In particular, the Vagrancy Act 1824 included four different types of penalisations. First, and perhaps at the core of the law, was its anti-poor components, which included the penalisation of those who refused to work, beggars, the homeless and unlicensed peddlers. Second, the law included a pronounced anti-immorality component, within which could be understood to fall its penalisation of 'prostitutes', fortune-tellers, public indecency, family desertion and public gambling. Third, the law included an anti-criminal component, which included its penalisation of those found with criminal instruments as well as its penalisation of those simply deemed suspicious. Finally, the law also contained an anti-migrant component, defined not so much by any of its substantive categories as by the procedural possibility of deportation that it authorised.

The anti-poor component of the law was that with the longest pedigree, constituting a central component of such laws from the fourteenth century Statutes of Labourers on. The purpose of this component of vagrancy law was never solely to punish the poor as such, but rather also to force the poor into work, both by penalising idleness and limiting workers' ability to move freely in search of work, as well as by diminishing their bargaining position and hence the terms upon which they might sell their labour. In the Vagrancy Act 1824, as noted, the component of vagrancy law took various forms, including the penalisation of alternative forms of livelihood – including begging, unlicensed street-selling and sex work (though the latter fits even more clearly in the following category) – as well as broader authorisation of the penalisation of the poor and marginalised.

While not new,[11] the anti-immorality component of the Vagrancy Act 1824 grew in prominence through passage of the Act itself, as well as during the decades that followed. Within the 1824 act, 'prostitutes', fortune-tellers, public indecency, family desertion and public gambling were all penalised, indicating the broad moral brush the law painted with, which penalised what were deemed anti-social, anti-familial and anti-Christian activities in similar manners. In subsequent years, in other times and places, other components would be added to this tradition including, for instance, the penalisation of 'obeah', a form of spiritual practice, throughout the Caribbean;[12] the penalisation of cross-dressing in British Guiana;[13]

[10] See 5 Geo IV c 83 (1824) ss 3–4.

[11] For more, see E Bristow, *Vice and Vigilance: Purity Movements in Britain Since 1700* (Lanham MD, Rowman & Littlefield, 1977); MJD Roberts, *Making English Morals: Voluntary Association and Moral Reform in England, 1787–1886* (Cambridge, Cambridge University Press, 2004); D Heath, *Purifying Empire: Obscenity and the Politics of Moral Regulation in Britain, India and Australia* (Cambridge, Cambridge University Press, 2010).

[12] For more, see D Paton, *The Cultural Politics of Obeah: Religion, Colonialism and Modernity in the Caribbean World* (Cambridge, Cambridge University Press, 2015); D Boaz, 'Fraud, Vagrancy and the "Pretended" Exercise of Supernatural Powers in England, South Africa and Jamaica' (2018) 5 *Law & History* 55.

[13] See British Guiana, Summary Jurisdiction (Offences) Act (1893). That provision has only very recently been successfully challenged. See *McEwan and others v Attorney General* [2018] CCJ 30 (AJ); Muri Assunção, 'Guyana Decriminalizes Cross-Dressing, 3 Years after International Court Ruled against Law' *NY Daily News* (11 August 2021).

and anti-'catamite' laws, which penalised male cross-dressing and homosexuality in jurisdictions such as Northern Nigeria and Sudan.[14]

The anti-criminal component of vagrancy law, which might also be termed the 'anti-vagabond' regime, also constituted a key component within the development of such laws over the nineteenth century. In the Vagrancy Act 1824 this component was most clearly reflected in what would later come to be known as the 'sus' clause, a provision authorising the detention of 'every suspected Person or reputed Thief, frequenting any River … or any Street … or any Place of public Resort … with Intent to commit Felony'.[15] The police power enhancing aim of this component of the law could be further discerned from the fact that a similar clause was included in the Metropolitan Police Act 1829, the act which first established a 'modern' police in England, which gave the police the power

> to apprehend all loose, idle, and disorderly Persons … disturbing the Public Peace, or whom he shall have cause to suspect of any evil Designs, and all Persons whom he shall find between Sunset and the Hour of Eight in the Forenoon lying in any Highway, Yard, or other Place, or loitering therein, and not giving a satisfactory Account of themselves.[16]

Similar clauses were included in subsequent police acts as well, while 'police regulations' around the empire were a frequent source for the further expansion of anti-vagrancy measures.[17]

The anti-migrant function of vagrancy laws, meanwhile, as noted, was not tied to any of the substantive components of the law. Rather, it grew out of the long connection between vagrancy law measures and pass requirements and the removal of non-permitted migrants those laws authorised, a power authorised by the Vagrancy Act 1824 as well.[18] Initially, when these laws were primarily domestic measures within England, these rules were applied to restrict movement around the country. By the early nineteenth century, however – and increasingly as time went on, especially in the colonial context – the relevant rules began to take on an international dimension. In British Hong Kong, for example, perhaps the primary function to which vagrancy laws were put, from the point of occupation on, was the discretionary removal of poorer members of the Chinese population.[19]

These four constituent parts of the Vagrancy Act 1824 would not remain bound to that measure alone: rather, vagrancy law was exported everywhere the British planted their flag, including the settler colonies as well as more purely imperial domains.[20] Initially, vagrancy laws served as an important vessel through which all

[14] See Sudan Penal Code (1899), s 448(2)(e); Human Rights Watch, 'This Alien Legacy: The Origins of "Sodomy" Laws in British Colonialism' (17 December 2008).

[15] 5 Geo IV c 83 (1824), s 4.

[16] 10 Geo IV c 44, s 7.

[17] For more, see Roberts, 'Discretion and the Rule of Law' (n 6).

[18] 5 Geo IV c 83 (1824), s 20.

[19] For more, see C Roberts and HWH Leung, 'Governance Through Vagrancy Law in Hong Kong, 1841–1941' in C Griffiths and L Korporowicz (eds), *English Law, the Legal Profession and Colonialism: Histories, Parallels, and Influences* (forthcoming 2024).

[20] For more, see Roberts (n 6).

such measures could be enforced and justified. As time went on, however, and local legal codes developed – as they did dramatically over the course of the nineteenth century around the British Empire – the subcomponent parts of vagrancy law were increasingly spun off into their own distinct legal provisions and regimes, including anti-homelessness, anti-begging, anti-street selling laws and numerous other minor regulations under which the poorer residents of cities might be punished; anti-prostitution and vice laws, dedicated anti-blasphemy and anti-obscenity laws, specific laws penalising homosexual acts and other anti-immorality measures; laws extending the discretionary powers of the police to apprehend, detain and punish suspicious persons as and when deemed necessary; and laws tightly governing and controlling migration, freedom of movement and freedom of residence. If anything, the police power-enhancing capacity of vagrancy laws was the subordinate regime on the basis of which such laws, and their successors in the form of loitering laws, were seen as most indispensable, and the police-power magnifying function of such measures remains closely linked to the ongoing force of vagrancy-type laws to the present day.[21] At the same time, the anti-immorality function of vagrancy laws was perhaps that which did the most to enable them to influence public discourse more broadly, as the following section explores.

Rhetoric and Ideologies of Social Contagion

The above developments in law were paralleled by developments in justificatory rhetoric and ideology. The rhetoric and ideologies considered here, which drew from and supported the vagrancy law model over the course of the century, were notable both for their fluidity and regularity. While in some ways the manner in which the threat of the poor was conceptualised shifted dramatically over the course of the period considered, in other ways – in particular, in terms of the close connection drawn between poverty, crime and immorality, as well as by reliance on a theory of social contagion – the same themes and approaches were consistently reiterated over time.

A word here at the beginning is appropriate as to the nature of the sources that follow, which explore developments not only in Britain, the British Empire and some (formerly) British settler colonies – the United States in particular – but also the evolution of ideas concerning and relating to social contagion in continental Europe, including especially France, Germany and Italy. In contrast to legal traditions, where national (/colonial) boundaries were relatively more significant, ideas flowed freely across borders in the nineteenth century. While the history below could be told by referring to the Anglo world alone, to do so would artificially exclude developments in ideology taking place in Britain's European neighbours which often transferred into Britain; those developments are hence referenced at

[21] See Roberts (n 6).

various points below, as and when they seem particularly pertinent to the history recounted. At the same time, while every national tradition's vagrancy law was to a certain extent unique, it should be clearly noted that vagrancy law was not a product of the British Empire alone – rather, every major power deployed or came to deploy vagrancy laws to similar effect over the course of the nineteenth and early twentieth centuries.

Early in the nineteenth century, in a manner which is not sufficiently recognised, the development of vagrancy law closely paralleled the growth of the new field of ethnography. 'Ethnography' was a scholarly approach initiated by German scholars in the eighteenth century, with the term first deployed by Johann Friedrich Schöpperlin and AF Thilo, before it was more widely popularised by August Ludwig von Schlözer and Christoph Wilhelm Jacob Gattere.[22] The concept was developed by French scholar Georg Bernhard Deppin, who characterised ethnography as field devoted to the study of the 'moral part' of geography and history, including the study of the question of 'indolence versus industry' in particular.[23] Insofar as one of the core targets of vagrancy law was the 'indolent' individual, early ethnography could be seen as a form of criminology addressed to the problems of 'vagrancy' in particular.

The object of focus of both ethnography and vagrancy law was crystallised in the early nineteenth century in various 'charitable' associations.[24] One prominent example was the 'Society for the Diffusion of Useful Knowledge which set out to train the working class in industry and self-discipline – building on and reinforcing the idea that the distribution of wealth was not the product of political economy, but rather of personal characteristics. As time went on, the Society sponsored a range of 'ethnographic' interventions including, for example, Edward Lane's 1860 study of the 'Egyptian character', Manners and Customs of the Modern Egyptians, which commented ad nauseum on the indolent nature of Egyptians.[25]

The domestic focus of an ethnographic lens in the period was particularly pronounced in the work of Henry Mayhew.[26] Mayhew's account presented the

[22] See H Vermeulen, *Early History of Ethnography and Ethnology in the German Enlightenment* (Lincoln, University of Nebraska Press, 2008).

[23] See GB Depping, *Evening Entertainments* (Philadelphia, A Towar, 1817), cited in T Mitchell, *Colonising Egypt* (Berkeley, University of California Press, 1988) 106.

[24] In addition to constituting a key component of these two fields, the idea of a close linkage between indolence and poverty was widely popular in the period, finding reflection in the work of major scholars of the period, such as Bentham and Malthus, as well. See T Bentham, *Outline of a Work Entitled Pauper Management Improvement* (London, R & A Taylor 1817) (first published 1798); T Malthus, *An Essay on the Principle of Population* (1989) (first published in 1798) 106, 112.

[25] E Lane, *Manners and Customs of the Modern Egyptians* (London, John Murray, 1860), cited in T Mitchell, *Colonising Egypt* (Berkeley, University of California Press 1988) 105–6.

[26] Mayhew described his task in his 1862 The Criminal Prisons of London and Scenes of Prison Life as 'ethnological' explicitly observing:

> We have thought the peculiarities of [criminals'] nature as worthy of study in an ethnological point of view, as those of the people of other countries, and we have learnt to look upon them as a distinct race of individuals, as distinct as the Malay is from the Caucasian tribe … An enumeration of the several natural orders and species of criminals will let the reader see that the class is multifarious, and surely, in a scientific point of view, as worthy of being studied as the varieties of animalcules.

poor of London in sharply civilisationally hierarchical terms, especially the lower rank of which he specifically referred to with the language of vagrancy: as he put it, the people of London constituted 'socially, morally, and perhaps even physically … two distinct races, viz., the wanderers and the settlers – the vagabond and the citizen – the nomadic and the civilized tribes'.[27] Elsewhere, Mayhew explored the distinguishing traits of the vagabond class, which included 'high cheek bones and protruding jaws', a tendency to use 'slang language', a 'repugnance to continuous labour' and a 'love of cruelty'. Overarchingly, Mayhew helped to normalise the idea of the existence of a separate, lesser class of 'vagrants' within British society, not only to the elites but also, given the mass popularity of his work, to the reading public at large.

Alongside the development of this ethnographic accompaniment of the vagrancy law legacy, which was often presented in the register of sympathetic paternalism, the mid-nineteenth century saw the dangerous nature of the lower, vagrant class highlighted by a number of authors who were clearly quite concerned with the threat they might pose to public order as well. In the 1840s the Chartist movement in England and simmering unrest in continental Europe, combined with the still-fresh memory of the French revolution, led to a number of characterisations that combined an emphasis on the 'degraded', 'barbaric' and 'savage' nature of the poorer segments of the population with an emphasis on the serious social and political threat they posed. In 1840, for instance, Eugène Buret, a French sociologist and economist, observed, using close to medical language to describe a social threat:

> In the very heart of the busiest centres of industry and trade [in England and France] you see thousands of human beings reduced to a state of barbarism by vice and destitution … The governments are rightly apprehensive. They fear lest formidable dangers may some day burst forth from amid these degraded and corrupted people.[28]

H Mayhew and J Binney, *The Criminal Prisons of London and Scenes of Prison Life* (London, Griffin, Bohn, 1862), 45. As Jones has observed, by the 1870s there was 'an insatiable middle-class demand for travellers' tales' in the British reading public, meaning stories about lower-class life in London; an increasingly impoverished Mayhew, amongst others, would, in Jones' telling, 'cate[r] for this appetite for the quaint, the picturesque, and the grotesque in London Characters (1870) – a sad decline from his former plan to complete a comprehensive social survey of London'. GS Jones, *Outcast London: A Study in the Relationship between Classes in Victorian Society* (Oxford, Clarendon Press 1971) 14. To what extent this was, in fact, a decline, rather than simply a differently pitched variation of his traditional body of work, is debatable. For more on the craze for 'explorers' stories in late nineteenth-century Britain, see P Keating (ed), *Into Unknown England 1866–1913: Selections from the Social Explorers* (Manchester, Manchester University Press, 1976).

[27] H Mayhew, *London Labour and the London Poor* (London, Griffin, Bohn and Co, 1861. As Mayhew put it elsewhere, he wanted to ensure that his readers would 'no longer confound the honest, independent working men, with the vagrant beggars and pilferers of the country', instead recognising that 'the one class is as respectable and worthy, as the other is degraded and vicious'. See Mayhew, *London Labour*, vol 4, and Mayhew and Binney, *Criminal Prisons* (n 26) at 87.

[28] E Buret, *Of the Distress of the Working Classes in England and France* (Paris, Paulin, 1840). As Chevalier has observed, immigrants to Paris in the 1820s were 'universally described in terms of what we should nowadays call racial or ethnic differentiation … The immigrants, alien as they were to the manners, customs, morality and laws of the community, were more than ever "misérables," wretched,

In Buret's account, that is, the urban poor were akin to a plague on their cities and their nations as a whole, from which a threat of broader infection was constantly present. The same year Honoré Antoine Frégier, a police official in Paris, writing on the population in Paris, hit upon a powerful general terminology through which to capture the sentiment of the authorities towards the threatening poor of the cities, whom he described as the 'dangerous classes':

> the poor and vicious classes have always been and will always be the most productive breeding ground of evildoers of all sorts; it is they whom we shall designate as the dangerous classes. For even when vice is not accompanied by perversity, by the very fact that it allies itself with poverty in the same person, he is a proper object of fear to society, he is dangerous.[29]

The strength of these negative characterisations can be seen by the fact that similar characterisations were utilised in the writing of leftist authors as well. In the same period Marx and Engels, in need of a revolutionary subject, worked to revive and romanticise the image of the 'proletariat', a term which had traditionally been used to refer to the poorest and worst off in society.[30] In the course of this positive re-characterisation of the image of a category that had previously been understood as broadly synonymous with that of the 'dangerous classes', however, Marx and Engels nonetheless chose to preserve a purely negative categorisation applied to the worst off in society, whom they rebranded as the 'lumpenproletariat'.[31]

barbarians, savages, nomads'. L Chevalier, *Laboring Classes and Dangerous Classes in Paris During the First Half of the Nineteenth Century* (New York, Howard Fertig 1973) 361.

[29] HA Frégier, *Des classes dangereuses de la population de la grande villes* (Paris, J.-B. Baillière, 1840). The above references are cited in D Taylor, 'Beyond the Bounds of Respectable Society: The "Dangerous Classes" in Victorian and Edwardian England' in J Rowbothan and K Stevenson (eds), *Criminal Conversations: Victorian Crimes, Social Panic, and Moral Outrage* (Colombus, Ohio State University Press, 2005) 5. Elsewhere, Frégier referred to the 'dangerous classes' as the 'proletarian' classes, which he described as typified by the 'ragpicker and nomad' – in short, the vagrant. While it seems reasonable to trace the more widespread use of the term 'dangerous classes' to Frégier, Wallerstein, citing Pierre Leon, suggests an earlier progeny, tracing the term to mid- to late-seventeenth century discourse, in which he suggests 'the two concepts working classes and dangerous classes began to be linked, developing "in the mind of the ruling classes" an association "between poverty and crime"'. I Wallerstein, *The Modern World System II: Mercantilism and the Consolidation of the European World-Economy, 1600–1750* (Berkeley, University of California Press, 1980) 125, quoting P Leon, 'Morcellement et emergence du monde ouvrier' in F Braudel and E Labrousse (eds), *Histoire Economique et Sociale de la France* (Paris, Presses Universitaires de France, 1970) 686.

[30] See R Bussard, 'The "Dangerous Class" of Marx and Engels: The Rise of the Idea of the Lumpenproletariat' (1987) 8 *History of European Ideas* 675, 678. There, Bussard observed the importance of the writings of Jean Charles Léonard Simonde de Sismondi and Felicité de Lamennais in the 1830s in transforming the idea of the proletariat. The disparaging image of the 'proletariat' may be seen, for example, in Granier de Cassagnac's *Histoire de classes ouvrières et des classes bourgeoises* (published in 1838), in which he referred to the proletariat as a cross between robbers and prostitutes (a cross between two figures typical of vagrancy law). See W Benjamin, *Charles Baudelaire: A Lyric Poet in the Era of High Capitalism*, H Zohn (trans), (London, Verso, 1983) 22.

[31] Marx and Engels gave further content to this term by using it to refer to the ignorant rabble most easily converted into reactionary agents, a deployment of the term that can be seen in *The German Ideology* (published in 1846), *The Communist Manifesto* (published in 1848), a November 1948 chapter

After the revolutionary tides of the 1840s were defeated and the century progressed, references to the 'dangerous classes' began to diminish. The terminology that arose was in some ways even more concerning, however. One term for the poorest members of society which became quite popular in the late nineteenth century, though its usage would not prove enduring, was that of the 'residuum', a reference to the substance left behind following a chemical process. Perhaps the first use of 'residuum' in the social context was its invocation by John Bright, a Liberal MP representing Birmingham, during parliamentary debates on the Second Reform Act of 1867. As Bright put it:

> At this moment, in all, or nearly all our boroughs, as many of us know, sometimes to our sorrow, there is a small class which it would be much better for themselves if they were not enfranchised, because they have no independence whatsoever, and it would be much better for the constituency also that they should be excluded, and there is no class so much interested in having that small class excluded as the intelligent and honest working men. I call this class the residuum, which there is in almost every constituency, of almost hopeless poverty and dependence.[32]

If 'residuum' had a utility, it was both in its scientific pretension as well as in its ability to dehumanise the poorest in society by rendering them into a purely material product, and a residual one at that. In the final decades of the nineteenth century the terminology of the 'residuum' was frequently found interlinked to an idea of the poor as something like a medical problem within the social body. In his 1884 *The Domestic Sanitary Arrangements of the Metropolitan Poor*, for instance, doctor and sanitary reformer John Tripe suggested an existential link between the residuum and their living conditions:

> The sanitary arrangements usually correspond with the houses; the water closets being dark, foul smelling; the water supply apparatus frequently defective, the supply generally insufficient; the cisterns dirty, being rarely cleaned out; the dustbins frequently broken and full, containing offensive refuse, even excrement, so that it is dangerous

by Marx in 'Neue Rheinische Zeitung', included in the volume of collected chapters *The Class Struggles in France 1848–1850* (published in 1850), in Engels' 'The Peasant War in Germany' published in (1850), and in Marx's *The Eighteenth Brumaire of Louis Napoleon* (published in 1852). In *The Eighteenth Brumaire*, Marx described the lumpenproletariat in the following terms:

> Alongside ruined roués with questionable means of support and of dubious origin, degenerate and adventurous scions of the bourgeoisie, there were vagabonds, discharged soldiers, discharged convicts, runaway galley slaves, swindlers, charlatans, lazzaroni, pickpockets, tricksters, gamblers, procurers, brothel keepers, porters, literati, organ grinders, rag-pickers, knife-grinders, tinkers, beggars; in short, the entirely undefined, disintegrating mass, thrown hither and yon, which the French call la bohème.

For more, see H Draper, 'The Concept of the "Lumpenproletariat"' in Marx and Engels 6 *Economies et Sociétés* (1972) 2286–2312; Bussard, 'The "Dangerous" Class' (n 30); N Thoburn, 'Difference in Marx: the Lumpenproletariat and the Proletarian Unnamable' (2002) 31 *Economy and Society* 434; M Cowling, 'Marx's Lumpenproletariat and Murray's Underclass: Concepts Best Abandoned?' in M Cowling and J Martin (eds), *Marx's Eighteenth Brumaire: (Post)Modern Interpretations* (London, Pluto, 2008).

[32] Parliamentary Debates, 3rd Series 636–37 (26 Mar 1867), cited in S Alexander, *Victorian Literature and the Physics of the Imponderable* (Pittsburgh, University of Pittsburgh Press, 2015) 51–52.

> to empty them. Houses in this state are frequently occupied by the residuum, many of whom are disgustingly filthy and destructive in their habits.[33]

Elsewhere, the 'residuum' began to be described in terms of spiritual and/or biological weakness. Professor Alfred Marshall described the residuum in 1885 as 'those who have a poor physique and a weak character – those who are limp in body and mind'.[34] Conservative polemicist William Hurrell Mallock described the residuum in similarly existential terms, observing:

> The right way, indeed, in which to regard [the unfortunate class] is, not as a product of [the modern industrial] system, but rather as something which has resisted it – not as a part of it, but as something which has failed to be absorbed by it; and the real problem for philanthropists and reformers is, not how to interfere with existing economic tendencies, but how, so far as possible, to bring the residuum under their influence.[35]

In all three writers, description of the poorest as the 'residuum' allowed for a tracing of the roots of contemporary urban poverty to the characteristics of the poor, mirroring and reiterating in different terms the traditional emphasis on their immorality, while continuing to occlude the need to contemplate broader structural, economic and political sources of society's inequalities.

The idea of the 'residuum' helped pave the way for more explicitly biological understandings of poverty, immorality and criminality as the nineteenth century drew to an end as well.[36] In many ways, however, the ethnographic tradition played an even more essential role in such regards. The Société Ethnologique, established by William Frederic in 1839, constituted one important link in the development of ethnology in the direction of the 'science of races'.[37] The 'science' of phrenology facilitated such developments as well, as illustrated for instance by the dispatch of the skulls of several 'thugs' – an Indian variant of the vagabond – to Edinburgh's Phrenological Society in 1833.[38] 'Eugenics' as such, the epitome of the biological understanding of 'race', poverty and immorality, was coined as a term by Francis Galton in 1883.[39] From there, the field grew rapidly, becoming widely influential by the first decade of the twentieth century.[40] In Britain, the Eugenics Educational

[33] J Tripe, *The Domestic Sanitary Arrangements of the Metropolitan Poor* (London, William Clowes, 1884), cited in Alexander, *Victorian Literature* (n 32) 63–64.

[34] See Sir C Dilke, Report of Proceedings and Papers of the Industrial Remuneration Conference (1885) 197, cited in Jones, *Outcast London* (n 26) 11.

[35] WH Mallock, *Classes and Masses: Wealth, Wages, and Welfare in the United Kingdom* (London, A & C Black, 1896), cited in Alexander, *Victorian Literature* (n 33) 63–64.

[36] For more on the manner in which the idea of the residuum supported the growth of eugenics, see P Mazumdar, 'The Eugenicists and the Residuum: The Problem of the Urban Poor' (1980) 54 *Bulletin of the History of Medicine* 204.

[37] See E Sibeud, 'The Metamorphosis of Ethnology in France, 1839–1930' in H Kuklick (ed), *A New History of Anthropology* (Hoboken NJ, Wiley-Blackwell, 2008) 97–98.

[38] See K Wagner, 'Confessions of a Skull: Phrenology and Colonial Knowledge in Early Nineteenth-Century India' (2010) 69 *History Workshop Journal* 27.

[39] F Galton, *Inquiries into Human Faculty and Its Development* (London, MacMillan, 1883).

[40] See M Adams (ed), *The Wellborn Science. Eugenics in Germany, France, Brazil, and Russia* (Oxford, Oxford University Press, 1990); S Khül, *The Nazi Connection: Eugenics, American Racism and German*

Society (later renamed the Eugenics Society) was founded, as a breakaway from the Moral Education League, in 1907.[41] Similar developments took place in the following decades in other parts of the British Empire as well.[42]

The growth of eugenics was closely paralleled by the growth of criminology, which ensured that the tendency towards crime, a key component of the vagrancy law legacy as a whole, would not be lost from the image of the lowest rungs of society within the biological understanding of human nature that was in vogue in the times. While criminology as such was a late nineteenth-century development, the idea that there was a close linkage between poverty and crime had, as the vagrancy law legacy suggests, long been established wisdom. Patrick Colquhoun, an important police theorist, provided one important articulation of the linkage at the beginning of the nineteenth century.[43] The linkage and its thorough indebtedness to the vagrancy law model were similarly emphasised by Thomas Plint, a well-off supporter of the Liberal party, in the mid-century, when he suggested that London possessed a class of dangerous criminals and proto-criminals which included 'not only the professional thief or burglar [but also] the whole rabble of the vagrant and dissolute classes, who labour by fits, and eke out subsistence by pilfering, and who are ever on the verge of a more serious breach of the law'.[44]

Criminological theory as such was popularised by the Italian Cesare Lombroso, who commenced his career in the 1870s before gaining widespread attention

National Socialism (Oxford, Oxford University Press, 1994); M Turda and P Weindling (eds), *Blood and Homeland: Eugenics and Racial Nationalism in Central and Southeast Europe, 1900–1944* (Budapest, Central European University Press, 2007); A Bashford and P Levine (eds), *The Oxford Handbook of the History of Eugenics* (Oxford, Oxford University Press, 2010); M Turda, *Modernism and Eugenics* (Cambridge, Cambridge University Press, 2010).

41 See P Mazumdar, 'The Eugenicists and the Residuum: The Problem of the Urban Poor' (1980) 54 *Bulletin of the History of Medicine* 204, 207. On the eugenics traditions in Britain broadly, see D McKenzie, 'Eugenics in Britain' (1976) 6 *Social Studies of Science* 499; GR Searle, *Eugenics and Politics in Britain 1900–1914* (New York, Springer, 1976); R Soloway, *Demography and Degeneration: Eugenics and the Declining Birthrate in Twentieth-Century Britain* (Chapel Hill, University of North Carolina Press 1990); L Bland, 'British Eugenics and "Race Crossing": A Study of an Interwar Investigation' (2006) 60 *New Formations* 66; L Bland and L Hall, 'Eugenics in Britain: The View from the Metropole' in Bashford and Levine (eds), *The Oxford Handbook* (n 40); D Stone, *Breeding Superman: Nietzsche, Race and Eugenics in Edwardian and Interwar Britain* (Cambridge, Cambridge University Press, 2017).

42 On developments in Kenya, see C Campbell, *Race and Empire: Eugenics in Colonial Kenya* (Manchester, Manchester University Press, 2007). On developments in South Asia, see S Hodges, 'South Asia's Eugenic Past' in Bashford and Levine (eds), *The Oxford Handbook* (n 40). On developments in South Africa, see S Dubow, 'South Africa: Paradoxes in the Place of Race' in Bashford and Levine (eds), *The Oxford Handbook* (n 40). On developments in the dominions generally, see D Paul, J Stenhouse and H Spencer (eds), *Eugenics at the Edges of Empire: New Zealand, Australia, Canada and South Africa* (London, Palgrave, 2018).

43 See, for example, P Colquhoun, *A Treatise on the Police of the Metropolis*, 7th edn (1806); Report of a Commission to Inquire as to the Best Means of Establishing an Efficient Constabulary Force in the Counties of England and Wales (1839). For academic commentary on Colquhoun, see Wiener, *Reconstructing the Criminal* (n 2); M Neocleous, *The Fabrication of Social Order: A Critical Theory of Police Power* (London, Pluto 2000); D Philips, 'Three "Moral Entrepreneurs" and the Creation of a "Criminal Class" in England, c. 1790s–1840s' (2003) 7 *Crime, History & Societies* 1 (2003).

44 See T Plint, *Crime in England: Its Relation, Character, and Extent as Developed from 1801 to 1848* (C Gilpin 1851), cited in Taylor, 'Beyond the Bounds' (n 29) 9.

across the world in the decades that followed.[45] Like many before him, Lombroso linked the figure of the criminal to that of the savage; his theory went further than those that had come before, however, in emphasising the innate, biological nature of the characteristics in question.[46] While Lombroso made his reputation on the basis of this insight, in many ways it was simply an idea whose time had come, as evidenced by the extent to which similar ideas were repeatedly voiced in Britain in the period without reference to Lombroso. Dr Bruce Thomson, for instance, a resident surgeon at Perth prison in Scotland, described the prisoners with whom he worked as 'a set of demi-civilized savages, who in hordes prey upon society … and, only connecting themselves with those of their own nature and habits … must beget a depraved and criminal class hereditarily disposed to crime'.[47] Luke Owen Pike, a lawyer and historian, emphasised familial inheritance as a key source of criminality in his A History of Crime in England.[48] Edmund Du Cane, a leading prison administrator, pondered whether or not criminals were 'examples of the race reverting to some inferior type … the type of what Professor Darwin calls "our arboreal ancestors"'.[49] Robert Anderson, who served for a time as head of England's Criminal Investigation Department, observed that 'the question should not be what the prisoner did … but what he is'.[50] Connecting this new insight back to the figure of the vagrant, Havelock Ellis, a prolific writer on psychology and sexuality and a strong believer in eugenics, emphasised the problematic existence of a 'great class of vagabonds among men, who also live on the borderlands of criminality, and who also present a larger proportion of abnormalities than even criminals'.[51] As Ellis further put it:

> We must be careful not to confuse vice and crime. At the same time we have to recognise that they both spring from the same root … [Both the criminal and the vicious

[45] On the rapid growth of criminology see D Garland, *Punishment and Welfare: A History of Penal Strategies* (Gower 1985) 77.

[46] See C Lombroso, *L'Uomo Delinquente*, 1st edn (Piedmont, Bocca, 1876); C Lombroso, *Criminal Man* (New York, Putnam's Sons, 1911); C Lombroso and G Ferrero, *La donna delinquent: la prostituta e la donna normale*, 3rd edn (L Roux 1915). On the history of criminology more broadly, see D Pick, *Faces of Degeneration: A European Disorder, c. 1848–1918* (Cambridge, Cambridge University Press, 1989); R Wetzell, *Inventing the Criminal: A History of German Criminology* (Chapel Hill, University of North Carolina Press, 2000); P Becker and R Wetzel (eds), *Criminals and their Scientists: The History of Criminology in International Perspective* (Cambridge, Cambridge University Press, 2006); RA Triplett (ed), *The Handbook of the History and Philosophy of Criminology* (Hoboken NJ, Wiley-Blackwell, 2017). The term 'born criminal' as such was coined by Lombroso's collaborator Enrico Ferri, in a chapter in L'Archivo di psichiatria, an 1880 compilation edited by Lombroso.

[47] J Thomson, 'The Hereditary Nature of Crime' (January 1870) XV *Journal of Mental Science* 489–90, cited in V Bailey, 'The Fabrication of Deviance: "Dangerous Classes" and "Criminal Classes" in Victorian England' in J Rule and R Malcolmson (eds), *Protest and Survival: The Historical Experience: Essays for EP Thompson* (New York, New Press, 1993) 245.

[48] Owen's work was published in 1873 and 1876. See P Knepper, 'Laughing at Lombroso: Positivism and Criminal Anthropology in Historical Perspective' in Triplett (ed), *History and Philosophy of Criminology* (n 46).

[49] ED Cane, 'Address on the Repression of Crime' (1875) Trans NAPSS 302, cited in Bailey, 'The Fabrication of Deviance' (n 47) 245.

[50] See Taylor, 'Beyond the Bounds' (n 29) 13.

[51] H Ellis, *The Criminal* (Newcastle-upon-Tyne, Walter Scott, 1890) 222.

> person are] anti-social because they are both more or less unfitted for harmonious social action, both, from organic reasons, more or less lazy. Criminals and prostitutes, as Féré remarks, have this common character, that they are both unproductive. This is true also of vagabonds, and of the vicious and idle generally, to whatever class they belong. They are all members of the same family.[52]

Ethnography, phrenology, the ideas of the dangerous classes and the residuum, eugenics and criminology all constituted forms of ideological and rhetorical support for the various initiatives advanced by the vagrancy law model. The gradual development of these different modalities of characterising and understanding the idle, immoral, savage and criminal poor helped a particular meta-discourse develop, moreover, in which the poor were understood not only as likely carriers of disease but a form of disease as such, to be 'treated' or 'cleansed' from the social body.

A degree of such analogisation could be seen in the 1837 decision *City of New York v Miln* by the New York Supreme Court. In that case, the court affirmed state 'police power' to obtain a list of all persons on board docking ships as a check against the immigration of the poor, writing:

> We think it as competent and as necessary for a state to provide precautionary measures against the moral pestilence of paupers, vagabonds, and possibly convicts, as it is to guard against the physical pestilence which may arise from unsound and infectious chapters or from a ship the crew of which may be laboring under an infectious disease.[53]

In his 1850 commentary on vagrants in England, Mayhew observed that they constituted 'a stream of vice and disease – a tide of iniquity and fever, continually flowing'.[54] Costermongers (public pedlars), meanwhile, Mayhew described as 'a social pestilence in the very heart of our land'.[55]

As the nineteenth century progressed, the idea of social contagion became increasingly influential. Drawing out the linkage to vagrancy, in particular, of the fear of 'contagion' on the part of authorities concerned with overseeing the poor in late-nineteenth century England Vorspan observes:

> A ubiquitous assumption underlying nineteenth-century social literature was the belief that immoral habits and behaviour patterns are communicable … The most common criticism of both the workhouses and the casual wards was that they were morally 'unclassified' and thereby facilitated the contamination of the virtuous workingman by the professional idler. Given sufficient exposure, the corruption of the innocent was inevitable; as Dr Stallard noted in 1866, 'no honest woman can hear the language used in the wards,

[52] H Ellis, *The Criminal* (n 51) 223.

[53] *New York v Miln*, 36 US 102, 142–43 (1837).

[54] H Mayhew, *The Morning Chronicle Survey of Labour and the Poor: The Metropolitan Districts*, P Razzell (ed), vol 3 (Abingdon, Routledge, 1980) 47.

[55] H Mayhew, *London Labour and the London Poor* vol 1 (n 27). On Mayhew's account generally, see AL Beier, '"Takin' It to the Streets": Henry Mayhew and the Language of the Underclass in Mid-nineteenth-century London' in AL Beier and P Ocobock (eds), *Vagrancy and Homelessness in Global and Historical Perspective* (Athens OH, Ohio University Press, 2008).

> or associate with the characters who habitually live there, without contracting infamy'. In 1880 a Poor Law guardian similarly observed that placing the idle and well-intentioned in one room tended to 'confirm a man in vagrancy'. The Fabians … denounced the casual wards in 1891 as 'permanent foci of moral infection' … Many unions, especially those in large midland and northern cities, tried to mitigate the possibility of contagion by providing for casuals to sleep and work in solitary confinement.[56]

Vorspan further notes how William Vallance, a poor law guardian clerk, observed in 1880 the 'contagious' nature of vagrant habits, 'how soon they are formed, and what a brief experience is needed to make them chronic'.[57] Another poor law guardian, the same year, discussed how 'vagrant epidemics oft owe their origin to certain plague spots from which the contagion spreads', leading to the "infect[ion of] everyone more or less with the social evil of vagrancy"'.[58] At times the felt political threat was emphasised in this context as well. As George Sims, the English writer, observed in 1889:

> The mighty mob of famished, diseased and filthy helots is getting dangerous, physically, morally, politically dangerous. The barriers that have kept it back are rotten and giving way … Its fevers and its filth may spread to the homes of the wealthy; its lawless armies may sally forth and give us a taste of the lesson the mob has tried to teach now and again in Paris.[59]

In the United States, Henry Martin Boies, a prominent criminologist, was particularly fond of medical metaphors. As he put it in 1901, for instance, '[i]t is evident … that the supreme function of the Science of Penology is the discovery of the infected members of society before their disease has become an actual offence'.[60] In his 1915 discussion of vagrancy, published in an early issue of the *Journal on Criminal Law and Criminology*, John Lisle observed how vagrants 'constitute a host in every large American city, living in disgusting filth, spreading disease by contagion and inheritance, giving examples of sexual immorality and every kind of dishonesty and crime', and how inadequate state policy had led to 'the contamination of every large city by the multitude of diseased immoral citizens, living in degradation, preying upon the charitable, breeding crime by example and inheritance, increasing the corrupt vote and tending to retard the advance of civilization physically, morally, mentally and hence socially'.[61]

Similar approaches could be observed around the British Empire. In regard to South Africa in the early twentieth century, Chanock has observed:

> Legislation [enacted] for the control of infectious diseases … was based on sweeping contaminated blacks out of contact with whites. There were similarities in the responses

[56] R Vorspan, 'Vagrancy and the New Poor Law in Late-Victorian and Edwardian England' (1977) 92 *English Hist R* 59, 68–69.
[57] Vorspan, 'Vagrancy' (n 56) 73.
[58] Vorspan (n 56) 74.
[59] G Sims, *How the Poor Live* (New York, Pictorial World 1883) 44.
[60] H Boies, *The Science of Penology* (New York, GP Putnam's Sons 1901) 66.
[61] J Lisle, 'Vagrancy Law Its Faults and Their Remedy' (1915) 5 *Journal of Criminal Law & Criminology* 498, 500, 511.

> to the 'crisis' of the rising crime rate in the new cities, where the increasing numbers of black urban residents lived in some places alongside poor whites. These were presented as remedies to infectious pollution as much as defenses against the challenges to social order.[62]

In this context the primary site of potential infection, 'the unsegregated racial frontier in the rapidly growing cities', was 'presented as an urban running sore', in which context the only appropriate 'treatment' for potentially degraded, vagrant whites was 'a long period of hard labour in a labour colony'.[63] After it took control of South West Africa following the First World War, South Africa adopted a segregation-based model there too, in which members of the local population were placed on reserves, 'the location of which had nothing to do with ancestral lands or ethnic heritage but everything to do with providing each magisterial district with a "holding tank" for surplus and redundant labor'.[64] Among other grounds, this policy was justified in the basis that:

> After providing for domestic and similar essential services at European centres, it is undesirable to allow surplus natives of various races to crowd into municipal locations … where, even under the best of control, they are liable to contract, or infect others with diseases … and in any case they generally deteriorate physically and morally, besides embarrassing the white population in regard to the use of commonage and water.[65]

In sum, the vagrancy law model was accompanied by enormous intellectual justificatory energy from the early nineteenth-century on. While the precise forms such justifications and modes of understanding the 'vagrant problem' took varied significantly over time, the approaches adopted were unified by a tendency to perceive poverty, immorality and criminality as closely connected. Frequently, moreover, a medical mode of thinking was employed as well, in which what were perceived and described as the negative characteristics of the populations in question were presented as communicable, necessitating carefully designed responses.

Ideational developments in this area, which may be described as governing through social contagion, may be understood as having played a significant role in the historical development of governance through contagion more broadly. The spread of ideas across borders was enabled by technological developments in transportation and communication, which also helped enable the development of expansive empires and the spread of similar legal approaches across those empires. While vagrancy law itself was enforced in a disaggregated way, through magistrates

[62] M Chanock, 'Criminological Science and the Criminal Law on the Colonial Periphery: Perception, Fantasy, and Realities in South Africa, 1990–1930' (1995) 20 *Law & Social Inquiry* 911, 917.

[63] Chanock, 'Criminological Science (n 62) 919, citing Transvaal Government, Report of the Indigency Commission (1908). As Chanock also notes, 'the report contains an extended, detailed, and approving discussion of labor colonies in Germany, Switzerland, and Belgium, which provided for long periods of detention for vagrants and which not only stopped the 'idle and vicious from contaminating each other' but prevented them from 'propagating their kind to prey upon the next generation', ibid.

[64] R Gordon, 'Unsettled Settlers: Internal Pacification and Vagrancy in Namibia' in C Greenhouse (ed), *Ethnography in Unstable Places* (Durham, Duke University Press, 2002) 63.

[65] South Africa Annual Report 1923, 13, cited in Gordon, 'Unsettled Settlers' (n 64).

and other low-level judicial agents, those agents were small cogs in an increasingly powerful, centralised system, that grew in strength, in terms of both its expanse and its ability to penetrate the lives of individuals, across the nineteenth century. Central to the vagrancy law model across time and space, moreover, was its ability to define and describe categories of the population, not in their own terms – and not even potentially in terms that would potentially have been discernible prior to the discretionary application of the law as such – but rather in the terms of a now global legal system centrally concerned with defining, controlling and circumscribing the poor.

Forced Sterilisation

Belief in eugenics and criminology, together with the idea of social contagion, helped to justify new, particularly bold 'solutions' to the long-existent vagrant problem. Eugenics in particular was linked to policies, including policies

> aimed to prevent life (sterilization, contraception, segregation, abortion in some instances); … aimed to bring about fitter life (environmental reforms, puériculture focused on the training and rearing of children, public health); [and] aimed to generate more life (pronatalist interventions, treatment of infertility, 'eutelegenesis'). And at its most extreme, it [was linked to policies and techniques aimed to] en[d] life (the so-called euthanasia of the disabled, the non-treatment of neonates).[66]

For present purposes, the connection of eugenics to sterilisation is particularly instructive. In various places around the world in the heyday of eugenics, the strength of the idea as such – or perhaps, the extent of the ideological cover it offered – was strong enough to see forced sterilisation take place in law and practice. The most significant development n the Anglo-world took place in the United States. As Reilly notes, a key wellspring of eugenicist thought and of the drive towards sterilisation in the United States 'was a once famous book about a large extended family in upstate New York who disproportionately populated the state's prisons', Richard Dugdale's *The Jukes*, published in 1877.[67] In the years that followed, the Eugenics Record Office, based in Cold Spring Harbor, Long Island, became 'the major intellectual center for eugenic policy, especially in regard to sterilization'.[68] Over the following decades several states passed laws limiting the rights of certain persons, including the 'mentally disabled' and the indigent, to marry.[69] In 1897 the first sterilisation bill was introduced in Michigan, though it

[66] P Levine and A Bashford, 'Introduction: Eugenics and the Modern World' in Bashford and Levine (eds), *The Oxford Handbook* (n 40).

[67] P Reilly, 'Eugenics and Involuntary Sterilization: 1907–2015' (2015) 16 *Annual Review Genomics & Human Genetics* 351, 355, citing R Dugdale, *The Jukes: A Study in Crime, Pauperism, Disease and Heredity* (New York, GP Putnam's Sons, 1877).

[68] Reilly, 'Eugenics and Involuntary Sterilization' (n 67).

[69] Reilly (n 67), citing H Bruinius, *Better for All the World: The Secret History of Forced Sterilization and America's Quest for Racial Purity* (New York, Vintage, 2007).

was not passed.[70] Despite lack of legal sanction, prison superintendents authorised sterilisation in several facilities in the period.[71] In 1907, Indiana passed the first forced sterilisation law.[72] California, Washington and Connecticut followed suit two years later, with California quickly becoming a leader in the field.[73] Institutions like the American Genetic Association, founded in 1913, and the Human Betterment Foundation worked to promote the effective implementation of eugenicist ideas in practice.[74] The theory was developed by Henry Laughlin, in particular, who called in 1914 for more measures to encourage the 'dysgenic' – a category that included the 'feebleminded', the 'insane', the 'criminalistic', the epileptic, the inebriated or the drug addicted, the diseased, the blind, the deaf, the 'deformed' and dependents, including orphans, 'ne'er-do-wells', 'tramps', the homeless and paupers.[75] While Indiana's forced sterilisation law was overturned by the Indiana Supreme Court in 1921,[76] after the US Supreme Court upheld Virginia's forced sterilisation measure in *Buck v Bell*[77] Indiana adopted a new law.[78] During the first third of the twentieth century 'state legislatures annually introduced scores of bills favoring sterilization of certain persons for eugenic reasons, newspapers and magazines published hundreds of chapters favoring eugenic programs and eugenics became a standard topic in high school biology texts'.[79] Such measures had widespread public support throughout the period – as Lombardo observes, '[e]very president from Theodore Roosevelt to Herbert Hoover was a member of a eugenics organization, publicly endorsed eugenic laws, or signed eugenic legislation without voicing opposition'.[80]

Outside the United States, while some government figures supported stronger measures – Winston Churchill, for instance, 'supported compulsory sterilization

[70] See S Hyatt, 'A Shared History of Shame: Sweden's Four-Decade Policy of Forced Sterilization and the Eugenics Movement in the United States' (1998) 8 *Indiana International & Comparative Law Review* 475, 489.

[71] Hyatt, 'A Shared History' (n 70).

[72] See P Reilly, *The Surgical Solution: A History of Involuntary Sterilization in the United States* (Baltimore, John Hopkins University Press, 1991).

[73] See S Trombley, *The Right to Reproduce: A History of Coercive Sterilization* (London, Weidenfeld & Nicolson, 1988) 51–52; AM Stern, 'From Legislation to Lived Experience: Eugenic Sterilization in California and Indiana, 1907–79' in P Lombardo (ed), *A Century of Eugenics in America: From the Indiana Experiment to the Human Genome Era* (Bloomington, Indiana University Press, 2011).

[74] See Trombley, *Right to Reproduce* (n 73) 59.

[75] H Laughlin, 'Report of the Committee to Study and Report on the Best Practical Means of Cutting Off the Defective Germ-Plasm in the American Population' (1914) Eugenics Record Official Bulletin Number 10A 10-44; H Laughlin, 'The Legal, Legislative and Administrative Aspects of Sterilization' (1914) Eugenics Record Official Bulletin Number 10B 115–20 (1914).

[76] See *Williams et al v Smith*, 131 NE 2 (Ind. 1921).

[77] 274 US 200 (1927).

[78] Reilly (n 67) 355.

[79] Reilly (n 67) 353.

[80] P Lombardo, 'Medicine, Eugenics, and the Supreme Court: From Coercive Sterilization to Reproductive Freedom' (1996) 13 *Journal of Contemporary Health Law & Policy* 1, 1. On the extent of sterilisation in the United States, see also W Kempton and E Kahn, 'Sexuality and People with Intellectual Disabilities: a Historical Perspective', 9 *Sexuality & Disability* 93 (1991). On later developments in the United States, see A Cohen, *Imbeciles: The Supreme Court, American Eugenics, and the Sterilization of Carrie Buck* (New York, Penguin, 2016).

and/or permanent segregation of the mentally deficient in colonies', in the hope that thereby 'their curse [would] di[e] with them and [would] not [be] transmitted to future generations'[81] – forced sterilisation never got far. On the other hand, there was support for the construction of various 'domestic colonies', including 'labour colonies for the "idle poor" and farm colonies for the "mentally deficient/ill"'.[82] The Eugenics Educational Society was a strong supporter of the 1913 Mental Deficiency Act[83] in England, for instance, which allowed for the 'feeble-minded' and 'moral defectives' to be kept in such 'colonies'.[84] Similar laws were passed in Australia and New Zealand.[85] While forced sterilisation was rejected in Britain, voluntary sterilisation was another matter, obtaining a degree of support in Britain in the inter-war period.[86] Across the British dominions, sterilisation got the furthest in Canada, in Alberta and British Colombia specifically.[87] Such measures were supported by figures such as the popular social democratic provincial premier Tommy Douglas, who argued in his master's thesis, 'The Problems of the Subnormal Family', for both sterilisation and the construction of colonies for those of low intelligence.[88] Across the empire, attention to eugenics-related issues typically took other forms, including a growing emphasis on demographic management throughout the inter-war period.[89] While sterilisation measures were proposed by the legislative council in Jamaica, the Colonial Office took a stance against the plan after public criticism.[90]

Both the idea of eugenics and technological developments were essential precursors to forced sterilisation, which could not have existed without them. However, the vagrancy law model and the form of governing through social contagion it helped to develop, and accustomise broad populations to, was essential to the possibility of these later developments. While an outcome as extreme as forced sterilisation was not an inevitable consequence of the vagrancy law tradition, it

[81] B Arneil, 'Liberal Colonialism, Domestic Colonies and Citizenship' (2012) 33 *History of Political Thought* 491, 581, citing M Gilbert, *Churchill and Eugenics* (The Churchill Center, 2009).

[82] Arneil, 'Liberal Colonialism' (n 81) 493.

[83] 3 and 4 Geo V c. 28.

[84] On the act and surrounding debates, see J Woodhouse, 'Eugenics and the Feeble-Minded: The Parliamentary Debates of 1912–14' (1982) 11 *Journal of the History of Education Society* 133. There was no accepted definition for feeblemindedness, but it was understood it could be deduced from certain forms of behaviour, including vagrancy, promiscuity, illegitimacy and immorality. See N Rose, *The Psychological Complex: Psychology, Politics and Society in England, 1869–1939* (London, Routledge, 1985) 108; L Bland, *Banishing the Beast: English Feminism and Sexual Morality, 1885–1914* (London, Penguin, 1995) 239–42.

[85] See S Garton, 'Eugenics in Australia and New Zealand: Laboratories of Racial Science' in Bashford and Levine (eds), *The Oxford Handbook* (n 40).

[86] See J Macnicol, 'The Voluntary Sterilization Campaign in Britain, 1918–39' (1992) 2 *Journal of the History of Sexuality* 422.

[87] See E Dyck, *Facing Eugenics: Reproduction, Sterilization, and the Politics of Choice* (Cambridge, Cambridge University Press, 2013).

[88] See Arneil, 'Liberal Colonialism' (n 81) 520.

[89] See K Ittmann, 'The Colonial Office and the Population Question in the British Empire, 1918–1962' (1999) 27 *Journal of Imperial & Commonwealth History* 55; K Ittmann, 'Demography as Political Science in the British Empire, 1918–1969' (2003) 15 *Journal of Policy History* 417.

[90] See Ittmann, 'The Colonial Office' (n 89) 66.

is hard to imagine so radical an approach would have been possible without the pathways laid by vagrancy law.

While forced sterilisation has by no means been eradicated,[91] it is at least subjected to far more forceful and consistent public criticism in the contemporary world. Forced sterilisation is instructive even in this regard, however, insofar as it represents one of the more extreme implications of the vagrancy law legacy, one rendered conceivable by the additional ideological support provided by the rise of eugenicist ideas. While forced sterilisation has come under challenge, however, other policies that were authorised by anti-vagrancy laws – including penalties for begging, homelessness, loitering, 'prostitution', homosexuality and even 'vagrancy' as such, together with strict, wealth and status-linked immigration controls – remain on the books in countless jurisdictions around the world. The metastasisation of the vagrancy law legacy in the early twentieth century which led to sterilisation laws – to say nothing of even more extreme policies of ethnic cleansing and extermination, which were by no means disconnected – has perhaps had the additional negative effect, even as such measures have been condemned, of serving to make invisible the more everyday components of the vagrancy law legacy, rendering the more mundane inequality contained therein relatively immune from challenges.

Conclusion

This chapter has argued that the nineteenth century saw the growth of what is termed herein the 'vagrancy law model'. That model had within it four different components: anti-poor, anti-immorality, anti-criminal and anti-migrant regimes. From its passage on, the Vagrancy Act 1824 served as an incubator of these repressive regimes, all of which were advanced in extensive part through vagrancy law initially, before they became their own distinct systems. Vagrancy law also helped to spawn, while also gaining legitimising support from, a variety of rhetorics and modes of thought that developed over the course of the nineteenth century. While the terms in which each mode of thought presented its insights varied, they were consistent in reaffirming the connection between poverty, criminality, immorality and a 'lower' form of existence vagrancy law already suggested. Cutting across all the different specific ideologies that developed in the period, moreover, was the overarching image and idea of vagrants as a form of 'social contagion'. This mode of dehumanising, medicalised understanding of the poorest in society as a form of disease in need of treatment and/or containment helped to justify some of the harshest measures which evolved within the broader context of the vagrancy law tradition, including forced sterilisation in particular. Even when not taken to such an extreme, however, the idea of social contagion in one way

[91] See OHCHR, UN Women, UNAIDS, UNDP, UNFPA, UNICEF & WHO, Eliminating Forced, Coercive and Otherwise Involuntary Sterilization: An Interagency Statement (2014). Available at: www.unaids.org/sites/default/files/media_asset/201405_sterilization_en.pdf.

or another motivated the policy measures adopted in the vagrancy law context, which alternated between disciplining, attempting to reform and simply removing the populations targeted.

This development in governance through 'social contagion', it is suggested, may be understood as a key part of the broader tradition of governing through contagion described by Chua and Lee. While vagrancy law was powerful precisely insofar as it could be enforced on the local level against 'petty' offenders, it was nonetheless closely linked to the centralisation of power, as both the expanse of vagrancy law and the resources devoted to its enforcement were closely linked to expansions in the power of the central authorities, whether within a more historically contained polity or in the context of the growing power of global empires across the nineteenth century. The spread of law and empire were both enabled by and helped to enable developments in communication, transportation and production technologies, on top of which some of the more extreme projects which the vagrancy law tradition helped to enable, including forced sterilisation in particular, depended centrally on technological developments. Across time and space, governance through social contagion of the vagrancy law sort was centrally concerned with what Chua and Lee term *inter/dysconnectedness* in the form of the coercive, top-down delineation of social categories, and the stigmatisation and attempted corralling of those who ended up on the wrong side of the lines drawn.

An appropriate coda to the developments surveyed here is provided by the United States' Immigration Act of 1917.[92] That Act showed not only how alive and well the vagrancy law model was in the early twentieth century United States, but also how extensively augmented it had been by the various ideological developments that had come to complement it in the meantime. Among others, the Immigration Act excluded 'idiots', 'imbeciles', 'feeble-minded persons', 'epileptics', 'insane persons', 'persons of constitutional psychopathic inferiority', 'persons with chronic alcoholism', 'paupers', 'persons afflicted with tuberculosis … or with a loathsome or dangerous contagious disease', 'persons … mentally or physically defective', 'persons who have been convicted of or admit having committed a felony or other crime or misdemeanour involving moral turpitude', 'polygamists', 'anarchists', 'prostitutes', 'persons who directly or indirectly procure or attempt to procure or import prostitutes', 'contract laborers' and 'persons likely to become a public charge'.[93] Here was a list fit to rival that assembled by the Vagrancy Act 1824 itself, utilising the same formula of loose affiliative construction and even employing several categories cribbed directly from the earlier vagrancy law tradition, albeit now combined with new threatening figures. The new law was different from the previous measure in one major respect, however: whereas the Vagrancy Act 1824 in England was nationally focused, the Immigration Act of 1917 in the United States was focused on the protection of international borders – reflecting not the twilight of vagrancy law but rather the increasing internationalisation of one component of its operation.

[92] Immigration Act of 1917, Pub L 64–301, 39 Stat 874.
[93] Immigration Act of 1917 (n 92).

7

The Oregon Citizen Assembly Pilot on COVID-19 Recovery*

*Participatory Governing Through Contagion***

STEPHANIE BURKHALTER AND ROBERT C RICHARDS JR

Introduction

In governing through contagion, state action to limit contagion's impact often entails totalising efforts of control, such as mask mandates, shelter-in-place and quarantine orders, school and business closures and policing of individuals through surveillance and monitoring. In conceptualising how governing through contagion can vary across time and place, Chua and Lee assert: 'The mode and degree of centralization of state infrastructures strongly influence the development of governing through contagion … The more centralized state infrastructures are, the more totalizing governing through contagion can become.'[1] In the case of Singapore in the COVID-19 era, governing through contagion approached totalisation in the early pandemic due to the high centralisation of the state, the high degree of cooperation in the national government between the executive and legislature and low political-party competition.[2] Further, inhabitants of Singapore were 'ready to spring into action' to support state and societal efforts to minimise the impact of contagion due to the process of normalisation and moralisation that they experienced most recently during the 2003 SARS epidemic.[3]

* The authors wish to note that their personal views and research are not affiliated to any organisations with which they are associated.

** We thank Professor John Gastil, Pennsylvania State University, for his leadership of the Oregon Citizens Assembly research project.

[1] LJ Chua and JJG Lee, 'Governing through Contagion' in VV Ramraj (ed), *COVID-19 in Asia: Law and Policy Contexts* (Oxford, Oxford University Press, 2021) 118.

[2] Chua and Lee, 'Governing through Contagion' (n 1); R Wai, 'Singapore's Response to COVID-19: An Explosion of Cases despite Being a "Gold Standard"' in SL Greer et al (eds), *Coronavirus Politics: The Comparative Politics and Policy of COVID-19* (Ann Arbor, University of Michigan Press, 2021).

[3] Chua and Lee (n 1) 122, 125.

In contrast, in early 2020 when COVID-19 emerged, the US was underprepared for governing through contagion in what would become the most impactful pandemic the country had ever experienced. The 1918 influenza pandemic, which very few could recall, was the last viral outbreak in the US near the scale of the COVID-19 pandemic.[4] According to public-health scholars, the US government's initial response to COVID-19 under Republican President Trump was woefully inadequate.[5] However, in the 'highly fragmented and decentralized' and 'politically polarized' US system of government, state and local governments, led by officials of different political parties, are authorised to act during a pandemic, which can produce quicker actions and heterogeneous policies.[6] States such as Oregon, which experienced early COVID-19 cases, quickly stepped into the gap in national policy response to implement variations of the governing-through-contagion rules and practices that are familiar to governments outside the US. These include: 'quarantine; physical distancing requirements; bans on large gatherings; stay-at-home orders; closures of schools, businesses, and public transport; masking requirements; and other measures'.[7]

In this chapter, we explore patterns of governing through contagion in the US state of Oregon in three historical periods, including the COVID-19 era. In contrast to highly centralised systems of government like Singapore's, within the US system of federalism, Oregon's state governing power is remarkably further decentralised, reflecting a tradition of settler-colonial 'pioneer' self-reliance, a limited state government and a culture of participatory governance among its people. As part of this culture, early in the COVID-19 pandemic several Oregon legislators asked Healthy Democracy, a non-profit organisation involved in participatory governance, to develop a process for gathering citizen input on policy matters concerning the state's response.[8] The result was an 'Oregon Citizen Assembly Pilot on COVID-19 Recovery' (ORCA), in which Oregon citizens participated as 'panellists' to discuss

[4] The 1918 influenza pandemic produced 675,000 US deaths. The H1N1pdm09 pandemic of 2009, the last US nationwide pandemic before COVID-19, yielded an estimated 60.8 million cases, 274,304 hospitalisations and 12,469 deaths. US Centers for Disease Control and Prevention (CDC), '2009 H1N1 Pandemic (H1N1pdm09 Virus)' (CDC, 11 June 2019). Available at: www.cdc.gov/flu/pandemic-resources/2009-h1n1-pandemic.html; US Centers for Disease Control and Prevention, '1918 Pandemic (H1N1 Virus)' (CDC, 20 March 2019). Available at: www.cdc.gov/flu/pandemic-resources/1918-pandemic-h1n1.html. The US avoided severe impact from the 2003 SARS outbreak, as only eight Americans contracted the virus. US Centers for Disease Control and Prevention, 'SARS Basics Fact Sheet' (CDC, 6 December 2017). Available at: www.cdc.gov/sars/about/fs-sars.html.

[5] PM Singer et al, 'Anatomy of a Failure: COVID-19 in the United States' in SL Greer et al (eds), *Coronavirus Politics: The Comparative Politics and Policy of COVID-19* (Ann Arbor, University of Michigan Press, 2021).

[6] Singer et al, 'Anatomy of a Failure' (n 5) 479–80.

[7] H Jarman, 'State Responses to the COVID-19 Pandemic: Governance, Surveillance, Coercion and Social Policy' in SL Greer and others (eds), *Coronavirus Politics: The Comparative Politics and Policy of COVID-19* (Ann Arbor, University of Michigan Press, 2021) 5; Ballotpedia, 'Government Responses to and Political Effects of the Coronavirus Pandemic, 2020 (Oregon)'. Available at: ballotpedia.org/Government_responses_to_and_political_effects_of_the_coronavirus_pandemic,_2020_(Oregon).

[8] J Gastil and others, 'Convening a Mini-Public During a Pandemic: A Case Study of the Oregon Citizens Assembly Pilot on COVID-19 Recovery' (2022) 3 *Digital Government: Research and Practice* 13:1.

potential state policy actions for addressing COVID-19 over seven two-hour sessions in July and August 2020.[9] Because of the danger posed by face-to-face interaction during the pandemic, the assembly took place entirely online.

Informed by Chua and Lee's perspective that subsequent periods of governing through contagion are shaped by the techniques of control used in prior periods,[10] we first describe governing through contagion in two earlier periods in Oregon: Contagious-disease epidemics of the 1770s–1850s instigated by Euro-American contact with Native American communities[11] and the 1918 influenza pandemic. We then address the COVID-19 era, with a particular focus on ORCA. In each period we apply the lens of the three major themes of governing through contagion: centralisation and technology of law, normalisation and technologies of moralisation and inter/dysconnectedness and the rearticulation of difference.

Epidemics of Measles, Smallpox and 'Fever and Ague' in the 1770s–1850s

Oregon's governing through contagion in the years of 'discovery' in the late eighteenth century until it became a US state reflects its origins as a coastal Pacific trading centre, its co-colonisation by Britain and the US and its ultimate incorporation as a US territory fuelled by migration of white Americans from the East.[12] The area in the Pacific Northwest that would become the state of Oregon in 1859 had long been settled by different bands of indigenous peoples from distinct ethnic groups, such as the Chinook and Tillamook on the Pacific coast, the Kalapuyans of the Willamette Valley, the Umpqua of the Rogue River Valley in the southwest and the Umatilla, Cayuse and Nez Perce in the east.[13] Prior to contact with Europeans, these Native communities had not encountered, and lacked immunity to, contagious diseases such as measles, smallpox and malaria.[14]

[9] The authors belonged to a research team led by principal investigator John Gastil, which observed and gathered data on ORCA.

[10] Chua and Lee (n 1) 115.

[11] In addition to the term *indigenous peoples*, we use the terms *Native Americans*, *American Indians*, and their variants interchangeably because those identifications are preferred by indigenous US residents. M Yellow Bird, 'What We Want to Be Called: Indigenous Peoples' Perspectives on Racial and Ethnic Identity Labels' (1998) 23 *American Indian Quarterly* 1.

[12] JH Tyler, *Leveraging an Empire: Settler Colonialism and the Legalities of Citizenship in the Pacific Northwest* (Lincoln, University of Nebraska Press, 2021).

[13] K Barber, '"We Were at Our Journey's End": Settler Sovereignty Formation in Oregon' (2019) 120 *Oregon Historical Quarterly* 382. In her analysis of colonialism in Oregon, Barber draws on the work of theorists of settler colonialism, such as P Wolfe, 'Settler Colonialism and the Elimination of the Native' (2006) 8 *Journal of Genocide Research* 387; L Veracini, 'Introducing *Settler Colonial Studies*' (2011) 1 *Settler Colonial Studies* 1; E Nakano Glenn, 'Settler Colonialism as Structure: A Framework for Comparative Studies of US Race and Gender Formation' (2015) 1 *Sociology of Race and Ethnicity* 52; and GH Whaley, *Oregon and the Collapse of the Illahee: US Empire and Transformation of an Indigenous World* (Chapel Hill, University of North Carolina Press, 2010).

[14] Tyler *Leveraging an Empire* (n 12); Whaley *Oregon and the Collapse of the Illahee* (n 13); R Boyd, *The Coming of the Spirit of Pestilence: Introduced Infectious Diseases and Population Decline among Northwest Coast Indians, 1774–1874* (Seattle, University of Washington Press, 1999) 264–65.

For competing imperial powers, access to the Columbia River (which separates present-day Oregon and Washington State) and the Pacific Coast was paramount, especially to facilitate the lucrative fur trade. In an 1818 treaty, the British and Americans asserted joint economic control over the area and prohibited either country from establishing a government.[15] Historian Katrine Barber describes this early period in Oregon as 'classic colonialism' in which white Euro-Americans exploited natural resources and relationships with indigenous people for profit on a temporary basis, 'ultimately returning to their country of origin'.[16] From 1818 to 1843, the only form of Western 'government' the people of Oregon Country would know came from the leadership of the British Hudson's Bay Company (HBC) at Fort Vancouver, a colonial outpost whose metropole was thousands of miles away and which had limited ability to enforce English common law.[17]

Early Euro-Americans were very much dependent on the local indigenous population for their knowledge of local lands and resources and created relationships with distinct bands of Native peoples through trade and marriage.[18] In 1805, William Clark, of the Lewis and Clark expedition, noted in his journal that the Clatsop, indigenous people who regularly traded with ships on the Pacific Coast near the mouth of the Columbia River, had experienced deaths due to a smallpox epidemic.[19] Almost all of the male HBC traders had relationships with local indigenous women, many of which were familial in 'custom of the country' marriages.[20] This interconnectedness of white and Native lives during the classic-colonialism period decimated populations of Native peoples through the spread of contagious disease.

While the US and Britain recognised that any permanent claims to land in Oregon should be legitimated through negotiations with the Indians, neither country prohibited settlements by non-Natives.[21] In the 1830s, white Protestant missionaries, such as Jason Lee (1834) and Marcus Whitman (1836), migrated to 'save' the 'heathen' Indians by converting them to Christianity.[22] Both Lee and Whitman reported to their East Coast sponsors that they were not very successful in their missions.[23] For Whitman, conversion required that an Indian accept the whole of the Biblical Gospel, keep a monogamous marriage and embrace a sedentary life of farming; however, Whitman found it almost impossible to translate the

[15] University of Washington, 'European Rivalry for the Pacific Northwest' (*Center for the Study of the Pacific Northwest*). Available at: www.washington.edu/uwired/outreach/cspn/Website/Classroom%20Materials/Pacific%20Northwest%20History/Lessons/Lesson%203/3.html; Whaley (n 13).

[16] Barber '"We Were at Our Journey's End" (n 13) 389.

[17] Whaley (n 13) 88; Tyler (n 12); T Marsh, *To the Promised Land: A History of Government and Politics in Oregon* (Corvallis, Oregon State University Press, 2012).

[18] Whaley (n 13).

[19] Whaley (n 13) 24–25.

[20] C Addis, 'The Whitman Massacre: Religion and Manifest Destiny on the Columbia Plateau, 1809–1858' (2005) 25 *Journal of the Early Republic* 221, 228–29.

[21] Tyler (n 12); Whaley (n 13).

[22] Addis 'The Whitman Massacre' (n 20); Marsh *To the Promised Land* (n 17) xii; Whaley (n 13).

[23] Addis (n 20); MJ Norton and J Booss, 'Missionaries, Measles, and Manuscripts: Revisiting the Whitman Tragedy' (2019) 107 *Journal of the Medical Library Association* 108; Whaley (n 13).

Gospel into the Cayuse and Nez Perce languages and, like many Native peoples in the region, the Cayuse were seasonally migratory and allowed polygamous marriage.[24]

American politicians, such as US senator Lewis Linn from Missouri, encouraged the migration of white settlers by introducing bills in Congress, the US national legislature, to provide those settlers with land claims in Oregon.[25] In the 1840s, streams of settlers followed the missionaries by migrating on the Oregon Trail, but the US government did not fully claim Oregon as a territory until 1848, two years after Britain ceded its land rights below the 49th parallel.[26] In 1843, frustrated Oregon settlers established a small 'provisional' government, incorporating elements of US and British law.[27] The provisional government awarded – with no legal basis in treaties with the Indians – land rights of 320 acres to any white man (or male Métis child with a white father) in the region who was at least 18 years old, adding another 320 acres if he was married.[28] Signalling that Oregon would not enter the United States as a so-called 'slave state', the provisional government banned slavery outright but also enacted white supremacy by prohibiting settlement by free Black people.[29] Though its official policy was to maintain friendly relations with local Native populations, the provisional government established a militia to control Indian challenges to settler land claims.[30]

The provisional government established in 1843 reflected a burgeoning settler-colonial system in which it was paramount that white settlers establish and enforce their property rights over those of indigenous peoples. As Evelyn Nakano Glenn argues, extermination of indigenous people for seizure of their lands is an essential component of settler colonialism and can be 'accomplished in a variety of ways: genocide, forced removal from territories desired by white settlers, and confinement to reservations outside the boundaries of white settlement … and assimilation'.[31] As Barber explains, Oregon 'settlers placed stock in the process of assimilation, championed extermination and forced removal, or held out hope for the providential "vanishing" of Native people' to facilitate resettlement of indigenous lands.[32]

[24] Whaley (n 13).

[25] Marsh (n 17) xii–xiii.

[26] It is estimated that over 250,000 migrants travelled the Oregon Trail to reach lands in the Oregon Territory and California between 1840 and 1860. Barber (n 13); Tyler (n 12); Whaley (n 13).

[27] Settlers refused to recognise the council systems of the local bands of Native Americans as more than informal and claimed Native Americans lacked governments with which they could establish diplomatic relations. B Mahoney, 'Provisional Government' (*Oregon Encyclopedia*, 24 May 2022). Available at: www.oregonencyclopedia.org/articles/provisional_govt_conference_in_champoeg_1843/; Addis (n 20); Tyler (n 12); Whaley (n 13).

[28] Mahoney 'Provisional Government' (n 27); Marsh (n 17).

[29] Mahoney (n 27); D Millner, 'Blacks in Oregon' (*Oregon Encyclopedia*, 31 January 2022). Available at: www.oregonencyclopedia.org/articles/blacks_in_oregon/; Tyler (n 12).

[30] Mahoney (n 27); Tyler (n 12); Whaley (n 13).

[31] Glenn 'Settler Colonialism as Structure' (n 13) 55.

[32] Barber (n 13) 395.

The epidemics that took the heaviest toll on Native communities occurred before the US territorial government was established in 1849. During this time, centralisation and legal technologies deployed to contain contagion were weak,[33] and historical records reveal little or no state action in response to epidemics in the region,[34] consistent with the 'less transparent but' nevertheless 'violent' settler-colonial strategy of allowing disease to facilitate the seizure of 'indigenous lands'.[35] This dysconnectedness is demonstrated in the decline of Native populations by almost 92 per cent by the 1850s.[36]

Colonists' technologies of moralisation reflected Western beliefs that contagious diseases could be prevented through inoculation and treated through various cures.[37] Indigenous theories of disease attributed illness to 'the intrusion of foreign objects into the body or witchcraft by malevolent individuals'.[38] Some Euro-American traders 'exploited the Northwest Indians' belief that the power to control medicine was potentially evil'[39] by falsely claiming that they held disease in small bottles, which they threatened to uncork to harm them.[40]

The 'fever and ague' epidemic in 1830 – the first time Native people in the region had been exposed to malaria – was devastating. To treat the disease, HBC agents provided their own employees and their families, including Indians, with quinine obtained from the Pacific trade.[41] Regarding other Native peoples, however, Fort Vancouver personnel 'dr[o]ve the Indians away instead of affording them the [medical] assistance they implored of us' because the fort lacked empty sickbeds.[42]

Traditional Native health practices, such as moving from low-lying riparian locations where mosquitoes bred to elevated areas and burning villages severely affected by contagion, may have limited disease spread.[43] Indians also created explanations and cures related to their beliefs, such as attributing a malaria outbreak to a shell and a stake placed by a Euro-American ship's captain in the

[33] Boyd *The Coming of the Spirit of Pestilence* (n 14); M Clark, *Eden Seekers: The Settlement of Oregon, 1818–1862* (Boston, Houghton Mifflin, 1981).

[34] For example, during the 1853 smallpox epidemic, records reveal observations of the US superintendent for Indian affairs in Oregon Territory regarding the epidemic's impact on Native communities, but no state response to the disease threat. Boyd (n 14) 160–61.

[35] P Frymer, *Building an American Empire: The Era of Territorial and Political Expansion* (Princeton NJ, Princeton University Press, 2017) 21.

[36] R Boyd, 'The Pacific Northwest Measles Epidemic of 1847–1848' (1994) 99 *Oregon Historical Quarterly* 6; Boyd (n 14) 4, 264–65; JDB DeBow, *The Seventh Census of the United States: 1850* (Public Printer 1853).

[37] AM Stern and H Markel, 'Commentary: Disease Etiology and Political Ideology: Revisiting Erwin H Ackerknecht's Classic 1948 Essay, "Anticontagionism between 1821 and 1867"' (2009) 38 *International Journal of Epidemiology* 31, 32.

[38] Boyd (n 14) 121; Norton and Booss 'Missionaries, Measles, and Manuscripts' (n 23).

[39] Addis (n 20) 228.

[40] Addis (n 20); Boyd (n 14) 46, 113–14; Whaley (n 13).

[41] Boyd (n 14); A Perry, *Colonial Relations: The Douglas-Connolly Family and the Nineteenth-Century Imperial World* (Cambridge, Cambridge University Press, 2015); Whaley (n 13).

[42] J McLoughlin, '[Letter to Arch McDonald, December 9, 1830]' in B Brown Barker (ed), *Letters of Dr John McLoughlin Written at Fort Vancouver 1829–1832* (Hillsboro, Binfords & Mort, 1948) 175.

[43] Boyd (n 14) 51, 97, 115.

Columbia River and then putting the stake and shell on trial, convicting them and ritualistically punishing them.[44]

For missionaries like the Whitmans, Indians' acceptance of Western medicine and hygiene practices was part of the process of 'civilizing' them, analogous to British colonial practices to 'civilize' the inhabitants of Singapore as documented by Chua and Lee.[45] When Marcus Whitman failed to cure many Cayuse during an outbreak of measles and dysentery in 1847, members of the Cayuse community executed him, his wife Narcissa and 12 other mission personnel. Approximately 40 per cent of the Cayuse people perished in the outbreak – disproportionately more than whites – and many Cayuse believed that Whitman, a medical doctor (te-wat), should have been more effective in preventing Cayuse deaths and may have even caused the outbreak.[46] Such a violent response to deaths from illness was not common, and subsequently the Cayuse Tribe denounced what they described as the actions of a few men. Nevertheless, the 'Whitman Massacre' and subsequent 'Cayuse Wars' influenced the US government's decision to support white settlers in their conflicts with Indians and officially claim Oregon Country as a territory in 1848.[47]

The impact of epidemics on Native populations followed by Indian 'wars' and white-militia violence boosted white Oregon settlers' claims to being the rightful owners of the land. In this context, governing through contagion was reflected in the settler government's passive response to disease among indigenous people unassociated with settlers through religion, trade or family. In communications with the national government and in the press, the settler government framed the non-assimilated Indians as a 'hostile' race who must be defeated to protect white property rights.[48] Oregonians successfully persuaded Congress to codify most of their land claims in the Oregon Donation Land Act of 1850 (ODLA).[49] As the land had not been officially surveyed and no formal treaties existed between the US and the Indians in Oregon Country, the ODLA was legally suspect.[50] Most treaties with the Indians whose ancestral homelands were located within the bounds of Oregon were not ratified until after statehood in 1859.[51] Nevertheless, following further decline of Native populations after a smallpox epidemic in 1853, in 1855–1856 the US began relocating Native peoples to reservations in the eastern part of the state, in the culminating expression of both settler-colonial power and dysconnection during this period.[52]

[44] Boyd (n 14) 113–15.
[45] Boyd, 'The Pacific Northwest Measles Epidemic of 1847–1848' (n 36); Chua and Lee (n 1) 123.
[46] Addis (n 20); Boyd (n 36) 16; Norton and Booss (n 23) 111; Whaley (n 13); Tyler (n 12) 58.
[47] Addis (n 20) 248.
[48] Tyler (n 12).
[49] Mahoney (n 27); Tyler (n 12); Whaley (n 13).
[50] Frymer *Building an American Empire* (n 35); Whaley (n 13).
[51] Tyler (n 12).
[52] TN Leavelle, '"We Will Make It Our Own Place": Agriculture and Adaptation at the Grand Ronde Reservation, 1856–1887' (1998) 22 *American Indian Quarterly* 433; R Spores, 'Too Small a Place: The Removal of the Willamette Valley Indians, 1850–1856' (1993) 17 *American Indian Quarterly* 171; Frymer (n 35) 137–40. On the geography of the ancestral homelands of Oregon's indigenous peoples,

The 1918 Influenza Pandemic

Oregon's response to the 1918 influenza pandemic reflected its political culture and the government that Oregonians created in 1859 on becoming a state. These embodied settler-colonialist ideas about the superiority of whites, the 'pioneer' spirit of frontier hardship, individualism and self-rule.[53] In their state constitution, Oregonians limited the formal powers of their government; for example, they made the legislature effectively part-time by restricting its regular sessions to 35 days a year in even-numbered years and 160 days in odd-numbered years, and they decentralised decision-making and enforcement powers to local-governmental entities, including local school districts and county sheriffs.[54] The exclusion of non-white people characterised the state into the twentieth century, such as laws that made it 'illegal for Blacks to be in Oregon or to own real estate, make contracts, vote, or use the legal system'.[55] In 1911, Oregonians further decentralised political power by adopting a system of direct, participatory democracy empowering citizens to write laws and vote on them through direct initiative and to vote on laws passed by the legislature in referenda.[56]

see E Guggemos, 'Indigenous History of Oregon' (Forest Grove OR, *Pacific University Libraries*, 16 November 2021). Available at: pacificu.libguides.com/indigenous. State and federal governments recognise nine sovereign reservations within the state of Oregon. Oregon State Government, Office of Tribal Affairs, 'Overview of the Nine Tribes'. Available at: www.oregon.gov/dhs/ABOUTDHS/TRIBES/Pages/Tribes.aspx. The authors note that the indigenous people of the region are resilient and that Native Americans who reside within the boundaries of the state of Oregon continue to thrive and make important contributions to the state.

[53] Barber (n 13) 385; Frymer (n 35) 280; Whaley (n 13).

[54] Oregon Constitution [1857] art IV, s 10(1a–1b); PA Diller, 'The Partly Fulfilled Promise of Home Rule in Oregon' (2008) 87 *Oregon Law Review* 939, 943; J Arnold, 'Mask Mandate Puts School Leaders in Impossible Situation' (*osba.org*, 10 August 2021). Available at: www.osba.org/News-Center/Announcements/2021/20210810Masks.aspx; 'Southwest Oregon School District Plans to Lift Mask Mandate' *Canby First* (Canby, 28 January 2022). Available at: www.canbyfirst.com/school-district-on-oregon-coast-moves-forward-with-to-lift-mask-mandate; J Parfitt, 'Douglas County Sheriff Pens Letter Opposing Governor Brown's Mask and Vaccine Mandates' (*kdrv.com*, 12 January 2022). Available at: www.kdrv.com/news/coronavirus/douglas-county-sheriff-pens-letter-opposing-governor-browns-mask-and-vaccine-mandates/article_06fab554-10a7-52c2-b520-611067b5e2fd.html.

[55] RA Clucas and M Henkels, 'Change and Continuity in Oregon Politics' in RA Clucas et al (eds), *Governing Oregon: Continuity and Change* (Corvallis, Oregon State University Press, 2018); Marsh (n 17) 142; Millner 'Blacks in Oregon' (n 29); A Rana, *The Two Faces of American Freedom* (Cambridge MA, Harvard University Press, 2010) 119–20. In 2021, the percentage of Black residents in the state (2.2%) was roughly the same as it was in 1919, and 74% of the residents identified as white and non-Hispanic. US Census Bureau, 'QuickFacts: Oregon' (1 July 2021). Available at: www.census.gov/quickfacts/OR. Expressly racially discriminatory provisions of Oregon's constitution and statutes are no longer on the books, as they were repealed during the twentieth century. See, for example, notes to Oregon Constitution [2022] art I, s 31; art II, ss 2, 6; art XV, s 8; notes to 11 Oregon Revised Statutes c 106 [2021]. Nonetheless, racial dysconnectedness in Oregon persisted into the twenty-first century, as explained below.

[56] Ballotpedia, 'History of Initiative and Referendum in Oregon'. Available at: www.ballotpedia.org/History_of_Initiative_%26_Referendum_in_Oregon; Clucas and Henkels 'Change and Continuity in Oregon Politics' (n 55); L Lipin, 'Populism in Oregon' (*Oregon Encyclopedia*, 12 May 2022). Available at: www.oregonencyclopedia.org/articles/populism_in_oregon/; Marsh (n 17); Oregon Secretary of State, *State Initiative and Referendum Manual* (Elections Division 2022). Available at: www.sos.oregon.gov/elections/Documents/stateIR.pdf.

When global interconnectedness during World War I brought the 1918 flu pandemic to Oregon, many of the state's efforts to respond were ineffectual due to resistance from citizens, businesses and, at times, government officials.[57] Among centralised legal pandemic-control measures were statewide orders closing schools and public meetings and municipal orders curtailing business hours, and imposing anti-crowding and ventilation rules on streetcars.[58] In early 1919, Portland's Consolidated Health Bureau took over hospitals, converted schools into hospitals and adopted anti-crowding and quarantine regulations, while Portland imposed a mask mandate.[59] Surveillance was also deployed: Portland deputised schoolteachers as public-health officers to inspect residences to enforce public-health regulations and sent nurses into schools to identify children for quarantine.[60]

In keeping with Oregon's political culture, there was substantial resistance to centralised legal interventions. In recent work on governing through contagion, Jack Jin Gary Lee and Lynette J Chua suggest that 'as [governing through contagion] develops, normalization-moralization tends to meet with resistance, embroiling state and subject in back and forth contestations'.[61] For example, in mid-November 1918, Portland's mayor re-opened theatres, schools and churches.[62] Portland's city council rejected its first mask-mandate proposal in 1919 and, when the mandate was subsequently adopted, Portland's health director opposed it, weakening enforcement.[63] As multiple public-health leaders departed for military service, the implementation of regulations was impeded.[64] Some streetcar workers were prosecuted for not enforcing social-distancing rules,[65] and Christian Scientists sought to end the ban on religious services.[66]

As part of their moralisation campaigns, public-health officials urged theatres to display infection-prevention messages, while encouraging residents to end

[57] 'Soldier En Route to Training Camp May Be Influenza Victim' *Oregon Daily Journal* (Portland, 4 October 1918) 4; 'Spanish Influenza Invades Portland' *Morning Oregonian* (Portland, 8 October 1918) 6.

[58] *Crane v School District No 14* [1920] 95 Or 644; IM Woolley, 'The 1918 "Spanish Influenza" Pandemic in Oregon' (1963) 64 *Oregon Historical Quarterly* 246, 248; 'Spanish Influenza Conditions in City Remain Unchanged' *Oregon Daily Journal* (Portland, 24 October 1918) 6; 'Improvement in Influenza Cases' *Oregon Daily Journal* (Portland, 26 October 1918) 3; 'Help Fight the Flu' *Morning Oregonian* (Portland, 4 November 1918) 6.

[59] 'Flu Safety Rules Draw More Tight' *Oregon Daily Journal* (Portland, 10 January 1919) 1, 4; 'Campaign Against Influenza Opened' *Morning Oregonian* (Portland, 11 January 1919) 9; 'Decline in Flu Cases Expected' *Oregon Daily Journal* (Portland, 16 January 1919) 1; 'Influenza Cases Show Big Decline' *Oregon Daily Journal* (Portland, 30 January 1919) 1.

[60] 'Principals and Teachers to Aid in Fighting Flu' *Oregon Daily Journal* (Portland, 7 November 1918) 4; 'Flu Safety Rules' (n 59) 4.

[61] JJG Lee and LJ Chua, 'Smallpox Vaccinations and the Limits of Governing through Contagion in the Straits Settlements, 1868–1926' 45 *Law and Policy* 335.

[62] Woolley 'The 1918 "Spanish Influenza" Pandemic in Oregon' (n 58) 257; 'Anti-Influenza Closing Order to Be Lifted on Sunday, Nov. 17' *Oregon Daily Journal* (Portland, 9 November 1918) 1, 11.

[63] 'Decline in Flu Cases Expected' (n 59) 1; Woolley (n 58) 254.

[64] Woolley (n 58) 248.

[65] 'Decline in Flu Cases Expected' (n 59) 5; 'Carmen Are Reprimanded' *Sunday Oregonian* (Portland, 3 November 1918) 7.

[66] 'Spanish Influenza Conditions in City Remain Unchanged' (n 58) 6.

public sneezing and avoid streetcars.[67] Portland's partial-lockdown order mainly offered exhortations, often reflecting middle-class norms, about public behaviour, such as 'Remember the three Cs – a clean mouth, clean skin, and clean clothes'.[68] Duties of teachers acting as health inspectors included 'distribut[ing] literature' bearing infection-prevention advice and teaching residents 'their shortcomings'.[69]

As state-based moralisation efforts were hampered by resource constraints, to help prevent contagion non-governmental organisations attempted to fill gaps. Some churches required masks at services and some businesses ordered employees to mask.[70] A retailer discouraged in-person shopping and advocated ordering by telephone, an emerging technology.[71] To foster social distancing, some stores and libraries removed tables and seating.[72] Perhaps partly due to internalisation of contagion-governance norms, after Portland schools reopened in mid-November 1918, 'many parents' were reluctant 'to permit their children to attend'.[73]

The importance of participatory institutions was illustrated when tens of thousands of Oregonians voted on several initiatives and referenda in the November 1918 election.[74] Dysconnectedness in pandemic governance was embodied in laws excluding non-white people from voting[75] and in the disproportionate impact of the pandemic on low-income and non-white workers. Treated under settler colonialism as 'undesirable exogenous others', Asian Americans in Oregon experienced racism, including segregated neighbourhoods, employment discrimination, violent expulsion from localities and attempts to outlaw Asian-American land ownership.[76] Mortality among Chinese people on the US Pacific coast due to the epidemic was

[67] Woolley (n 58) 248; 'Influenza in City Is Under Control' *Morning Oregonian* (Portland, 9 October 1918) 7.

[68] 'Help Fight the Flu' (n 58) 6; CA Connolly and ME Gibson, 'The "White Plague" and Color: Children, Race, and Tuberculosis in Virginia 1900–1935' (2011) 26 *Journal of Pediatric Nursing* 230.

[69] 'Principals and Teachers to Aid in Fighting Flu' (n 60) 4.

[70] 'Flu Masks Will Be Required by Church' *Oregon Daily Journal* (Portland, 19 January 1919) 1; '"Flu" Serum Demands Now Being Supplied' *Morning Oregonian* (Portland, 25 October 1918) 11.

[71] Meier and Frank Co., 'Store Opens at 9:00 A.M. – Closes at 3:30 P.M.' *Morning Oregonian* (Portland, 5 November 1918) 20; Woolley (n 58) 253.

[72] Meier and Frank Co., 'Store Opens at 9:00 A.M.' (n 71) 18; Woolley (n 58) 253.

[73] Woolley (n 58) 257.

[74] Oregon Secretary of State, *Proposed Constitutional Amendments and Measures (with Arguments) to Be Submitted to the Voters of Oregon at the General Election Tuesday, November 5, 1918*. Available at: www.web.archive.org/web/20130328184643/https://library.state.or.us/repository/2010/201003011350161/ORVPGenMari1918.pdf; Oregon Secretary of State, 'Initiative, Referendum and Recall: 1916–1921' in *Oregon Blue Book* (Oregon Secretary of State 2016). Available at: www.web.archive.org/web/20160303171619/http:/bluebook.state.or.us/state/elections/elections13.htm; Oregon Secretary of State, 'Initiative, Referendum and Recall: 1922–1928' in *Oregon Blue Book* (Oregon Secretary of State 2016). Available at: www.web.archive.org/web/20160303173704/http:/bluebook.state.or.us/state/elections/elections14.htm. However, none of these ballot measures concerned the 1918 pandemic.

[75] K Jensen, '"Neither Head nor Tail to the Campaign": Esther Pohl Lovejoy and the Oregon Woman Suffrage Victory of 1912' (2007) 108 *Oregon Historical Quarterly* 350; Rana *The Two Faces of American Freedom* (n 55); B Yasui, 'The Nikkei in Oregon, 1834–1940' (1975) 76 *Oregon Historical Quarterly* 225.

[76] Nakano Glenn 'Settler Colonialism as Structure' (n 13) 60; Woolley (n 58) 249; Yasui 'The Nikkei in Oregon, 1834–1940' (n 75) 238.

disproportionately high.[77] Some physicians engaged in price gouging,[78] limiting working-class patients' access to health care. Indigent patients sought treatment at the makeshift hospital in Portland's civic auditorium, which had higher rates of mortality than other hospitals and housed a segregated 'Japanese ward, attended by a Japanese physician'.[79] Anti-Asian racism would re-emerge strongly during the next major pandemic Oregon faced, that of COVID-19.[80]

Oregon's COVID-19 Response

By 2020, many Oregonians' values had changed and the population had become more diverse, with 25 per cent identifying as non-white.[81] Oregon had expanded suffrage to non-whites and in the 1950s began overturning other explicitly racist laws.[82] Contemporary Oregonians in cities such as Portland are known for progressive values such as anti-racism, post-materialism and social democracy.[83] Oregon's political culture continues to prioritise participatory governance and decentralised state government. The government reflects vigorous political-party competition between Republicans from more rural areas in the eastern and southern parts of the state and Democrats from cities in western Oregon.[84] As the worldwide COVID-19 pandemic was emerging, in February 2020, Republican lawmakers walked out of the legislative session in an effort to thwart quorum rules to slow the Democrats' lawmaking agenda.[85]

By early March 2020, when the first COVID-19 cases were identified, Oregon's elected and appointed officials 'found themselves having to quickly invent and implement new policies and figure out how to communicate those decisions to the public'.[86] To prevent people from spreading disease in the absence of a vaccine, Oregon's government turned to non-pharmaceutical interventions such as 'lockdown' and mask mandates, as recommended by the WHO.[87]

[77] CEA Winslow and ZW Koh, 'The Mortality of the Chinese in the United States, Hawaii, and The Philippines' (1924) 38 *China Medical Journal* 877, 885.

[78] '"Flu" Serum Demands Now Being Supplied' (n 70) 11.

[79] Woolley (n 58) 250, 256.

[80] S Tonthat, 'Report Reveals a Surge in Anti-Asian Crimes in Oregon' (*OPB*, 25 July 2022). Available at: www.opb.org/article/2022/07/25/report-reveals-a-surge-in-anti-asian-crimes-in-oregon/.

[81] A Buylova, RL Warner and BS Steel, 'The Oregon Context' in RA Clucas and others (eds), *Governing Oregon: Continuity and Change* (Corvallis, Oregon State University Press, 2018); US Census Bureau (n 55).

[82] Millner (n 29).

[83] Buylova, Warner and Steel 'The Oregon Context' (n 81); Rana (n 55) 328–36.

[84] Clucas and Henkels (n 55); Marsh (n 17).

[85] D Roberts, 'Oregon Republicans Are Subverting Democracy by Running Away. Again' *Vox* (29 February 2020). Available at: www.vox.com/energy-and-environment/2020/2/29/21157246/oregon-republicans-walk-out-climate-change-cap-trade-democracy.

[86] Jarman 'State Responses to the COVID-19 Pandemic' (n 7) 51.

[87] Jarman (n 7) 51; World Health Organization, 'Coronavirus Disease (COVID-19) Pandemic'. Available at: www.who.int/emergencies/diseases/novel-coronavirus-2019.

From 8 to 12 March 2020, Oregon's governor, Kate Brown, centralised the governmental response by issuing executive orders that declared a public-health emergency, closed schools, prohibited public gatherings including religious services and ordered all residents to stay at home.[88] Two weeks later, she closed businesses in which social distancing was not feasible and required social distancing or remote working in other businesses.[89] This executive action was followed up in June 2020 by a statewide mask mandate.[90]

To keep residents housed and self-sufficient and to protect the state's economy from collapse, the governor and state legislature suspended evictions and foreclosures and barred creditors from garnishing government relief payments.[91] However, although Democrats controlled both legislative chambers and the governorship, Oregon neither extended its 'short' legislative session nor held a special session to pass COVID-19-related laws.[92] Thus, for its initial legal response, the state relied on statewide and local COVID-19 executive orders requiring mainly local enforcement.

As in the 1918 pandemic, implementation of some COVID-19 control measures was hampered by opposition from state or local government personnel. The statewide mask mandate was opposed by some county commissions and sheriffs as well as by several local school districts, while some state and local government employees sued to block the governor's public-employee vaccination mandate.[93] The Oregon Health Authority, an executive agency, attempted moralisation through its COVID-19 portal, providing data about cases, education about hygiene and prevention and updates on mandates.[94] The Governor's official portal also

[88] Oregon Executive Orders 20-03 (8 March 2020), 20-05 (12 March 2020), 20-05 (12 March 2020), 20-07 (17 March 2020); Oregon Health Authority, 'Oregon Announces First Presumptive Case of Novel Coronavirus' (28 February 2020). Available at: www.oregon.gov/oha/ERD/Pages/Oregon-First-Presumptive-Case-Novel-Coronavirus.aspx.

[89] Oregon Executive Order 20-12 (23 March 2020).

[90] A Green, 'Oregonians Will Be Required to Wear Masks Statewide – Not Just in Select Counties – Starting Wednesday' *The Oregonian* (Portland, 29 June 2020). Available at: www.oregonlive.com/coronavirus/2020/06/oregonians-will-be-required-to-wear-masks-statewide-not-just-in-select-counties-starting-wednesday-governor-says.html; Oregon Temporary Administrative Order PH35-2021 (11 August 2021), codified as Oregon Administrative Rules 333-019-1025 (7 February 2022).

[91] Oregon Executive Orders 20-11 (22 March 2020), 20-56 (28 September 2020), 21-14 (20 September 2021), 20-18 (17 April 2020); OR HB4213 (enacted 30 June 2020), HB4204 and HB4212 (enacted 7 July 2020), HB4401 (enacted 23 December 2020), HB2009 (enacted 25 September 2021). For a partial list of Oregon's legal responses to COVID-19 in 2020, see Ballotpedia 'Government Responses to and Political Effects of the Coronavirus Pandemic, 2020' (n 7).

[92] Ballotpedia, '2020 Oregon Legislative Session'. Available at: www.ballotpedia.org/2020_Oregon_legislative_session. In 2021, the Oregon state legislature held its regular 'long session' of 135 days, plus two shorter special sessions. Ballotpedia, '2021 Oregon Legislative Session'. Available at: www.ballotpedia.org/2021_Oregon_legislative_session.

[93] J Much, 'Marion County Votes to Oppose Brown's COVID Mask Mandate' *Portland Tribune* (Portland, 22 August 2021). Available at: www.pamplinmedia.com/pt/9-news/519498–415007-marion-county-votes-to-oppose-browns-covid-mask-mandate-; Parfitt 'Douglas County Sheriff Pens Letter' (n 54); Arnold 'Mask Mandate Puts School Leaders in Impossible Situation' (n 54); 'Southwest Oregon School District Plans to Lift Mask Mandate' (n 54); *Johnson v Brown* [2021] No. 3:21-cv-1491-SI (D Oregon).

[94] See www.govstatus.egov.com/OR-OHA-COVID-19; CH Park, R Richards and J Reedy, 'Assessing Emergency Information Sharing between the Government and the Public during the COVID-19 Pandemic: An Open Government Perspective' (2022) 45 *Public Performance and Management* R 828.

communicated information about COVID-19 prevention measures and related executive orders.[95]

To enhance the sense of collective challenge and encourage compliance with mandates, state agencies and civil-society organisations quickly adopted the moralisation campaign centred on the slogan 'We're all in it together'.[96] In addition, many Oregon employers implemented their own employee-vaccine requirements.[97] There was some evidence of Oregonians' internalisation of these norms, such as student-council representatives at local schools expressing support for a proposed student vaccine mandate.[98]

While these efforts helped residents feel connected, they also masked inequality and dysconnectedness by positing an unspecified 'we' who were working together to defeat the contagion.[99] Oregon leaders evinced awareness of the dysconnectedness present in prior periods of governing through contagion and in current conditions, which 'combined inclusion with the persistence of previous prejudices' concerning race and class.[100] Thus officials were immediately concerned about preventing the evictions of renters and the foreclosure of homes.[101] Further, the Oregon Health Authority acknowledged equity gaps in differences in case exposure, access to treatment and hospitalisation rates for severe illness between racially minoritised populations and whites.[102]

Illustrating dysconnectedness as resistance, in early 2021 Republicans in the state legislature walked out to protest some of Governor Brown's COVID-19 policies and draw attention to rural residents' vaccine access.[103] As in 1918, some churches sued to block the state lockdown order.[104] Residents objected to the statewide mask mandate through demonstrations, hearings and letters to legislators.[105]

[95] Office of the Governor, 'Building a Safe and Strong Oregon'. Available at: www.coronavirus.oregon.gov/Pages/default.aspx.

[96] See, for example, Oregon Community Foundation, 'We're All in This Together, Oregon' (23 April 2020). Available at: www.youtube.com/watch?v=i-EaR6qDYpA.

[97] K Davidson, 'Following Supreme Court, Oregon Won't Adopt Vaccine-or-Test Rule for Big Businesses' (*OPB*, 14 January 2022). Available at: www.opb.org/article/2022/01/14/oregon-puts-brakes-vaccine-mandate-after-supreme-court-strikes-biden-policy/.

[98] E Miller, 'Portland Public Schools Staff Recommend Six-Month Delay for Student Vaccine Mandate' (*OPB*, 15 November 2021). Available at: www.opb.org/article/2021/11/15/portland-public-schools-covid-19-vaccine-mandate-delay/.

[99] L Bowleg, 'We're Not All in This Together: On COVID-19, Intersectionality, and Structural Inequality' (2020) 110 *American Journal of Public Health* 917; F Sobande, '"We're All in This Together": Commodified Notions of Connection, Care and Community in Brand Responses to COVID-19' (2020) 23 *European Journal of Cultural Studies* 1033.

[100] Rana (n 55) 324.

[101] As Chua and Lee note, low-income workers faced a disproportionate impact from the COVID-19 contagion, as they are more likely to be in jobs that expose them to disease and to lose jobs when businesses shut down and supply chains are disrupted. Chua and Lee (n 1) 128.

[102] Oregon Health Authority, '2020 COVID-19 Data Review (reissued 7/13/22)' *COVID-19 Weekly Report* 5 (Salem, 13 July 2022), www.oregon.gov/oha/covid19/Documents/DataReports/2020-Annual-Data-Report.pdf.

[103] Roberts 'Oregon Republicans Are Subverting Democracy' (n 85); Ballotpedia, '2021 Oregon Legislative Session' (n 92).

[104] *Elkhorn Baptist Church v Brown* [2020] 366 Or 506.

[105] N Pate, 'An Estimated 1,000 People Gather at Oregon Capitol to Oppose Mask, Vaccine Mandates' *Statesman Journal* (Salem, 19 August 2021). Available at: www.statesmanjournal.com/story/news/

Echoing the past, these protests featured the settler-colonial rhetoric of 'rugged individualism' and self-rule.[106] Moreover, reflecting what Lee and Chua call 'endemic inter/dysconnectedness', some resistors to Oregon's COVID-19 prevention measures exhibited further radicalisation by joining the insurrection against the US national government in January 2021.[107]

Despite the state's commitment to participatory governance, however, Oregon offered citizens few opportunities to collaborate in developing contagion-governance policies.[108] Consequently, ORCA provided Oregonians a notable opportunity to shape governance during contagion.

Oregon Citizen Assembly

Responding to some Oregon legislators' call for public input on pandemic-recovery policies, two non-partisan citizen-participation organisations conducted ORCA.[109] Participants were 36 Oregon residents, selected by stratified random sampling and generally representative of the state population.[110]

Participants were charged with developing recommendations for state lawmakers regarding recovery from the pandemic.[111] In July and August 2020, participants deliberated in seven two-hour online sessions, featuring facilitated plenary and small-group discussions.[112] After testimony from issue experts and

local/2021/08/14/hundreds-gather-oregon-capitol-oppose-mask-vaccine-mandates-schools-kate-brown-coronavirus-covid-19/8116023002/; R Manning, 'Mask Opponents Press Oregon Health Authority to Abandon Indoor Face Covering Requirements' (*OPB*, 20 January 2022). Available at: www.opb.org/article/2022/01/20/mask-opponents-tell-oregon-to-abandon-mask-requirements/; Jeff Golden, 'Response to Face Mask Opposition' (*Senator Jeff Golden Homepage*). Available at: www.oregonlegislature.gov/golden/Documents/Response%20to%20Face%20Mask%20Opposition.pdf.

[106] Frymer (n 35) 280. At one rally, Oregon protestors displayed '"Don't tread on me" flags', symbols of rugged individualism since the eighteenth century. Pate 'An Estimated 1,000 People Gather at Oregon Capitol to Oppose Mask, Vaccine Mandates' (n 105); HF Rankin, 'The Naval Flag of the American Revolution' (1954) 11 *William & Mary Q* 339, 343.

[107] Lee and Chua 'Smallpox Vaccinations and the Limits of Governing through Contagion' (n 61) 3; S Olmos and C Wilson, 'At Least 3 Men from Oregon Protest Appear to Have Joined Insurrection at US Capitol' (*OPB*, 10 January 2021). Available at: www.opb.org/article/2021/01/10/oregon-washington-protest-insurrection-david-anthony-medina-tim-davis/.

[108] Park, Richards and Reedy (n 94).

[109] Gastil and others 'Convening a Mini-Public During a Pandemic' (n 8).

[110] Of 36 ORCA participants – whose average age was 51 – 56% were female, 69% white, 8% African American, 8% Asian American, 8% Native American, and 5.5% Latinx/Hispanic. Thirty per cent of panellists had an undergraduate degree or graduate education, 20% had a secondary-school diploma or less education, 42% worked full-time, 21% were part-time workers or unemployed, and 21% were retired. Gastil and others (n 8). Forty-two per cent of panellists identified as or leaned Democratic, 31% were or leaned Republican, 77% lived in metropolitan regions, and 22% in rural areas. Healthy Democracy, '2020 Oregon CA Demographic Profile', healthydemocracy.org/wp-content/uploads/2020-Oregon-CA-Demographics-Profile-200709-merged.pdf.

[111] Park, Richards and Reedy 'Assessing Emergency Information Sharing' (n 94).

[112] Healthy Democracy, '2020 Oregon Citizen Assembly Pilot on COVID-19 Recovery'. Available at: www.healthydemocracy.org/what-we-do/local-government-work/oregon-assembly-on-covid-recovery/.

legislators, panellists deliberated to develop principles and recommendations on education and housing, published in late August 2020.[113]

To investigate ORCA, the research team observed and recorded Assembly sessions, surveyed and interviewed participants and analysed ORCA's principles and recommendations.[114] Qualitative data were analysed using content analysis concerning themes of governing through contagion.[115] Relevant qualitative results follow.

Diversity, Agency, and Deliberation in ORCA

Several panellists reported ORCA enabled them to exercise agency – to 'have my voice heard'[116] or 'tak[e] some action'[117] – regarding pandemic-recovery policy. For some panellists, exercising agency involved their 'civic duty'.[118]

Ten of twelve participants interviewed spoke of ORCA panellists' diversity. Appreciating their diverse viewpoints and backgrounds,[119] panellists characterised themselves as constituting a good representation of the state's population[120] and lauded their ability to deliberate across social differences to produce recommendations serving the public interest.[121] One panellist praised ORCA for being:

> such a diverse group and from all over the state … and how we collectively came together to try to compromise … and to come up with good positive suggestions that worked not just for one area but for the whole state.[122]

Another participant identified credibility as an outcome of ORCA, characterised as a deliberation generating well-informed recommendations which lawmakers should 'take … seriously'.[123]

Inter/Dysconnectedness in ORCA

Interconnectedness and dysconnectedness, particularly concerning class, were additional prominent themes of ORCA. A large share of panellists were working class – two-thirds of ORCA participants lacked an undergraduate degree

[113] Gastil and others (n 8); Park, Richards and Reedy (n 94).
[114] Gastil and others (n 8).
[115] Park, Richards and Reedy (n 94); Chua and Lee (n 1).
[116] Transcript: Participant Interview 9, 1 (this and subsequent transcripts are on file with authors).
[117] Transcript: Participant Interview 11, 2.
[118] Transcript: Participant Interview 3, 21; see also Transcript: Participant Interview 1, 12.
[119] See, for example, Transcripts: Participant Interview 1, 2, Participant Interview 4, 2.
[120] See, for example, Transcripts: Participant Interview 3, 3, Participant Interview 9, 6.
[121] Transcript: Participant Interview 5, 55–56.
[122] Transcript: Participant Interview 1, 2.
[123] Transcript: Participant Interview 6, 4.

and 20 per cent had a secondary-school diploma or less education[124] – and many revealed they rented their homes. Moreover, several participants were landlords. Inter-class conflict, particularly between renters, on the one hand, and landlords and homeowners, on the other, could have divided participants. Yet ORCA panellists reached across class and other divisions to collaborate on recommendations benefiting all Oregonians, though class dysconnectedness periodically surfaced.

Participation in deliberation can promote systemic thinking through social learning, in which participants explore relationships among multiple facets of an issue.[125] During ORCA, participants became aware of the systemic nature of their focal issues, especially housing. In early sessions, participants spoke of discrete aspects of housing. By ORCA's sixth week, however, participants discussed housing as a system of interrelated problems:

> Panelist 1: 'When people can't pay rent, the landlords can't pay their mortgage, and a lot of these issues are systemic, and so when one system starts to collapse, it's a domino effect across the entire economy.'
>
> Panelist 2: 'That's what I said. Exactly.'
>
> Several Panellists: [Indicate agreement].[126]

This 'systemic consciousness' coincided with increased cohesion in ORCA's groups and with panellists' feeling responsible for their issues – all forms of interconnectedness.

Regarding group cohesion, as ORCA panellists explored issues in depth, their groups came 'together in a cohesive manner'.[127] One participant likened this cohesiveness to 'kinship with the people in the group' arising from in-depth discussion and collaboration 'on a common cause'.[128] For another participant, group cohesiveness involved perspective taking and mutual identification:[129] 'I felt like people were embracing other viewpoints. They weren't just tolerant of them. They were … open and willing to then take some of that in and make it their own.'[130]

Moreover, several participants stated they had come to feel responsible for their focal issues.[131] For one ORCA panellist, this sense of responsibility for the housing issue arose from participants' realisation, through deliberation, of their interconnectedness with that issue: 'that they knew people that this [that is, housing insecurity] had already happened to. Or that it was going to happen to'.[132]

[124] Gastil and others (n 8).

[125] JO Kenter, MS Reed and I Fazey, 'The Deliberative Value Formation Model' (2016) 21(B) *Ecosystem Services* 194.

[126] 'ORCA Week 6: S2 and S3, Housing, Brainstorm Questions for Final Witnesses and Presentation by Final Witnesses' [video recording] 8:35–9:17 (on file with authors).

[127] Transcript: Participant Interview 5, 9–10.

[128] Transcript: Participant Interview 11, 7.

[129] Kenter, Reed and Fazey 'The Deliberative Value Formation Model' (n 125).

[130] Transcript: Participant Interview 6, 18.

[131] Transcripts: Participant Interview 5, 13–14, Participant Interview 8, 7, Participant Interview 11, 6–7.

[132] Transcript: Participant Interview 10, 10.

These feelings of responsibility resemble the type of responsibility that, according to Chua and Lee in their conceptual chapter, subjects experience post-contagion while '[s]taying with dysconnectedness'.[133] Motivated 'to resist and survive' to find 'ways to live and die well with all' forms of life,[134] subjects with this sense of responsibility experience enhanced agency and a novel awareness of the interrelatedness of human and nonhuman beings.

Like those described by Chua and Lee, ORCA panellists' feelings of responsibility arose when reflecting on post-pandemic existence and they coincided with increased agency and a newfound, systemic understanding of issues. Yet the type of responsibility experienced by ORCA panellists also differs from that delineated by Chua and Lee. First, whereas the latter involves resistance to contagion-governance conditions of 'near totalization',[135] ORCA panellists' sense of responsibility reflected citizens' assertion of their capacity for participatory governance during relatively free civil-society discussions under conditions of incomplete, decentralised governance. Second, whereas Chua and Lee's sense of responsibility arose in the absence of supporting institutions, ORCA panellists experienced their feelings of responsibility within a tradition and institutions of participatory governance that are central to Oregon's political culture.

Patterns of interconnectedness and dysconnectedness also appear in ORCA's principles and recommendations. The second principle states, 'without appropriate, secure housing, the fabric of our entire community will feel the drastic results'; the third principle holds, 'health and economy are closely integrated: we need to prioritize funding and policies that promote healthy people'; while the fourth principle asserts, 'Employment and housing go hand in hand'.[136] These principles exhibit a systemic view that housing problems have community-wide effects, jobs and small businesses are essential to secure housing, and residents require protection from infection to fill those jobs, run those businesses and maintain the economy.

Some ORCA recommendations likewise exhibit a systemic understanding of housing. The fourth housing recommendation enjoins unaffected residents to meet housing needs 'through volunteering or donating'.[137] Similarly, the seventh recommendation endorses an eviction ban to protect those susceptible to homelessness, while acknowledging others in the housing system – landlords – with a stake in vulnerable residents' need for shelter. Nonetheless, class dysconnectedness still manifests in the injunction that 'payments should be made directly to landlords to ensure … that the help [people] are receiving is going to housing',[138] which evokes the stereotype of irresponsible poor residents.[139]

[133] Chua and Lee (n 1) 131.
[134] Chua and Lee (n 1) 123, 125, 131.
[135] Chua and Lee (n 1) 123.
[136] Oregon Citizen Assembly Pilot on COVID-19 Recovery (ORCA), 'Core Principles and Policy Recommendations' (*Healthy Democracy*) [1]. Available at: www.healthydemocracy.org/wp-content/uploads/OR-CA-Final-Principles-Recommendations.pdf.
[137] ORCA 'Core Principles and Policy Recommendations' (n 136) [2].
[138] ORCA (n 136) [2].
[139] B Lott, 'Cognitive and Behavioral Distancing from the Poor' (2002) 57 *American Psychologist* 100.

The sixth housing recommendation – 'establishing community gardens in … empty lots' as 'spaces to grow food or put people to work' – links the pandemic-instigated housing crisis with Oregon's structural housing crisis which has spawned myriad vacant lots.[140] ORCA panellists viewed those lots as community assets, whose development could address food-system and labour needs. The final housing recommendation – 'prioritize compensation for essential workers … to ensure that others have what they need'[141] – likewise acknowledges the interconnectedness of essential-workers' labour with other community-members' needs.

Discussion and Conclusion

Cultivated in a settler-colonial polity in which white settlers monopolised political participation, Oregon's participatory-governance institutions grew more inclusive and egalitarian during the twentieth and twenty-first centuries, with universal adult suffrage, direct-democratic elections and innovations like the Citizens' Initiative Review and ORCA moving politics closer to inclusive and equal self-rule.[142] ORCA afforded panellists a multi-faceted experience of participation in contagion governance. Although state officials offered Oregonians few opportunities to influence COVID-19 policy,[143] ORCA panellists exercised agency by contributing well-informed recommendations on pandemic-recovery policy, echoing Oregonians' agency in direct-democratic elections during the 1918 pandemic. Acknowledging their diversity, which rendered them a microcosm of Oregon's population, ORCA participants enjoyed an intensive experience of interconnectedness with the democratic polity, as embodied by their fellow panellists.

ORCA deliberations enabled social learning, featuring perspective-taking fostered by personal storytelling about COVID-19.[144] This learning granted participants a systemic understanding particularly of housing with a sense of responsibility for addressing that issue, reflecting an inclusive, egalitarian form of self-rule.[145] ORCA panellists' systemic consciousness and feelings of responsibility also paralleled Chua and Lee's account of subjects' post-pandemic sense of responsibility rooted in 'staying with dysconnectedness' but supported by participatory-governance traditions and institutions.

Further, ORCA panellists engaged in structured deliberation – designed to encourage civil interaction – and bridged dysconnectedness to develop

[140] ORCA (n 136) [2]; JA Ramaley, 'Working Together Differently: Addressing the Housing Crisis in Oregon' (2017) 28[2] *Metropolitan Universities* 22.

[141] ORCA (n 136) [2].

[142] J Gastil and KR Knobloch, *Hope for Democracy: How Citizens Can Bring Reason Back into Politics* (Oxford, Oxford University Press, 2020); Rana (n 55) 14.

[143] Park, Richards and Reedy (n 94).

[144] J Gastil, *The Group in Society* (SAGE 2010); Kenter, Reed and Fazey (n 125); LW Black, 'Deliberation, Storytelling, and Dialogic Moments' (2008) 18 *Communication Theory* 93.

[145] Rana (n 55) 336.

recommendations serving the public interest.[146] For some panellists, deliberation enhanced the credibility of ORCA's recommendations, consistent with theories of deliberative legitimacy.[147] Nonetheless, at times those recommendations reinscribed social dysconnectedness by expressing middle-class stereotypes of the poor.[148] This persistence of class hierarchy is another vestige of settler colonialism, which required property ownership for full social inclusion.[149] That race was not a fault line of dysconnectedness stemmed from participants' perceptions that racial justice was orthogonal to ORCA's focal issues, perhaps due to facilitators' and witnesses' failure to explain those issues' racial dimensions and to media framings of racism as a criminal-justice matter.[150]

In conclusion, we find that Oregon's political culture and structure of government shaped governing through contagion in each of the three periods we examined. Oregon is an example of how totalisation during governing through contagion is never 100 per cent complete.[151] A tradition of limited government meant that centralisation and state enforcement of legal technologies were relatively minimised, although they increased in the COVID-19 era with the comprehensiveness of global models of pandemic response. In the context of decentralisation, polarised party competition and a culture of participatory governance, techniques of normalisation and moralisation that produce voluntary compliance became relatively important. In future pandemics, one can expect legal orders and moralisation efforts to produce pockets of resistance or 'counter-conduct', especially among Republicans, churchgoers who seek in-person services and rural people.[152]

Reflecting Oregon's origin as a settler-colonial state, dysconnectedness of racial and class difference is indicated in different periods of governing through contagion. In the COVID-19 period, however, policymakers were much more attuned to the disparate impact of contagion on racially minoritised and working-class populations and were able to tailor policy and practice to help these populations in ways that had not characterised governing through contagion in prior periods.

The opportunity for participatory governing provided by ORCA gave a sense of agency to individuals who, faced with the exigencies of the security modality of power, valued having a say in the protective measures and legal rules enacted by their government on their behalf. As the panellists worked through different

146 S Burkhalter, J Gastil and T Kelshaw, 'A Conceptual Definition and Theoretical Model of Public Deliberation in Small Face-to-Face Groups' (2002) 12 *Communication Theory* 398.

147 JS Fishkin, *When the People Speak: Deliberative Democracy and Public Consultation* (Oxford, Oxford University Press, 2009).

148 Lott 'Cognitive and Behavioral Distancing from the Poor' (n 139).

149 Rana (n 55) 52.

150 ORCA observational notes, week 3, breakout group 1, 63–64 (on file with authors); M Samayoa, 'Black Lives Matter Demonstrations Are Not a Big Factor in Oregon's COVID-19 Spike' (*OPB*, 26 June 2020). Available at: www.opb.org/news/article/black-lives-matter-demonstrations-covid-19-cases-oregon/.

151 Chua and Lee (n 1); M Foucault, '1 March 1978' in *Security, Territory, Population: Lectures at the College De France, 1977–1978* M Senellart (ed) G Burchell (tr) (London, Picador, 2004).

152 Foucault '1 March 1978' (n 151).

ways to potentially limit the impact of a pandemic, they created connectedness while exposing dysconnectedness, especially along lines of class. Those with more resources in the form of time, income or home ownership have flexibility to adapt to stringent state policies, such as the closing of schools and businesses. Those who are renters, are jobless or are essential workers live closer to the edge of personal disaster in which state policies creating a safety net are critical. Through ORCA, citizens took collective responsibility for the pandemic's effects on people from diverse backgrounds without being legally forced by a government or intentionally moralised to do so. This process demonstrated that citizens could exercise some agency in the face of increasing state power during governing through contagion.

PART III

Authoritarianism and Governing Through Contagion

8

Advancing a Politics of Social Division and Governing Through Contagion in Texas, USA

NOLAN KLINE AND NATHANIEL WEBB

Introduction

In the United States, COVID-19 was a political flashpoint and a source of social and political division. Rather than a single unified approach to address the pandemic, individual states instead responded based on the political whims of their governors and legislators. Consequently, in states controlled by Republican governors, there were fewer measures to prohibit the spread of the SARS-CoV-2 virus than in states led by Democrats. Moreover, the political differences in COVID-19 responses became conflated with other dividing lines, including a newly resurging debate on the rights of lesbian, gay, bisexual, transgender and otherwise queer identifying individuals. Politicised by the Trump administration, the COVID-19 pandemic became yet another partisan issue,[1] and the policies, attitudes and behaviours associated with it were linked to individuals' partisan identities and views on other matters. Such political tensions exacerbated by COVID-19 were highly prominent in the state of Texas, a battleground for numerous social and cultural issues, including abortion, LGBTQ+ rights and immigration.[2]

Though often portrayed by American media and political commentators as a solidly politically conservative state,[3] in recent years, Texas has become a place where progressive politicians are hopeful about eroding its conservative footing. The COVID-19 pandemic opened up new terrain for ongoing struggles for

[1] SK Gadarian, SW Goodman and TB Pepinsky, *Pandemic Politics: The Deadly Toll of Partisanship in the Age of COVID* (Princeton NJ, Princeton University Press, 2022).

[2] S Ayres, 'Exclusive Spectrum News/Ipsos poll: Texans See their Sstate as a Political Battleground' *Spectrum News 1*. Available at: spectrumlocalnews.com/tx/south-texas-el-paso/news/2021/12/01/texans-see-their-state-as-a-political-battleground.

[3] A Serwer, 'How Texas Turned Purple' (*The Atlantic*, 2020). Available at: www.theatlantic.com/ideas/archive/2020/11/texas-turning-blue/616978/; W Goodwyn, *Morning Edition* (National Public Radio, 2022).

political power in Texas, as conservative state leaders and progressive municipal authorities clashed over how to respond to the pandemic.[4] The confluence of continuous political struggles and deeply politicised responses to COVID-19 also gave rise to ever-more exclusionary laws and policies, championed by conservative lawmakers who wanted to reassert their conservative political bona fides. The battle for governor between two conservative politicians perhaps best illustrates this phenomenon. In the Fall of 2021, during a surge of COVID-19 cases,[5] Texas State Senator Don Huffines released a Twitter video complaining about the webpage of the Texas Department of Family and Protective Services. Huffines, a challenger to the incumbent Republican Governor of Texas, Greg Abbott, argued that the state agency was 'promoting transgender sexual policies', even though the website simply provided links to trans-affirming organisations.[6] Months earlier, Huffines criticized Abbott's pandemic response, claiming the Governor was too slow to fully reopen the state's economy. In response to these claims, Abbott ordered information about LGBTQ+ people be removed from the website of the Texas Department of Family and Protective Services[7] and ordered a ban on COVID-19 vaccine mandates, including mandates issued by private employers.[8]

As the Huffines-Abbott feud over LGBTQ+ issues and COVID-19 practices show, in Texas, much like other conservative US states, rather than attending to an ongoing public health crisis and slowing the spread of an infectious respiratory disease, government leaders enacted and enforced laws and policies that buttressed social division. In this chapter, we emphasise how laws and policies implemented during the COVID-19 pandemic can reinforce what Chua and Lee describe as dysconnectedness and therefore advance authoritarian controls beyond responses to a particular pandemic. Because pandemics of life-threatening diseases such as COVID-19 are events laden with grave moral significance, governmental responses, or the intended lack thereof, tend to be moralised in terms of pre-existing patterns of political polarisation and social dysconnectedness. To examine how the COVID-19 pandemic provided the stage for a range of policies that performed the politics of social division, we focus on Texan legislative and executive measures to restrict abortion rights, LGBTQ+ rights, political representation, reinforce xenophobic policies and, at the same time, enhance firearm access during the pandemic. Taken together, these deliberate failures to respond to a public health crisis and efforts to heighten partisanship and social differences

[4] See, for example, *State of Texas v City of Austin, Texas, County of Travis, Texas, Steve Adler* Price, VL District Court of Travis County, Texas.

[5] Our World In Data, 'Daily New Confirmed COVID-19 Deaths per Million People' (Oxford, University of Oxford, 2022). Available at: www.ourworldindata.org/explorers/coronavirus-data-explorer.

[6] A Waller, 'State Agency Removed Online Resources for LGBTQ Youth after Complaints from a Republican Challenging Gov. Greg Abbott, Emails Show' *The Texas Tribune* (12 October 2021). Available at: www.texastribune.org/2021/10/12/texas-lgbtq-resources-department-family-protective-services/.

[7] Waller, 'State Agency' (n 6).

[8] R Allen, 'Texas Gov Greg Abbott Bans any COVID-19 Vaccine Mandates – including for Private Employers' *The Texas Tribune* (11 October 2021). Available at: www.texastribune.org/2021/10/11/texas-greg-abbott-covid-19-vaccine-mandate/.

reveal how pandemics can be strategic moments for elected officials to tighten their grip on power by exploiting social division.

Background: Texas' Inconsistent Responses to COVID-19

Governor Abbott's inconsistent responses demonstrate how the chief executive's office employed state authority to implement strategies of control against COVID-19, shifted its stance toward emphasising individual responsibility and even criminalised certain strategies of control, depending on whether the position at hand was politically advantageous. When COVID-19 was first detected in Texas on 3 March 2020, Governor Abbott hesitated to issue stay-at-home orders or close businesses, leaving this decision up to the municipalities.[9] Subsequently, on 19 March 2020, he issued an executive order closing schools and businesses with exceptions for essential businesses, or businesses deemed so important that society would not be able to function without them.[10] However, in less than a month, on 17 April 2020, he decided to reopen the state incrementally.[11] Five months into the pandemic, he placed the responsibility for reducing the spread of COVID-19 on local businesses and municipalities.

Furthermore, after initially following public health guidance to mandate mask wearing in public areas to mitigate the rampant spread of COVOD-19 across Texas,[12] Governor Abbott switched his position to score political points with his far-right electoral base, as he and the Texas Republican Party promoted individual responsibility as the state's primary response to COVID-19. By March 2021, he lifted capacity limitations on businesses, allowing indoor activities to return to pre-pandemic levels.[13] In May of the same year, he went one step further. He implemented an executive order that prohibited municipalities and local public health authorities from implementing mask mandates and specified punishments for those who ignored the order.[14] The punishments included fines for local governments or government officials that attempted to impose a mask mandate of up to $1,000.[15] He also permitted in-person schooling to resume, at the same time restricting schools from taking any form of precautionary COVID-19 measures.

[9] The Texas Newsroom, 'How We Got Here: A Timeline of Gov. Greg Abbott's COVID Policies' (*National Public Radio*, 2021). Available at: www.houstonpublicmedia.org/articles/news/politics/2021/08/20/406474/how-we-got-here-a-timeline-of-gov-greg-abbotts-covid-policies.

[10] The Texas Newsroom 'How We Got Here' (n 9).

[11] The Texas Newsroom (n 9).

[12] The Texas Newsroom (n 9); P Svitek, 'Gov Greg Abbott Orders Texans in Most Counties to Wear Masks in Public' *The Texas Tribune* (2 July 2020). Available at: www.texastribune.org/2020/07/02/texas-mask-order-greg-abbott-coronavirus/.

[13] The Texas Newsroom (n 9).

[14] Allen, 'Texas Gov Greg Abbott' (n 8).

[15] Governor Greg Abbott, *Executive Order No GA-36 relating to the prohibition of governmental entities and officials from mandating face coverings or restricting activities in response to the COVID-19 disaster.* (2021).

The discourse of individual responsibility would continue throughout the subsequent waves of COVID-19. When COVID-19 vaccines were made available to all adults in March of 2021, Abbott initially allowed businesses to require their employees to be vaccinated. However, in October of 2021, he changed his mind. He issued an executive order that banned all businesses from imposing such a requirement, probably a direct rebuke to President Biden's order that all businesses with at least 100 employees must require their workers be vaccinated.[16]

Governor Abbott's contradictory responses to COVID-19 were partly shaped by his political challengers. Throughout the pandemic, he received criticism from individuals seeking to push his office further right politically, including the Lieutenant Governor Dan Patrick and Abbott's primary election opponent Don Huffines. Huffines criticized Abbott's response to COVID-19 during each stage of the pandemic and even called for Abbott to prohibit any form of vaccination requirement for schools, businesses or local governments.[17] Lieutenant Governor Patrick used his position of power within the Texas government to champion economic interests over human health and wellbeing, even intimating that he and other older individuals in the state, who were often described as being at higher risk for COVID-related death, would be willing to die if it meant the economy would thrive.[18] Facing pressure from his own government and party, Abbott repeatedly yielded to arguments that championed discourses of individual responsibility and prioritised economic interests.

Restricting Reproductive Rights, LGBTQ+ Rights and Political Representation While Expanding Gun Access

Texas' responses to COVID-19 reveal only one layer of how Abbott and other elected officials prioritised political interests over public health. In addition to the inconsistent COVID-19 responses described above, during the pandemic, the Texas government engaged in law and policy-making that had nothing to do with COVID-19 strategies of control but rather advanced their politics of division. The Texas case, therefore, demonstrates the ways in which governments and political leaders can take advantage of already deadly contagious outbreaks to achieve authoritarian aims that can exacerbate social exclusion or dysconnectedness and result in fatalities and other forms of suffering.

The Texas legislature meets once every two years – an atypical pattern for most US states since most state legislatures meet annually.[19] In addition to regular meetings, special sessions can be held for extraordinary circumstances that require governmental action. In 2019, the state's regular session was held January to May,

[16] Abbott, *Executive Order No GA-36* (n 15).

[17] Abbott (n 15).

[18] A Samuels, 'Dan Patrick says "there are more important things than living and that's saving this country"' *The Texas Tribune*, Available at: www.texastribune.org/2020/04/21/texas-dan-patrick-economy-coronavirus/.

[19] Texas House of Representatives, 'About Us' (n.d.). Available at: www.house.texas.gov/about-us.

before the COVID-19 pandemic occurred. In 2020, the legislature did not meet, even though the circumstances would have called for a special session to respond to the COVID-19 crisis. Indeed, across the US, many states called special sessions to specifically respond to the pandemic, but Texas was not one of them.[20] When the 2021 regular session started, it began on 12 January and ended on 31 May.[21] Three additional special sessions – the focus of this section – were then called.

Special sessions in Texas have occurred in 59 out of 89 legislative sessions. Only the Governor can call special sessions, and they can last for up to 30 days.[22] During his eight years as Governor, Abbott called a special session only once before 2021. In 2021, he called three special sessions. The first special session was called on 8 July and ended on 6 August. Immediately after the first special session, the second special session was called on 7 August, and ended 2 September. Finally, the third session was called on 20 September and ended on 19 October.[23] The focus of these special sessions was not to address the ongoing COVID-19 crisis in Texas, fuelled by comparatively low vaccination rates[24] and limited efforts to reduce transmission. The first and second were supposed to respond to 'election integrity'[25] and the third purportedly to respond to the distribution of federal COVID-19 funds administered to the state.[26] However, each of the three special sessions advanced the Governor and his party's divisive politics: during the first two sessions, the Republican-controlled legislature introduced anti-abortion legislation; in the third session, it put forth anti-trans and redistricting legislation that would constrain voting for people of colour.

Anti-Abortion Legislation: The 'Heartbeat' Bill

The most notorious legislative measure that the Texas government passed during the pandemic was an aggressive anti-abortion bill known as the 'heartbeat' bill. The right to an abortion has historically been a politically contentious issue in

[20] National Conference of State Legislatures, 'Coronavirus and State Legislatures in the News' (2021). Available at: www.ncsl.org/research/about-state-legislatures/coronavirus-and-state-legislatures-in-the-news.aspx.

[21] Legislative Reference Library of Texas, 'Texas Legislative Sessions and Years' (2022). Available at: www.lrl.texas.gov/sessions/sessionyears.cfm.

[22] *The Texas Constitution* (1876) Legislative Reference Library of Texas, 'Special sessions topics: 87th 1st C.S.' (2021). Available at: www.lrl.texas.gov/sessions/specialsessions/specialSessionTopics.cfm?legSessionID=87-1; Legislative Reference Library of Texas, 'Special sessions topics: 87th 2nd C.S.' (2021). Available at: www.lrl.texas.gov/sessions/specialsessions/specialSessionTopics.cfm?legSessionID=87-2.

[23] Legislative Reference Library (n 21).

[24] E Mathieu, H Ritchie and E Ortiz-Ospina, 'A Global Database of COVID-19 Vaccinations' (2021). Available at: www.ourworldindata.org/covid-vaccinations?country=USA.

[25] P Svitek, 'Gov. Greg Abbott Announces Special Legislative Session Starting Saturday, Covering Elections, Federal COVID-19 Funding, Quorum Rules' *The Texas Tribune* (2 October 2021). Available at: www.texastribune.org/2021/08/02/greg-abbott-texas-special-legislative-session.

[26] Legislative Reference Library of Texas, 'Special sessions topics: 87th 3rd C.S.' (2021). Available at: www.lrl.texas.gov/sessions/specialsessions/specialSessionTopics.cfm?legSessionID=87-3; C Pollock and J Barragán, 'Texas Legislators Pass Most – but Not All – of Gov. Greg Abbott's Priority Measures in Final Flurry of Lawmaking' *The Texas Tribune* (19 October 2021). Available at: www.texastribune.org/2021/10/19/texas-legislature-redistricting-property-tax-vaccine-mandates/.

the United States. Even though the landmark Supreme Court case of *Roe v Wade* guaranteed people capable of pregnancy the right to an abortion in 1973, opponents of the decision, including Republican political leaders, mobilised to get the case overturned.[27] These contentions did not abate but persisted throughout the pandemic.[28]

Prior to the COVID-19 pandemic, Texas maintained some of the strictest abortion laws in the United States.[29] With some exceptions, abortions after 20 weeks of fertilisation were illegal and the law placed a number of burdens on healthcare providers, insurance providers and patients. Healthcare providers were required to: (1) pay additional fees for cremating the remains of foetuses from abortions, (2) have an association with a hospital within a 30-mile radius, which constrained abortion access in rural communities and (3) follow specific protocols from the state when performing abortions.[30] Comprehensive health insurance plans were not allowed to include abortion services; instead, these services required an additional plan for abortion coverage, creating a burden for both insurance providers and patients.[31] Patients seeking an abortion carried the most significant burden and formed the focus of most laws prior to 2019, including laws that required a sonogram 24 hours before the procedure and mandated providers give biased information related to abortions during the patient's initial visit.[32] Under the 'Women's Right to Know' Act, providers are required to give patients an information booklet containing medically questionable claims that abortion increased the likelihood of developing breast cancer, infertility or mental health issues such as depression or suicidal ideation.[33] These efforts, as social and health scientists have shown, are intentional interventions by the state to entangle medical providers in its performance of political power[34] – in this case, by optimising the health and wellbeing of foetuses at the expense of women as a population.[35]

During the COVID-19 pandemic, the Texas legislature utilised the special sessions to enact laws that further restricted access to abortion.[36] Most notably,

[27] M Ziegler, *After Roe: The Lost History of the Abortion Debate* (Cambridge MA, Harvard University Press, 2015).

[28] In 2022, the effort to rollback reproductive rights and the ability to receive an abortion, specifically, was achieved through the *Dobbs v Jackson Women's Health Organization*, which overturned the right to an abortion.

[29] ACLU Texas, 'A Recent History of Restrictive Abortion Laws in Texas' (2022). Available at: www.aclutx.org/en/recent-history-restrictive-abortion-laws-texas.

[30] ACLU Texas 'A Recent History' (n 29).

[31] ACLU Texas (n 29).

[32] ACLU Texas (n 29).

[33] A Pattani, 'Abortion Booklet Revisions Called Even More Inaccurate' *The Texas Tribune* (27 July 2016). Available at: www.texastribune.org/2016/07/27/state-proposes-changes-abortion-information-bookle/; Texas Department of Health and Human Services, *A Woman's Right to Know* (2016).

[34] M Buchbinder, 'Scripting Dissent: US Abortion Laws, State Power, and the Politics of Scripted Speech' (2016) 118 *American Anthropologist* 772.

[35] S Rodrigues, 'A Woman's "Right to Know"? Forced Ultrasound Measures as an Intervention of Biopower' (2014) 7 *International Journal of Feminist Approaches to Bioethics* 51.

[36] SB 8 went into effect shortly after passing, and additional laws were passed, including 'trigger laws', or laws that a legislative body passes that will go into effect when a particular condition allows

a law commonly referred to by its bill name, Senate Bill (SB) 8, made abortions illegal after six weeks post-fertilisation. It also created a 'bounty hunter' system that allowed any individual (other than certain public employees) to file a lawsuit against abortion providers and/or individuals receiving an abortion and awarded successful plaintiffs at least $10,000 from defendants.[37] The new law, therefore, effectively recruited all citizens into the state's anti-abortion surveillance network, transforming them into capillaries of state power, following Foucault's understanding of carceral power.[38]

In addition, other laws passed during this time made it illegal for abortion providers to not care for a foetus in certain circumstances[39] and restricted government entities from partnering with healthcare facilities that provide abortions or are affiliated with those that provide abortions.[40] These laws may disproportionately affect women of colour, who, compared to white women, already have elevated maternal mortality rates, lack access to reproductive services and are more likely to have an unplanned pregnancy. Moreover, all these laws passed during the pandemic portended more to come. Although abortion access enjoys broad support from the population, conservative lawmakers continued to press forward with restricting abortion access.[41] Following the reversal of *Roe v Wade* in 2022, the Texas legislature implemented a law that makes performing an abortion a felony punishable by up to a lifetime prison sentence and civil penalties of no less than $100,000 plus attorney's fees.[42]

Anti-LGBTQ+ Legislative Efforts

LGBTQ+ issues also dominated the Texas state legislative agenda during the pandemic. House Bill 25, passed and signed into law in October 2021, combined much of the content of thirty bills that were introduced but not passed during the

for it. For example, HB 1280, designed to ban abortions when the constitutional right to abortion was overturned, went into effect on 25 August 2022, following the US Supreme Court decision of *Dobbs v Jackson*. The full text of HB1280 is available at: www.capitol.texas.gov/tlodocs/87R/billtext/html/HB01280I.htm.

[37] Huffman, *SB 6* (87(2) edn, 2021); E Bowman, 'As States Ban abortion, the Texas Bounty Law Offers a Way to Survive Legal Challenges' (*National Public Radio*, 2022). Available at: www.npr.org/2022/07/11/1107741175/texas-abortion-bounty-law.

[38] J Rouse, 'Power/Knowledge' in *The Cambridge Companion to Foucault*, Gary Gutting (ed) (Cambridge, Cambridge University Press, 1994); M Foucault, 'Prison Talk: an Interview' (1977) 16 *Radical Philosophy 10–15.*

[39] ACLU Texas (n 29).

[40] ACLU Texas (n 29); D Blumenthal and L Zephyrin, 'Texas's New Abortion Law Will Harm People of Color, Further Entrench Racist Policies' (*The Commonwealth Fund*, 2021). Available at: www.commonwealthfund.org/blog/2021/texass-new-abortion-law-will-harm-people-color-further-entrench-racist-policies.

[41] S McCammon, 'Poll: One year after SB 8, Texans express strong support for abortion rights' (*National Public Radio*, 2022). Available at: www.npr.org/2022/09/01/1120472842/poll-one-year-after-sb-8-texans-express-strong-support-for-abortion-rights.

[42] E Klibanoff, 'Texans who Perform Abortions Now Face Up to Life in Prison, $100,000 Fine' *The Texas Tribune*. Available at: www.texastribune.org/2022/08/25/texas-trigger-law-abortion.

regular session. According to Texas's largest LGBTQ+ political advocacy organisation, Equality Texas, thirteen out of those 30 bills targeted transgender youth:[43] six banned transgender people from participating in sports teams that aligned with their gender identity; another six prohibited healthcare facilities from providing affirmative services to transgender youth, such as prescribing puberty blockers, providing hormone therapy, or conducting gender-affirming surgeries; and one stopped people from amending their birth certificates to match their gender identity. The remaining bills focused on LGBTQ+ people generally and included powers that would have enabled the state government to pre-empt local non-discrimination ordinances, religious exemptions that would have provided for exceptions to anti-discrimination laws based on 'sincerely held religious beliefs' and provisions that would have criminalised HIV transmission and perceived exposure to the virus.[44]

Authored by legislators who introduced some of these bills during the regular session, House Bill 25 also restricted the sports participation of transgender youth. The 30 bills introduced during the regular session had either failed to meet procedural deadlines or were defeated in committees run by Democrats. During the special session, however, Republicans managed to direct House Bill 25 to a committee under their party's control and ensure its eventual passage through the legislature. Furthermore, in February 2022, Texas Attorney General Ken Paxton declared that provision of transgender-affirming care was a form of child abuse and ordered state agencies to investigate parents who organised gender-affirming care for their children for child abuse and to bring charges against them.[45] Overall, then, despite most bills failing, their content – restricting sports participation and banning gender affirming care – advanced through House Bill 25 and through the Attorney General's directives.

House Bill 25 represented a concerted effort by conservatives to send symbolic messages of exclusion to LGBTQ+ people while COVID-19 infections were rising.[46] It demonstrated that LGBTQ+ identities, especially transgender identities, remained a source of political capital for these politicians in Texas. This is an observation later confirmed by the Republican Party of Texas's changes to its political platform in 2022. Those changes included a section on 'Homosexuality and Gender Issues' that claims that 'homosexuality is an abnormal lifestyle choice' and 'we oppose all efforts to validate transgender identity'.[47]

[43] Equality Texas, 'Legislative Bill Tracker' (2022). Available at: www.equalitytexas.org/legislative-bill-tracker.

[44] Equality Texas (n 43).

[45] K Paxton, *Opinion No KP-0401* (Attorney General of Texas 2022); J Leahy, 'Texas Attorney General Declares Gender-affirming Medical Care for Transgender Kids 'Child Abuse' *KERA*. Available at: www.keranews.org/news/2022-02-22/texas-attorney-general-declares-gender-affirming-medical-care-for-transgender-kids-child-abuse.

[46] NS Kline and others, 'Mapping Transgender Policies in the US 2017–2021: The Role of Geography and Implications for Health Equity' (2023) 80 *Health & Place* 102985.

[47] M Patrick et al, *Report of the Permanent 2022 Platform & Resolutions Committee* (2022). Available at: www.texasgop.org/wp-content/uploads/2022/06/6-Permanent-Platform-Committee-FINAL-REPORT-6-16-2022.pdf.

Restricting Political Representation Through Redistricting

In addition to limiting reproductive and LGBTQ+ rights during the pandemic, the Texas legislature shrunk the political representation and weakened the vote of racially minorised people through what is known in the United States as 'redistricting'. This case of redistricting demonstrates how the Texas legislature exercised its congressional powers to privilege White populations and, correspondingly, maintain the advantage of political Conservatives. The increase in White representation did not align with the state's population growth and arguably contributed to the political disenfranchisement of people of colour.

In the United States, each state allocates legislative power by drawing up its own congressional districts. Each district within a state may elect members to the US House of Representatives, one of the houses of the bicameral Congress, which is the federal legislature. Redistricting is a process whereby the state redraws congressional district lines by making adjustments according to a decennial census that may reflect changing population demographics within the state's districts.[48] Federally mandated,[49] redistricting is meant to ensure the equitable representation of individuals across legislative districts.[50] In Texas, redistricting occurred in 2021 following the 2020 United States census. Gerrymandering, or redrawing congressional districts in a manner that favours one party, class or group of people, including a racial group, is unconstitutional in the United States.[51] Nevertheless, it still occurs and requires legal action to rectify.[52] If gerrymandering is shown to have occurred, states are required to redraw their districts. As of May 2023, 73 court cases had been filed challenging congressional and legislative maps in 27 states.[53]

According to the 2020 census, the Texas population grew substantially over the last ten years, with the majority of the growth stemming from people of colour.[54] However, when the Texas legislature redrew the congressional district lines during the pandemic special sessions, it heavily favoured White representation over populations of colour. For example, it removed the only congressional district that had a majority Black population, leaving Texas with no majority

[48] The Texas Legislative Council, 'Redistricting Process'. Available at: www.redistricting.capitol.texas.gov.

[49] The Texas Legislative Council 'Redistricting Process' (n 48).

[50] ACLU, 'What is Redistricting and Why Should We Care?' (2021). Available at: www.aclu.org/news/voting-rights/what-is-redistricting-and-why-should-we-care.

[51] JA Curiel and T Steelman, 'A Response to 'Tests for Unconstitutional Partisan Gerrymandering in a Post-Gill World' in a Post-Rucho World' 19 *Election Law Journal: Rules, Politics, and Policy* 101.

[52] RL Engstrom, 'Partisan Gerrymandering: Weeds in the Political Thicket' 101 *Social Science Quarterly* 23.

[53] Brennan Center for Justice, 'Redistricting Litigation Roundup' (2021). Available at: www.brennancenter.org/our-work/research-reports/redistricting-litigation-roundup-0.

[54] A Ura et al, 'People of Color make up 95% of Texas' Population Growth, and Cities and Suburbs are Booming, 2020 Census Shows' *The Texas Tribune* (12 October 2021). Available at: www.texastribune.org/2021/08/12/texas-2020-census.

Black congressional district.[55] Additionally, it reduced the number of congressional districts with a majority Hispanic/Latinx population from eight to seven.[56] To make matters worse, the Texas 2020 census might have already undercounted its burgeoning Hispanic/Latinx communities. Leading up to the 2020 census, the Trump administration attempted to add a question about citizenship status.[57] The addition of this question had the potential to undercount Latinx individuals who were undocumented or have other precarious immigration statuses. Fearing arrest and deportation, such individuals might have hesitated to respond to the census, potentially decreasing their political representation and the congressional representation of cities and districts with higher proportions of their populations. These concerns, along with significant pushback from congressional lawmakers and activists, resulted in the omission of this question from the 2020 census. Nevertheless, at the height of the pandemic in 2020, media attention on this census question might still have discouraged some individuals with precarious immigration statuses from filling out the census, leading to an underreporting of Hispanic/Latinx population numbers in Texas.[58]

Expanding Gun Access

Whereas the above three legislative efforts focused on restricting rights to enhance social exclusion, the fourth during the pandemic aimed at expanding gun rights, specifically by allowing people to carry concealed handguns without a licence.[59] In August 2019, two mass shootings happened back to back in Texas: one in El Paso and another in Midland/Odessa, which claimed the lives of 30 individuals in total.[60] The El Paso shooting resulted in 23 people being murdered and 23 others being injured, most of whom were Latinx. In this deadliest attack on Latinx people in contemporary US history, the shooter was motivated by xenophobic and white nationalist ideologies adopted by far-right political Conservatives in the US.[61]

[55] Ura et al, 'People of Color' (n 54).

[56] J Barragán, A Livingston and C Astudillo, 'Texas reduces Black and Hispanic Majority Congressional Districts in Proposed Map, Despite People of Color Fueling Population Growth' *The Texas Tribune* (24 September 2021). Available at: www.texastribune.org/2021/09/24/texas-congressional-redistricting.

[57] M Wines, 'A Census Whodunit: Why Was the Citizenship Question Added?' *The New York Times* (30 November 2019). Available at: www.nytimes.com/2019/11/30/us/census-citizenship-question-hofeller.html.

[58] GR Sanchez, 'What are the Consequences of the Latino Undercount in the 2020 U.S. Census?' (Washington DC, Brookings Institute, 2022). Available at: www.brookings.edu/blog/how-we-rise/2022/03/24/what-are-the-consequences-of-the-latino-undercount-in-the-2020-u-s-census/.

[59] *Gun Laws* (Texas State Law Library, 2021). Available at: https://guides.sll.texas.gov/gun-laws/carry-of-firearms.

[60] K McGee and J McCullough, 'Confronted with Mass Shootings, Texas Republicans have Repeatedly Loosened Gun Laws', *The Texas Tribune* (24 May 2022). Available at: www.texastribune.org/2022/05/24/texas-gun-laws-uvalde-mass-shootings.

[61] M Pskowski, 'As El Paso Struggles to Heal, Walmart Shooter's Rhetoric Builds in GOP' *El Paso Times* (4 August 2022). Available at: www.elpasotimes.com/story/news/2022/08/04/el-paso-walmart-shooting-patrick-crusius-gop-rhetoric-invasion/7585100001.

Shortly after the two mass shootings, Governor Abbott and Lieutenant Governor Dan Patrick indicated that they were open to increasing background checks for stranger-to-stranger sales.[62] These proposed changes to Texas firearm laws would have been a small but necessary step towards safer gun laws, but the discussion around them was short-lived. Following significant political pressure from the Republican Party and gun-rights activists, Abbott backed away from any restrictions related to gun laws despite broad support within the Texas population for expanded background checks.[63]

Two years later, in 2021, the Texas legislature still had not taken any action to enhance background checks. Instead, the state passed a law for 'constitutional carry'.[64] House Bill 1927, which was signed in June 2021, effectively gives individuals in Texas the right to obtain and carry a gun without a permit.[65] The law eliminated the requirement for residents to obtain a licence to carry a handgun if they are not already prohibited from having a firearm in their possession due to another state or federal law. Meanwhile, conservative lawmakers in Texas opposed gun legislation that would prevent numerous cases of mass shootings within the state. Despite a largely conservative base in Texas, a majority of voters indicated that they preferred stricter gun laws and, since 2019, no more than 20 per cent of voters have indicated that they wanted to relax gun laws.[66] Nonetheless, in the special sessions held during the pandemic, the Republican-led legislature pushed forward efforts to reduce restrictions to firearm access.

House Bill 1927 passed into law and went into effect on 1 September 2021. In less than year, another mass shooting occurred in Texas. On 24 May 2022, a teenager shot and killed 17 children and two teachers at Robb Elementary School in Uvalde, Texas.[67] Upon turning 18 – the legal age for the purchase of a rifle in Texas – the teenager purchased an AR-15 semi-automatic assault rifle in the same week that he carried out the mass shooting.[68] Before turning 18, he had attempted to buy weapons on multiple other occasions but was denied purchase.[69] Arguably, the deaths of children and teachers at Robb Elementary could have been avoided had the Texas legislature enacted more restrictive gun

[62] McGee and McCullough 'Texas Republicans have Repeatedly Loosened Gun Laws' (n 60).

[63] McGee and McCullough (n 60); The Texas Politics Project, 'Background Checks on All Gun Purchases (June 2022)' (The University of Texas at Austin, 2022). Available at: www.texaspolitics.utexas.edu/polling/search/topic/gun-control-27.

[64] McGee and McCullough (n 60).

[65] M Schaefer, *HB 1927* (2021).

[66] The Texas Politics Project, 'Should Gun Laws be More or Less Strict? (August 2022)' (The University of Texas at Austin, 2022). Available at: www.texaspolitics.utexas.edu/polling/search/topic/gun-control-27.

[67] C Astudillo, R Oxner and E Neugeboren, 'What We Know, Minute by Minute, about How the Uvalde Shooting and Police Response Unfolded', *The Texas Tribune* (27 May 2022). Available at: www.texastribune.org/2022/05/27/uvalde-texas-school-shooting-timeline.

[68] R Oxner, 'Uvalde Gunman Legally Bought AR Rifles Days before Shooting, Law Enforcement Says' *The Texas Tribune* (25 May 2022). Available at: www.texastribune.org/2022/05/25/uvalde-shooter-bought-gun-legally.

[69] Astudillo, Oxner and Neugeboren 'What We Know' (n 67).

laws instead of legislation that expanded access to firearms. Specifically, the legislature could have passed a ban on assault rifles, such as AR-15s, the type of weapon used in the Robb Elementary shooting or followed nine other states and the District of Columbia and regulated access to high-capacity magazines – an ammunition storage and feeding device.[70]

Doubling Down on Xenophobia

For Governor Abbot and other Texas elected officials, COVID-19 also introduced an opportunity to reinforce xenophobic attitudes. Critically, they did so by interfering with essential supply chain activities that had been disturbed due to the pandemic under the guise of dealing with immigration matters. In the US, the disruption of global supply chains due to the spread of the virus,[71] movement in several labour markets, shifts in demand for certain goods and climate crises such as droughts, resulted in shortages of electronic goods, vehicles, food, hygiene items and other commodities.[72] In Texas, Governor Abbott arguably aggravated these pandemic-related supply issues when he issued a directive for longer safety inspections of vehicles entering Texas from Mexico. The inspections extended a routine entry into lengthy crossings, some lasting as long as 30 hours,[73] thus delaying the entry of Mexican goods into the US.

Abbott's directive can be regarded as a protest against President Joe Biden's reversal of Title 42, the Trump administration's pandemic immigration policy.[74] Title 42 empowered immigration authorities to prohibit immigrants, including asylum seekers, from entering the US on the grounds of curbing the spread of infectious diseases.[75] Abbott's directive, along with the superseded Title 42, therefore illustrates how politicians made use of health concerns to enforce anti-immigration

[70] R Oxner, 'Uvalde Gunman Legally Bought AR Rifles Days before Shooting, Law Enforcement Says' *The Texas Tribune* (25 May 2022). Available at: www.texastribune.org/2022/05/25/uvalde-shooter-bought-gun-legally.

[71] P Chowdhury et al, 'COVID-19 Pandemic Related Supply Chain Studies: A Systematic Review' 148 *Transportation Research Part E: Logistics and Transportation Review* 102271.

[72] B Klayman and P Lienert, 'Analysts Forecast US Vehicle Shortages as Supply Chain Woes Persist' Reuters (28 June 2022). Available at: www.reuters.com/business/autos-transportation/analysts-forecast-us-vehicle-shortages-supply-chain-woes-persist-2022-06-28; K Teague, '10 Grocery Items That Might Be Hard to Find in Your Local Store' CNET. Available at: www.cnet.com/culture/10-grocery-items-that-might-be-hard-to-find-in-your-local-store.

[73] A Wallace and V Yurkevich, 'Rotting Fruit, Spoiled Vegetables: How Texas Just Made the Supply Chain even Worse', CNN Business. Available at: www.cnn.com/2022/04/16/economy/texas-mexico-abbott-border-economic-impact/index.html.

[74] Office of the Texas Governor, *Operation Lone Star Mission Expands As Biden Ends Title 42 Expulsions* (2022).

[75] J Gramlich, 'Key facts about Title 42, the Pandemic Policy that has Reshaped Immigration Enforcement at U.S.-Mexico Border' (Pew Research Center, 2022). Available at: www.pewresearch.org/fact-tank/2022/04/27/key-facts-about-title-42-the-pandemic-policy-that-has-reshaped-immigration-enforcement-at-u-s-mexico-border.

policies in the US[76] and how contagious outbreaks could become moments of renewed xenophobia and nativism.[77]

As a result of Abbott's directive, approximately $240 million of fresh produce rotted in trucks and did not reach grocery stores, creating a shortage of retail food.[78] In statements about the directive, Abbott explained that it was a direct response to what he viewed as failed immigration policies from President Biden.[79] Frustrated with Texas' supply-chain politics and policies, governmental authorities in Mexico announced they would no longer use Texas as a trade corridor and would shift to New Mexico, a move that will result in an estimated loss of $4.23 billion in Gross Domestic Product for Texas.[80]

Conclusion: Pandemic as an 'Unurgent' Crisis Compared to Legislating Division

The COVID-19 pandemic created new forms of strategies of control that relied on the law to regulate, even normalise-moralise, behaviours to ward off the SAR-CoV-2 virus, as the introduction to this volume and Chapters 2, 3, 4 and 7 have demonstrated. In contrast, in Texas, rather than trying to mitigate the potentially deadly effects of the pandemic, the legislature restricted reproductive rights, sexual and gender minority rights and political representation, while expanding firearm access in ways that could worsen gun violence; while the Texas administration advanced xenophobic and anti-immigration policies. Although the preceding chapters remind us that COVID-19 strategies of control could also bring about dysconnectedness,

[76] AL Fairchild, 'Policies of Inclusion: Immigrants, Disease, Dependency, and American Immigration Policy at the Dawn and Dusk of the 20th Century' 94 *American Journal of Public Health* 528.

[77] LJ Hardy, 'Connection, Contagion, and COVID-19' (2020) 39 *Medical Anthropology* 655; L Eichelberger, 'SARS and New York's Chinatown: the Politics of Risk and Blame During an Epidemic of Fear' (1982) 65 *Social Science & Medicine* 1284; TT Reny and MA Barreto, 'Xenophobia in the Time of Pandemic: Othering, Anti-Asian Attitudes, and COVID-19' (2020) 10 *Politics, Groups, and Identities* 209.

[78] S Nowlin, 'Texas Gov. Greg Abbott's Border Slowdown Ruined Millions of Dollars in Food. Texas Consumers will Pay', *San Antonio Current* (18 April 2022). Available at: www.sacurrent.com/news/texas-gov-greg-abbotts-border-slowdown-ruined-millions-of-dollars-in-food-texas-consumers-will-pay-28678151; S Al-Arshani, 'Texas Gov. Greg Abbott's Truck Inspection Policy Created a Logjam at the Border that Resulted in $240 Million of Spoiled Produce' (2022). Available at: www.businessinsider.com/texas-gov-greg-abbott-truck-inspection-policy-creates-logjam-2022-4.

[79] Sergio Martínez-Beltrán, 'Gov. Abbott is Again Adding Truck Inspections Along the Border. Critics say He's Playing Politics'. *Texas Public Radio* (29 June 2022). Available at: www.tpr.org/border-immigration/2022-06-29/gov-abbott-is-again-adding-truck-inspections-along-the-border-critics-say-hes-playing-politics.

[80] M Vermeulen, 'Mexico Axes Texas Trade Route in Response to Abbott's Overreach' *Texas Signal* (6 May 2022). Available at: www.texassignal.com/mexico-axes-texas-trade-route-in-response-to-abbotts-overreach; S. Nowlin, 'Mexico Says Major Rail Project will Bypass Texas as Payback for Abbott Slowing Border Trade', *San Antonio Current* (2 May 2022). Available at: www.sacurrent.com/news/mexico-says-major-rail-project-will-bypass-texas-as-payback-for-abbott-slowing-border-trade-28793518.

the laws and policies that Texas politicians passed and implemented during the pandemic made no attempt to curb the contagion but rather represented deliberate politics of social exclusion. In fact, these politicians not only passed unpopular legislation but also restricted local municipalities from protecting their populations from COVID-19. To be clear, we are not advocating for particular forms of COVID-19 strategies of control; rather, we show that instead of using their legislative and executive powers to focus on fighting off COVID-19, Texas politicians took advantage of the pandemic as a morally charged backdrop for their own politically divisive aims.

Although the laws and policies examined in this chapter could have been proposed and put into effect without the COVID-19 pandemic, the timing of the proposals and the special sessions highlight a problematic phenomenon. Texan political leaders reacted with urgency by calling the special sessions to uphold, even strengthen, social divisions with laws and policies disconnected from the broader electorate's positions but not to address a public health crisis. If they were interested in addressing the COVID-19 crisis, they would have prioritised the wellbeing of the Texas population rather than finding ways to amplify the state's authoritarian controls at the special sessions.

This problematic phenomenon also raises questions regarding the US's approach to pandemic-related governance at large. Historically, individual states have held 'police powers' to ensure the health of their populations, which can include measures such as quarantine, isolation and compulsory vaccination.[81] At the time of writing, as the COVID-19 pandemic persists and as Texas still lags in comparison to the national average of vaccination rates,[82] US states continue to operate with a patchwork-like of strategies of control at municipal, county, state and federal levels. The Texas case therefore suggests that this approach could lead to an abdication of responsibility by state and local governments. Even more broadly, the Texas case indicates a need to trace not only multiple levels of governing through contagion but also seemingly unrelated law – and policy-making initiatives within a given jurisdiction during contagious outbreaks. Especially in the event of a pandemic when control over contagion is a matter of life and death, a wide range of governmental policies, particularly those that regulate social welfare and inclusion, may become highly moralised even when they do not have an immediate impact on the disease in question. We have demonstrated such patterns of moralisation in conservative-dominated Texas, where the pandemic heightened the stakes of partisan politics. It is inadequate for health and social scientists to pay attention to strategies of control that are intentionally targeted at the contagion in question; they must also follow how politicians and ruling elites continue to deliberately marginalise disadvantaged social groups for political gain in these moments of public health crises.

[81] EP Richards, 'A Historical Review of the State Police Powers and their Relevance to the COVID-19 Pandemic of 2020' 11 *Journal of National Security Law & Policy* 83.

[82] Mathieu, Ritchie and Ortiz-Ospina 'A Global Database of COVID-19 Vaccinations' (n 4); LO Gostin, '*Jacobson v Massachusetts* at 100 years: Police Power and Civil Liberties in Tension' 95 *American Journal of Public Health* 576.

9

Governing Through Contagion in the Authoritarian Context and the Case of China

MARK SIDEL

This chapter explores 'governing through contagion' in the particular context of authoritarian Asia. Here I focus on China as a case study about how COVID-19 governance, 'governing through contagion', has worked alongside the authoritarian governance that long preceded it and which has grown more restrictive in recent years.

In China, as in some other parts of authoritarian Asia, the governing regime has not needed to govern through contagion to take and maintain strict control of their societies; in China, the authorities already had firm authoritarian control. But that does not mean that governing through contagion has been meaningless. This chapter details how even in such authoritarian environments as China, COVID-19 strategies of control have significantly enhanced the state's supervision and surveillance of both domestic and overseas civil society and non-governmental activity. Such strategies, layered upon existing broader authoritarian governance, have led to different forms of resistance: citizen resistance against harsh COVID-19 rules; overseas support for attempts to provide legal aid to COVID-19 victims and families in China; and the cautious emergence of carefully worded suggestions for less harsh and more facilitative civil society regulation in the future.

In China, COVID-19-based restrictions have played out and enhanced the state's already fearsome capacity through what the editors' term juridical modalities – bodily and fiscal sanctions – and security modalities, the coordination of political and social relationships. Authoritarian states such as China used the mechanisms of governing through contagion as an additional mechanism to control populations during the COVID-19 era. At the same time, authoritarians seeking to govern and control civil society possessed ample means to control society and quiet dissent well before COVID-19 enabled them to use additional tools for political control purposes. Asia's authoritarian regimes did not need COVID-19 for control but have found the additional tools deployed during the pandemic to be helpful in the additional controls they sought to impose. They have added so much substantial repressive and administrative capacity during the Xi Jinping era and through COVID-19 that they will continue to have available to use into the future.[1]

Here I illustrate these points through the examination of policy in one undeniably authoritarian state, the People's Republic of China. I discuss the imposition of control over overseas civil society activities and funding in China that began well before COVID-19 – that has served as the basis for COVID-19-related controls on this branch of social power alongside additional 'governing through contagion' measures. I indicate that the same dynamic is at work with respect to the domestic civil society sector, layering significant additional COVID-19 restrictions upon a robust and dynamic process of regime control of domestic non-governmental organisations. I bring this story up to date with a discussion of the use of COVID-19-era repressive mechanisms, along with other tools of repression available to the state, in the late COVID-19 period in China. Then I discuss how 'governing through contagion', layered upon existing broader authoritarian governance, has led to new forms of resistance in China and from outside the country.

Governing External Civil Society in China Through Authoritarian Law and Policy, with Supplemental 'Governing Through Contagion'

In the five years since China's overseas NGO legal and political framework came into effect in January 2017, the Chinese Ministry of Public Security has assumed full policy control over the work of overseas (including Hong Kong, Macao and Taiwan) NGOs, foundations, think tanks and business associations in China. Those authoritarian, security-based controls have only tightened over time. Those five years have seen increasing controls and restrictions on overseas non-profits seeking to operate in China and have included intensive pre-COVID-19 constraints on Chinese universities, research institutions and other institutions working on non-profit and philanthropic projects and academic exchanges.[2]

In 2014 the new Chinese National Security Commission tasked the Ministry of Public Security with rapidly developing a framework for controlling and managing the work of overseas non-profit organisations in China. Within a year the

[1] See, for example, Y An and T Zhang, 'Pandemic State-Building: Chinese Administrative Expansion Since 2012', Yale Law & Policy Review, forthcoming 2024. A version of this paper is available at https://papers.ssrn.com/sol3/papers.cfm?abstract_id=4356026:.

[2] On the Chinese context, see, for example, M Sidel, 'Securitizing Overseas Nonprofit Work in China'(2021) 2 US-Asia Law Institute (USALI) Perspectives, NYU Law School. Available at: www.usali.org/usali-perspectives-blog/securitizing-overseas-nonprofit-work-in-china; M Sidel and H Ming, 'Party, State, Civil Society and Covid-19 in China', (2021) 12 *Nonprofit Policy Forum* 199–211; H Hu and M Sidel, 'Civil Society and COVID in China: Responses in an Authoritarian Society'(2020) 49 *Nonprofit and Voluntary Sector Quarterly* 1173.

ministry presented a draft Overseas NGO Law to the National People's Congress. It was adopted in April 2016 with only one significant amendment – a new Article 53 that partially exempted university and research collaborations with overseas educational and research organisations from the new law. Those matters were left to a separate stream of earlier Ministry of Education and State Council regulations.

The idea of contagion did play a role in these original developments, although the general idea of foreign contagion long predates COVID-19 in Chinese Communist Party and government policy. The more general idea of foreign contagion – the contagion of ideas and power and money – is never far away from Chinese Communist Party ideology and policy when it comes to limiting and controlling the activities of outside groups and governments in China and funding by overseas NGOs and foundations. Those overall 'anti-contagion' policies have waxed and waned over time as a result of intense policy debates within China. There have been significant periods of time in the Chinese reform era when the contagion idea – the notion that the work of foreign NGOs, foundations and think tanks represents a contagious danger to China and its development path – was temporarily subsumed to the idea that overseas NGOs, foundations and think tanks could be harnessed to Chinese policy and did not represent a significant danger. However, in the Xi Jinping period, the danger from foreign ideas, power and money was thought to be greater than the idea of useful contributions from abroad; the Overseas NGO Law and framework quickly took shape in 2014 and 2015 and was formally enacted in 2016.

This new framework for controlling overseas NGO, foundation and other non-profit work in China gave the Ministry of Public Security overall control over the approval and management of overseas non-profit activity in China as part of the 'securitisation' of this area under the auspices of China's new National Security Commission. Only two channels were permitted for foreign non-profit work in China: registering representative offices, which required a long approval process, and obtaining a temporary activity licence, for which approval was somewhat more streamlined and activities were even more significantly constrained.

These were all pre-COVID-19 constraints. Each overseas organisation was required to have an official sponsor to vet and supervise its activities and to be responsible to the security authorities. Dedicated public security offices and staff for handling overseas non-profit matters were quickly formed and now exist down to the rural county and urban district level in some parts of China. In the five years since the Overseas NGO Law took effect in January 2017, over 600 representative offices of NGOs, foundations, think tanks and business associations have been set up in China under the new securitised framework; about half of these are relatively uncontroversial and unchallenging (in political terms) business and trade associations. More than 4,000 temporary activity filings (generally one-year renewable projects) have been made, although the total number of overseas groups involved is considerably less than 4,000 because some overseas organisations carry out multiple projects and have made multiple filings.

The result has been authoritarian control and monitoring of overseas non-profit activity from the neighbourhood and village level to the top of China's governance structure to a degree that was almost unimaginable a decade earlier. Dedicated public security offices and staff for handling overseas non-profit matters now exist down to the rural county and urban district level in some parts of China and to the provincial and municipal levels throughout the country.

Most of the activities permitted to overseas NGOs, foundations and other non-profit groups in China are in areas encouraged by the Chinese government, such as education, health and poverty alleviation. Very few programmes and projects are now possible in less-favoured areas such as civil society development, legal reform, women's rights, LGBT rights and other rights-related matters. A number of overseas groups active in China before the Xi Jinping era have left China or have sharply curtailed their activities. These restrictions and constraints are all in keeping with China's pre-COVID-19 intensive focus on overseas and domestic non-profits as service providers who do not engage in advocacy – what may be termed 'more third sector, less civil society'.

Even Authoritarians have Exceptions to Restrictive Policies – Though COVID-19-era 'Governing Through Contagion' Can Make Restrictions Even Easier

When the Chinese Overseas NGO Law was enacted in 2016, China's sometimes influential research and higher education sector objected to including all their projects with overseas NGOs, foundations, think tanks and business associations in the new Ministry of Public Security-directed framework. That is not because China's intellectual institutions had any illusions about autonomy from the security forces. But they sought to maintain a separate, preexisting channel for obtaining Ministry of Education and State Council approval for cooperative projects with overseas non-profits, foundations and think tanks. They hoped this might help them maintain some distance from security forces in running their own affairs. The resulting compromise was expressed in Article 53 of the final law, which maintained the regulation of overseas academic exchanges through existing State Council and Ministry of Education regulations rather than making those exchange relationships fully subject to the new Overseas NGO Law.

Outside China, Article 53 was sometimes called a 'carve-out' from the Overseas NGO Law, but to my knowledge it was never called that in China. It was the so-called 'carve-out' that never was. Any significant autonomy from security force supervision in the Xi Jinping era was a myth that could be ended at any point or gradually. Authoritarian lawmakers, as in Xi Jinping's China, do not so much 'carve out' or make things 'exempt' as they treat certain subjects differently for a while but always with the option to close further doors.

Over the past several years Article 53's recognition of a separate and preexisting regulatory stream for overseas academic exchanges, and somewhat more autonomy for universities and research institutions to work with overseas non-profit institutions, has been whittled down by the Ministry of Public Security and the current highly restrictive Chinese political atmosphere. This was accomplished in a number of coordinated ways, both before and during COVID-19:

- In 2018 and 2019 the Ministry of Public Security began an intensive series of joint meetings and trainings to bring universities and research institutions into the Overseas NGO Law framework at the provincial, municipal and sub-provincial level throughout China.
- Consistent with political shifts in China, the role of Communist Party committees in Chinese universities and research facilities has been substantially strengthened, along with the roles of internal security bodies within universities and research agencies that report to the party.
- New regulations have been issued from Beijing and provincial governments and within academic and research institutions, significantly restricting online and in-person international academic exchanges and overseas travel. Chinese academics are now regularly told by party, security and academic officials, both within and outside their institutions, to decline invitations to collaborate or travel or are refused permission when they seek it. (COVID-19, of course, has exacerbated that isolation, but the policies would not allow much exchange at this point even if COVID-19 were no longer a significant issue.)
- Universities and research centres around China have promulgated highly restrictive new regulations on the approval and management of activities with overseas non-profit organisations that mandate a bewildering array of steps for even small projects to be approved. Those include approvals by multiple levels of both the party and academic leadership of academic institutions, separate review by security bodies within those institutions and review of projects and Chinese project personnel by both public security and education agencies outside the universities.
- In 2023, these new requirements for universities and research institutes, who were initially treated more 'leniently' mean that, in some cases, the controls on these institutions are even more restrictive; they are preventing a number of overseas foundation and NGO activities from moving forward.

The result, for academic exchanges and research work with China, is not a separate stream of regulation that facilitates university and research collaborations abroad, but a dual stream of regulation – security and educational – that, in effect, cuts off most of that exchange. What continues, tenuously, are some non-sensitive research projects and the fraying remnants of personal ties between Chinese intellectuals and their counterparts overseas – relationships that sometimes continue to result in useful academic work even in these highly restrictive times.

However, for the most part, political and educational restrictions in China, combined with the almost complete integration of Chinese academic institutions into the Overseas NGO framework, have shut down most collaborations with overseas academic institutions, non-profit organisations and foundations. That is one important legacy of the Overseas NGO Law as it reaches five years of securitised control. Interestingly for our purposes, most of this authoritarian control has taken place outside the framework of 'governing through contagion'.

Certainly, COVID-19 restrictions have strengthened a regime of virtual isolation between Chinese universities and research institutions and their counterparts abroad. Among other measures, those 'governing through contagion' prohibitions on entry, requirements for quarantine and bans on significant meetings have helped to further break down academic and research ties between China and countries and regions outside the PRC. However, authoritarian policies and rules pre-dated COVID-19 and provided – particularly in their ever-tightening enforcement – more than sufficient power to do the job of regulating the work of Chinese academics and researchers.

Overseas Pandemic Aid to China in a Time of Contagion: Fully Governed by Pre-contagion Restrictive Regulation, not by 'Governing Through Contagion'

For another example of how authoritarianism did not need to govern through contagion but was well-equipped with the tools to govern and control when the pandemic hit and then used 'governing through contagion' to further strengthen control, take the related example of aid to China during COVID-19. The COVID-19 crisis that enveloped Wuhan, Hubei Province and some other parts of China in late 2019 and early 2020 might, in another era, have encouraged China to temporarily relax constraints on international aid and engagement. In the current Chinese political environment, such relaxation of constraints was not going to happen. China accepted some overseas aid at the beginning of the COVID-19 crisis but almost entirely on the restrictive political and legal terms laid down in the Overseas NGO Law and framework enacted in 2016. 'Governing through contagion' was not primarily used as the means for social control of overseas aid.[3]

In two other major disasters in recent Chinese history, China's response has been different. In 1976 the Tangshan earthquake hit, killing hundreds of thousands of people and destroying a major city in Hebei Province. An autarkic, authoritarian China in the midst of a bitter political struggle before Mao Zedong's death rapidly and forcefully declined overseas aid.

[3] This section is adapted and updated from Mark Sidel, 'Overseas NGOs and Foundations and Covid in China: Using a Securitized Framework in a Time of Crisis' (2021) 14 *EURICS* (European Institute for Chinese Studies) Briefs/Analyses, August 2021. Available at: www.eurics.eu/upload/document/20210729020749_eurics-july-august-2021.pdf.

It was a different China 32 years later in 2008, when the Wenchuan earthquake destroyed parts of Sichuan, killing at least 69,000 people, injuring hundreds of thousands more and levelling homes, schools and hospitals across a wide area. The Wenchuan earthquake occurred at a time of cautious civil society expansion as well as policy rivalry about the constraints over both domestic charitable organisations and the large number of overseas organisations that sought to work with China. In that political and policy context, China welcomed overseas assistance after Wenchuan through significant domestic regulation.

In the absence of national rules for work by overseas NGOs and foundations, China's acceptance of foreign assistance in 2008 had to be brokered by rapid but careful national policy making. The Ministry of Civil Affairs and other agencies adopted special relaxed regulatory measures to facilitate the process. A limited number of local partners, vetted and approved by the state, then distributed the foreign aid. Overall, in 2008–2009, China received Wenchuan-related aid from about 170 countries and more than 20 international and regional organisations, as well as about $8 million from the UN's Central Emergency Response Fund.[4]

By 2020, when COVID-19 shook China, the situation was quite different in political and regulatory terms. Chinese policy towards overseas NGOs and foundations had significantly hardened by 2020, as it had towards domestic civil society. On the overseas side, this culminated in 2016 with the enactment of the Overseas NGO Law of the PRC and its strict constraints on the work of overseas (including Hong Kong and Taiwan) NGOs, foundations, think tanks and other non-profits in China. A resurgent, suspicious authoritarian central government now had a fully-fledged, hard-edged regulatory regime in place to manage COVID-19-related aid. That pre-COVID-19 hardened regulatory fortress was sufficient to manage offers of foreign assistance in the COVID-19 era and did not require the use of COVID-19-specific rules or 'governing through contagion'.

By early 2020, the Overseas NGO Law had already been in place for three years, implemented on a national basis by the Ministry of Public Security in Beijing and by province-level and lower public security bureaux throughout the country. That framework mandated a 'two masters' system: for each overseas NGO and foundation seeking to work in China, a professional Chinese partner organisation would approve work plans; the relevant public security unit was also required to approve the organisation's plans and presence in China. As discussed above, this framework generally allowed overseas NGOs, foundations and other non-profits to be active in China only through representative offices or one-year (often renewable) 'temporary activities' projects.

COVID-19 donations from abroad in 2020 and 2021 were fully handled under that pre-COVID-19 regulatory stream that requires the double approval of overseas NGO activity in China. No 'governing through contagion' framework was required, though it

[4] Ministry of Foreign Affairs, 'Assistance to China after the Wenchuan earthquake' (12 May 2008). Available at: www.new.fmprc.gov.cn/ce/ceun/eng/zt/earthquake20080512/t478049.htm.

helped to emphasise the severity of the issues and the need for control. Unsurprisingly, China used that existing overseas NGO framework, the Overseas NGO Law, under full public security control to deal with offers of assistance to help with the COVID-19 outbreak in China in early 2020 and beyond. Unlike after Wenchuan in 2008, when there was little effective regulation already governing foreign charitable activity in China, in 2020 significant new regulations and policies were not enacted to govern the import of overseas aid. The existing, comprehensive, restrictive framework for overseas NGOs and foundations served to govern this process and limit the role that these overseas charitable organisations could play. In that new environment, China was generally offered and expressed a preference for immediate relief and supplies distributed through approved local partners, rather than assistance that raised policy questions and sought to expand participation in policy making.

Within those constraints, a number of overseas groups were active with donations and programmes in the early months of the COVID-19 outbreak. Overseas giving platforms and intermediaries (which largely did not exist for aid to China in 2008) brought in millions of dollars. One of the largest donation intermediaries, the San Francisco-based Give2Asia, raised about $10 million for China's COVID-19 relief in the first several months after the outbreak in Wuhan.[5] Give2Asia was able to raise and distribute those funds because it had already been fully registered under the Overseas NGO Law to work in China. The aid directed through Give2Asia went almost entirely to and through large local Chinese NGOs that were already approved partners.

But this work was not within Give2Asia's 2020 work plan that had been submitted to its professional supervisory unit and its regulatory public security unit in 2019. Channelling that aid to domestic, already vetted NGO partners required 'expedited approvals' from both agencies. Those approvals to send aid came very rapidly. That pattern was repeated in other cases, including the Gates Foundation and other donors, NGOs or intermediaries. Already existing rules, not governing through contagion, governed this process.

Most of the larger donations appear to have come through a relatively small number of registered offices rather than through the 'temporary activities' provisions of the existing and fully applied Overseas NGO Law framework. For example, the China Medical Board, registered with an office in China since 2017 under the ONGO Law, committed $2 million to support its Chinese partners in COVID-19 relief, equipment, capacity building and research.[6] The Gates Foundation, also registered in China since 2017 under the ONGO Law, committed $110 million in early 2020 for COVID-19-related relief and research.[7]

[5] Give2Asia, 'Donors give US$10 Million to Support COVID-19 Health Workers, Patients in China' (6 Jan 2020).

[6] China Development Brief, 'China Medical Board Donates 200M USD to Support the Struggle Against the COVID-19 Epidemic' (22 Feb 2020). Available at: www.chinadevelopmentbrief.org/reports/china-medical-board-donates-200m-usd-to-support-the-struggle-against-the-covid-19-epidemic/.

[7] China Development Brief, Gates Foundation Pledges $100 Million to Support Coronavirus Relief Efforts (10 Feb 2020). Available at: www.chinadevelopmentbrief.org/reports/gates-foundation-pledges-100-million-to-support-coronavirus-relief-efforts/.

In addition to large donations from groups with registered offices in China under the Overseas NGO Law, a significant number of donations for COVID-19 relief and recovery also came from organisations that received approval for more limited 'temporary activities' projects in this area. The Ministry of Public Security website for temporary activities, made available in English via the ChinaFile NGO project, lists well over 100 COVID-19-related temporary activity projects approved in 2020 and early 2021. Those ranged across the world – from the Brazil-Guangdong Natives Association to the China Enterprises Chamber of Commerce in Malaysia and many countries and organisations in between. Approvals began as early as 23 January 2020, indicating rapid facilitation by both partner organisations and public security. Many of these donations went to organisations in Hubei, where the COVID-19 outbreak was centred, but many others went to Guangdong, where many of the donor organisations have their roots.

For the Chinese political and public security leadership, the Overseas NGO Law securitised framework has held up well under both non-crisis and crisis conditions. Special methods to govern through and using contagion have not been needed. The existing, applied Overseas NGO Law framework has served to enable aid to flow into China that China could vet, approve and limit in advance, constraining and channelling that assistance to relief and services through approved domestic partners and avoiding the chaotic vitality of the post-Wenchuan era or the autarky of the post-Tangshan time.

Governing Through Contagion and Domestic Control of Civil Society in the COVID-19 Era

All of this is not to say that COVID-19-era controls and regulation – what we are here calling and discussing as 'governing through contagion' – played no role in social control of civil society and citizen action in China during the crisis. It certainly did. Existing regulations layered with COVID-19 controls have limited the range of domestic Chinese charitable organisations that can receive domestic and foreign donations for COVID-19 relief; the existing regulations layered with COVID-19 controls have provided a preference for state-related and state-approved agencies (such as Red Cross organisations or the charity federations approved at the central and provincial levels) to receive philanthropic assistance; and the existing regulations layered with 'governing through contagion' have served to limit and require sometimes onerous approvals for a range of local services and charitable actions by nongovernmental groups in many areas of China. In many cases COVID-19-era regulations, 'governing through contagion', has added special force to those restrictions. Domestic charitable groups have been prevented from undertaking service activities due to lockdown, quarantine, approval and other measures. Domestic nongovernmental groups have been denied the possibility of advocacy through a combination of pre-COVID restrictions and those applied during the pandemic.

Approvals of new charitable organisations under the Chinese Charity Law enacted in 2016 have further slowed during COVID-19, at least in part because of COVID-19-era restrictions and slowdowns.

In other words, on the domestic side of the civil society ledger, 'governing through contagion' has had a role to play. Restrictions were always tight on the domestic charitable and nongovernmental groups, going back to beginning of the Xi Jinping era in 2012 and formalised in a 2016 Communist Party document and the 2016 Charity Law. However, 'governing through contagion', both the general means of emergency-based lockdowns, quarantines, digital controls that constitute 'governing through contagion' in China and more specific COVID-19-era regulations on charitable work, did significantly restrict civil society and citizen action since 2020.

Does 'Governing Through Contagion' and Existing Authoritarian Regulation Help to Foment 'Resistance Through Contagion' in China?

If the Chinese Party-state has been able to govern forcefully during the pandemic through a combination of pre-COVID-19 authoritarian law and COVID-19-era 'governing through contagion', has this combination of methods of authoritarian rule helped to spark some opposition in China? I submit that it has, and I provide examples of two forms of resistance below. Other examples of resistance are certainly possible to identify, and both Chinese and non-Chinese scholars are working on these issues.[8] One form of resistance is a form of soft raising of other views, the raising of implicit and careful objections, by mainstream Chinese academics and other figures that we cannot and will not call resistance but which appears to have been influenced by the experience with China's severe 'governing through contagion', 'Zero Covid' approach. The second is a form of fully-fledged 'resistance through contagion' organised by Chinese dissidents abroad and at home.

The first raising of careful questions – which I would not call resistance – is the implicit debate emerging on the amendment of China's omnibus Charity Law, which was first enacted in 2016 and which has proven to be a useful tool for restricting and suppressing civil society activity. Yet, at the same time, China needs charitable and social organisations to provide social services and, when permitted, to offer policy perspectives and analysis. In recent years, very cautiously, some Chinese observers have begun to question whether such regulation of charitable activity in China amounts to over-regulation at a level that restricts and prevents

[8] See, eg, the discussion of Chinese resistance measures in L Crout, 'The Consent of the Governed: Resistance as Constituent Power' (forthcoming, 2024) *Washington University Law Review*.

even the kind of robust service delivery and neighbourhood relief that China's leaders indicate that they wish to see.[9]

The second, more explicit, form of 'resistance through contagion' is evident in the activities and online speech of many angry Chinese citizens and Chinese dissidents during COVID-19. Occasionally these activities have developed into a more organised 'resistance through contagion'. These more formal 'resistance through contagion' efforts were almost immediately dismantled by the authorities, usually through a combination of available pre- COVID-19 authoritarian rules that can squash citizen action and through pandemic-specific contagion measures. As with the control of civil society discussed above, the Chinese state was armed with the political and regulatory measures it needed to crush attempts to organise opposition in the COVID-19 era. Yet, governing through contagion helped and provided extra tools to suppress newer forms of civil society from arising.

Among the most striking and sustained attempt at organised resistance in China in the COVID-19 era has been the attempt by a group of Chinese lawyers and activists overseas and in China to organise legal aid and mobilise legal advocacy for COVID-19 victims in China and against state policy. As the prominent Chinese activist Lu Jun has described,[10] in March 2020 some 18 lawyers in China and abroad came together to form the Legal Aid Group for Covid Victims. Over the next year or so they published a research report on COVID-19 testing and treatment, sought to provide legal aid and provided legal opinions to victims and sought compensation for them against provincial governments (for not informing citizens initially of the scope and seriousness of the pandemic) and private actors.

The legal opinions issued by the Legal Aid Group for Covid Victims included documents on a range of issues: 'whether Covid-19 is eligible for work injury benefits in private enterprises'; 'funeral expenses and pensions for retirees after death from Covid-19'; the legal treatment and benefits for civil servants who died from COVID-19; and hospital refusals to provide nucleic acid test results. They released 'Guidelines for filing Covid-19 Cases', helped clients to draft complaints and 'assisted 8 [survivors of Covid] victims to file lawsuits [in the] Wuhan Intermediate Court, Hubei Provincial High Court, and … Supreme Court' against insurance companies, hospitals, employers and local governments. The group also proposed 'hold[ing] officials responsible for misconduct and create[ing] a Covid-19 compensation fund' and 'protect[ing] … recovered Covid-19 patients from employment discrimination' and tried to make open government applications to national, provincial and local agencies seeking disclosures: on pandemic policies; on the death of COVID-19 martyr D Li Wenliang in Wuhan; and on the names and positions of government officials punished for COVID-19-related policy errors.

[9] I discuss these incipient matters in more detail in M Sidel, 'Rebooting China's Charity Law' (2022) 2 *US-Asia Law Institute (USALI) Perspectives*, NYU Law School. Available at: www.usali.org/usali-perspectives-blog/rebooting-chinas-charity-law.

[10] Lu Jun, 'Rights Defending through Legal Means, NGOs' Roles, and CCP Spies in the Era of Epidemic: A Case Study of the COVID Victims Legal Aid Group', (unpublished 2022).

The Legal Aid Group for Covid Victims carried out its work and communication primarily through social media. The government's response was rapid and sustained, often using pre-COVID-19 authoritarian measures and regulations that were fully available to security forces in China. Social media accounts and messages were blocked, and social media was used to threaten and attack organisers. Victims and potential litigants were beaten and summoned by the police, who threatened their family members and friends, while their bank accounts were frozen. The lawyers involved were given warnings by local bureaux of justice and the police. Leaders were especially targeted. Lu Jun concludes, perhaps optimistically: 'Legal means still work. NGOs still work. CCP spies still work, too.'[11]

The methods used to crush this pandemic-based outbreak of resistance to contagion and the state were methods that were almost entirely available and in effect beforehand. They included social media and censorship regulations, detention regulations and other pre-existing mechanisms. While resistance was attempted during and through contagion, the methods used to deal with it demonstrate primarily the pre-existing power of the Chinese state, supplemented by the prohibitory, lockdown, quarantine and other measures that have been utilised as part of 'governing through contagion'.

These patterns continued in the second half of 2022. A variety of administrative and other mechanisms to control the population – most available before and into the pandemic and some related to COVID-19 controls – remained in place. But gradually resistance increased within China, culminating in the 'blank paper' protests and small-scale street protests that took place before and after the Twentieth Congress of the Chinese Communist Party in October 2022. After nearly three years of harsh, rolling COVID-19 restrictions around China, both enforcement and resistance were mounting, and the authorities were taking back control over the small-scale, grassroots, mutual-aid activities that had sprung up to help communities in the midst of COVID-19.

These events culminated with the 'blank paper' protests of November and early December 2022, when small bands of Chinese citizens took to the streets in a number of Chinese cities to protest COVID-19 restrictions and, in some brave cases, to press for broader political change. The Party responded quickly, rolling back many COVID-19 policies, ending most lockdowns and allowing most domestic travel. But the pre-COVID-19 and prohibitory, lockdown and sanction policies remained in place, ready for use when the authorities wanted to use them. The enforcement of this wide range of administrative policies was relaxed in December 2022, but the measures themselves were not abrogated.

By early 2023, as COVID-19 restrictions were on the wane in China, the Party-state struck back against the late-2022 protesters. A wide range of participants in the 'blank paper' and other resistance activities were rounded up by the authorities. Some were detained for several days; others are still held pending charges or

[11] Lu Jun, 'Rights Defending' (n 10).

have already been charged. The message is clear: Pre-COVID and COVID-19-era 'governing through contagion' measures remain in place. They may be enforced more or less strictly depending on Party policy. Harsh instruments of sanction remain available, bolstered by COVID-19-era measures, to take retribution against those who publicly resist the Party-state, and these were utilised in early and mid-2023.

Conclusion: Governing Through Contagion in the Authoritarian Context

As the editors of this volume indicate, 'governing through contagion' and its legal rules have often meshed effectively with regulatory restrictions that took effect in the now seemingly distant pre-COVID-19 era. In the authoritarian context, as I have sought to show here, that meshing of pre-COVID-19 and COVID-19-era restraints has proven to be even more effective from the point of view of authoritarian regimes. In China and other authoritarian or increasingly authoritarian states, the regulatory mix of controls often includes both robust pre-COVID-19 measures and COVID-19-era lockdowns, quarantines, digital controls, geographic blockades and other constraints. In the authoritarian context, strict pre-COVID-19 restrictions may be enough to virtually fully control both domestic and overseas civil society activity. However, 'governing with contagion' has provided some new, supplementary tools for a new era that have also been used by authoritarians in the unending quest to constrain and to mould civil society and citizen action.

Although space prevents extensive discussion of comparative dynamics in other Asian states, let me at least raise some developments in another Asian state run by a single Communist Party, the Socialist Republic of Vietnam. The Vietnam case is somewhat similar to the Chinese case, in significant part because of the political power exercised by a Communist Party. In Vietnam, the COVID-19 era restrictions on domestic civil society groups and on foreign support for civil society and COVID-19 relief in Vietnam has relied primarily on pre-COVID-19 restraints on domestic activity and on restrictive frameworks for the control of foreign philanthropy and NGOs in Vietnam. These restrictive frameworks were tightened in pre-pandemic recent years to the point that contagion-specific measures or regulation have not, for the most part, been needed by the Vietnamese authorities to constrain the activities of domestic civil society groups and the funding and activities of overseas groups that would like to be active in Vietnam. Yet 'governing through contagion' has at times been useful for the state too, operating as a supplement to existing strict regulatory measures.[12] While Vietnamese individuals and businesses have been impacted by COVID-19 regulations, quarantines

[12] On the Vietnamese case, see a considerably longer discussion in Son, Doan and Sidel, 'State, Civil Society and Covid in Vietnam' (2022) *Alliance*. Available at: www.alliancemagazine.org/analysis/philanthropy-after-covid-what-can-we-learn-from-vietnam/.

and other restrictions, the aspects of life that the Vietnamese authorities most care about – such as civil society and public participation – were well-covered by pre-existing policy and law and, at the same time, exacerbated and further constrained by the state's COVID-19 restrictions.

A mixture of pre-COVID-19 authoritarian regulation and COVID-19-era restrictions thus serve Party-states well. When resistance grew in China in late 2022, the Chinese authorities relented on many of the COVID-19 restrictions. However, the resistance was not the only cause of that policy shift – Chinese authorities had been preparing to relax some COVID-19 policies and restrictions in any case. After policies shifted, and the Chinese Party-state began using its regulatory and administrative tools to punish the protesters of late 2022, it was mostly pre-existing administrative and criminal regulations that served as the basis for enforcement.

Crises in authoritarian China can produce a variety of responses by the Chinese Party-state. In earlier eras, such as the Tiananmen protests of 1989 and the Sichuan Wenchuan earthquake of 2008, citizen action grew rapidly in the absence of immediate repressive action by the authorities. Then – 4 June 1989 and after in China and after some time in Sichuan in 2008 – the Party-state stepped in to quell resistance while carefully taking note of who the protesters were and what they were demanding.

COVID-19 was different. The Chinese authorities, already well along a repressive path in the Xi Jinping era and with domestic security at the forefront of their agenda, were determined not to lose control of this situation, even briefly, as they had done in 1989 and 2008. Pre-COVID-19 prohibitory and criminal controls had already been ramped up and utilised in the years before COVID-19 struck in 2020. New COVID-19 controls added to that package of measures. The combination of pre-COVID-19 and 'governing through contagion' measures enabled the Chinese Party-state to maintain control during the height of the pandemic, then to permit and carefully observe limited protests in late 2022 and to change its direction on COVID-19 – and, finally, utilising the measures available, to crack down on protesters in 2023.

10

Governing Through Contagion and the Limits of Law

LYNETTE J CHUA AND JACK JIN GARY LEE

The preceding nine chapters in this volume have shown us the multifarious nature of legal power, its diverse agents and its effects. Seen across these chapters, law's relation to contagion and authoritarian control cannot be taken for granted. In Chapters 8 and 9, the authors remind us of how governments can establish or enhance their authoritarian hold on power by amending laws in the time of pandemic. Kline and Webb write about the state of Texas in the United States, a Western liberal democracy, whereas Sidel comments on China, a country typically described as illiberal. Although they consider two contrasting governments, the authors demonstrate that the spread of contagion, by heightening a sense of risk and producing new rationales for discrimination, endowed political elites with the opportunity to enhance law as their weapon of control against othered, excluded groups.

In yet another political context, the convergence of contagion, law and authoritarian control took on a different expression. Examining imperial governance in the face of perceived social ills, Roberts highlights how fears about the spread of poverty, sexual immorality and other 'vices' resulted in the control and criminalisation of marginalised groups through the enactment of the 'vagrancy law model'.[1] Subsequently carried over into post-colonial jurisdictions, the punitive logic of such laws points to another way that law, authoritarianism and (social) contagion are interlinked in the politics of dysconnectedness.

By contrast, as discussed in other chapters, legal power has been mediated or overwhelmed by the interventions of non-human agents, such as the physical environment, infrastructures and technologies. For example, we could look to Rose's observations of how the jurisdictional borders of the telegraph and quarantine stations between empires depended on the changing contours of their natural environments; Nainani's theorisation of the use of sewage infrastructures as technologies for governing through contagion 'from below'; and Godden's prescient

[1] This volume, ch 6.

discussion of how the continuous accumulation of pandemic wastes troubles the systems used for waste disposal and recycling, pushing them past their limits.[2]

Likewise, human actors can help produce intended and unintended consequences when they come into contact with legal power. Yang, Ho and Tan's chapter on Section 23 of Singapore's Infectious Diseases Act reveals how the discriminatory force of legal provisions can be magnified when law's subjects interpret the law in ways that reinforce their stigmatisation.[3] While law moralises by defining norms and sanctioning conduct, the effects of such moralisation are also shaped by the pre-existing moral understandings and rules that undergird human interactions. Such recursive dynamics of social and moral change feature in Roach Anleu and Sarantoulias' examination of the visual landscape of the pandemic, where mask and social-distancing directives manifested in a plethora of official and unofficial signs that re-orientated human actors toward new understandings of safety and duty.[4] Law's moral force may also take place through the open-ended, imperfect practice of democratic deliberation. For instance, in their critical study of the settler-colonial US state of Oregon, Burkhalter and Richards highlight how residents revitalised their state's long-standing but historically exclusionary tradition of participatory governance in online discussions of social policy responses to the pandemic.[5]

Together, the nine preceding chapters demonstrate the contingency of legal power: law's effectiveness hinges on a constellation of human *and* non-human agents that may place limits on its design and intentions. Furthermore, found across a range of polities, governing through contagion does not necessarily portend an authoritarian turn even if it generates new but familiar modes of difference and exclusion. These insights raise questions about the politics of governing through contagion, and how law, power and contagion operate in conjunction.

In this final chapter of *Contagion, Technology and Law at the Limits*, we conclude with lessons on the relationship between law, power and contagion, especially the limits and possibilities of law as a technology of rule. Inspired by the preceding chapters and informed by our ongoing historical ethnography on Singapore, we draw attention to two points on the power of law itself.

(i) Integral to governmental responses to contagion, law plays a potent but mediated role in human efforts to combat infectious diseases through the ages. According to GTC analyses, law is both a boon and bane as states seek to counter the deadly risks posed by outbreaks of infectious disease. The more political actors seek to establish or consolidate legal infrastructures for the unobstructed exercise of power, the more they deploy other technologies that moralise, discipline and thus normalise conduct aimed at curtailing contagion. However, as we show in this volume, the effects of this complex system of

[2] This volume, chs 1, 2 and 3, respectively.
[3] This volume, ch 5.
[4] This volume, ch 4.
[5] This volume, ch 7.

control are tempered. At first glance, our observation on the mediated power of law may seem nothing new. Law and society studies already recognise the Janus-faced nature of law.[6] However, we focus on the often-misconstrued role of law in public health governance and emphasise the impact of non-human actors. With the other chapters in this volume, we highlight how law can meet and be confounded by uncontrollable, unanticipated patterns of behaviour from not only living creatures like humans, animals and microorganisms but also non-living things like physical infrastructure and medical technology. In other words, law's power relies on its interactions with humans *and* non-humans.

(ii) Resistance, ingrained in any project of GTC, tends to produce unintended, inequitable consequences that compound existing forms of inequality – what we term endemic inter/dysconnectedness. These consequences bring to light the insidious side of law when humans put it to use, alongside other technologies, to regulate populations and public health. As states seek to control and defeat contagious diseases, their efforts at moralising conduct and normalising new regulatory norms tends to encounter subjects' indifference, non-compliance and even refusal, generating irreducible tension and contestation between state and subjects. At times, such actions can be disruptive, undermining hegemony and power – a theme often celebrated in law and society scholarship.[7] However, perceived or actual resistance can provoke governmental responses that deepen the social imbalances and inequities that already exist between groups in a given society.

These two sets of insights indicate how law can unsettle the extension of state power. Even in profoundly disruptive events like the COVID-19 pandemic, what has resulted was not a state of emergency without end. Rather, we saw restless state machinations to constantly devise new forms of legal technology while jettisoning old ones – witness the changing regulations regarding the use of masks over the COVID-19 pandemic – to outwit the waves of contagion and the problems posed by the restless agencies of humans and non-humans.

We elaborate on these two sets of insights by referring to our larger study of colonial and postcolonial Singapore,[8] specifically our analysis of smallpox vaccination over the late-nineteenth to early twentieth century as well as the recent COVID-19 vaccination campaign.[9] The colonial government's approach to smallpox inoculation bears lessons because it helped frame modern legislation concerning vaccination,

[6] See, for example, LJ Chua, 'Legal Mobilization and Authoritarianism' (2019) 15 *Annual Review of Law & Social Science* 355; MW McCann with G Lovell, *Union by Law: Filipino American Labor Activists, Rights Radicalism, and Racial Capitalism* (Chicago, University of Chicago Press, 2020).

[7] SE Merry 'Resistance and the Cultural Power of Law' (1995) 29 *Law and Society Review* 11.

[8] LJ Chua and JJG Lee, 'Governing through Contagion' in VV Ramraj (ed), *Covid-19 in Asia: Law and Policy Contexts* (New York, Oxford University Press, 2021).

[9] JJG Lee and LJ Chua 'Smallpox Vaccination and the Limits of Governing Through Contagion in the Straits Settlements, 1868–1926' (2023) 45 *Law & Policy* 331–52.

particularly in terms of the ways the colonial state countered resistance in extending vaccination across populations. Indeed, smallpox vaccination, originating in the use of the cowpox virus, was the first effort by modern states to systematically inoculate populations, providing the origin of the word *vaccine*.[10]

Certainly, there are major dissimilarities between the earlier colonial project of smallpox vaccination and the contemporary case of COVID-19 vaccination. For one, the former involved a colonial state, whereas COVID-19 implicates a post-colonial nation-state. For another, the respective viruses, variola and SARS-CoV-2, behave differently although they are both potentially fatal to humans upon infection. Transmitted primarily via droplets through the air and on surfaces, variola leads to fever, aches and skin sores that later manifest as rashes, pustules and, eventually, scabs.[11] SARS-CoV-2, according to current evidence, spreads through aerosol and droplets; people with COVID-19 experience a wide range of symptoms, such as fever, coughing, respiratory problems and body aches.[12] In addition, vaccination as technology and a strategy of control has improved vastly between these two contagious episodes. In colonial Singapore, smallpox vaccination first used an arm-to-arm approach, harvesting lymph containing the 'vaccine virus' – as it was called – from inoculated humans and injecting it into the unvaccinated subject. Only later did the colonial government turn to lymph obtained from calves. Whereas some COVID-19 vaccines, such as CoronoVac and Sinopharm, kept to an older method that uses inactivated SARS-CoV-2 virus, others such as Pfizer-BioNTech and Moderna utilise messenger ribonucleic acid (mRNA) technology to deliver instructions to the human body so that it can produce a protein of the virus and train the immune system's response.[13]

Nevertheless, we found across both cases the aforementioned insights on the relationship between law and public health governance: namely, the mediated operation of law and the compounded negative consequences of resistance to law and other technologies deployed in GTC. We organise our discussion of how law both enables and impedes power along the three themes of GTC: centralisation and technology of law; normalisation and technologies of moralisation; and inter/dysconnectedness and rearticulation of difference.

Centralisation and Technology of Law

Although we emphasise the critical role of law in GTC, we simultaneously stress that law is an insufficient condition for establishing control over outbreaks. This is especially the case when we scrutinise the complex realities of contagious episodes,

[10] S Blume and B Baylac-Paouly, 'Introduction' in S Blume and B Baylac-Paouly (eds), *Immunization and States: The Politics of Making Vaccines* (New York, Routledge, 2021), 2–3.

[11] See www.who.int/health-topics/smallpox.

[12] See www.who.int/health-topics/coronavirus.

[13] See www.who.int/emergencies/diseases/novel-coronavirus-2019/covid-19-vaccines.

where the deployment of legal and other technologies – no matter how centralised or expansive – often prove to be for naught due to breakdown or non-compliance.

Smallpox vaccination is a case in point. Even for a directly ruled territory like the Crown Colony of the Straits Settlements, where the governor controlled lawmaking without legislative or judicial checks, the state was cautious about implementing its policy of mandatory vaccination. Authorities in Singapore took well over 50 years (1868–1926) to establish a regular, extensive regime of smallpox vaccination involving both children and adults. Unlike their heavy-handed, immediate imposition of quarantine and other methods of control during contagious outbreaks, officials in Singapore and the rest of the Straits Settlements were stymied by the resistance that they encountered in vaccinating various subject populations, and they often blamed 'native prejudices' for their failures.[14] Although the 1868 Vaccination Ordinance (VO) specified the mandatory vaccination of children in coordination with the registration of their births,[15] parents would often avoid the reach of the government's Vaccinator or not register the birth of their children. It was one thing for the colonial state to legally mandate a policy of mandatory vaccination; it was another for officials to carry out law's dictates.

Officials also struggled with inadequacies of the supply of 'vaccine virus' for most of the 1800s. Success rates of vaccinations improved and stabilised only after vaccine supply and technology improved in the late 1800s with the use of cow lymph sourced from other colonies. In 1915, colonial authorities expanded its vaccination requirements in a comprehensive public health law, the Quarantine and Prevention of Diseases Ordinance (QPDO), requiring compulsory vaccination and revaccination for prison inmates, the institutionalised poor and adults arriving on ships from China and India; and, with the amended QPDO of 1926, they ordered re-vaccination – now known to us as 'booster shots' – for all children upon their turning seven years of age.[16]

In the case of COVID-19 vaccination, although independence transformed Singapore's state infrastructures into a Westminster-style parliamentary government, post-colonial legislators and executives built upon the colonial legal scaffolding to respond quickly to public health crises. Moreover, since independence in 1965, the People's Action Party has dominated the Parliament and cabinet: this alignment of executive and legislative power facilitated the government's nimble use of centralised legal technologies to combat contagion. At the beginning

[14] We place the term, 'native prejudice,' in quotation marks because it conveys officials' tendencies to morally dismiss any 'native' objections to vaccination as prejudice rather than possibly being based on reason or legitimate convictions. We also do so for the term, 'native', because British officials used it loosely to indicate non-European populations rather than indigeneity.

[15] Straits Settlements Ordinance No 19 of 1868.

[16] Straits Settlements Ordinance No 33 of 1915; Straits Settlements Ordinance No 3 of 1926. Even though the colonial government did order the vaccination of adults as early as 1890, it only did so in an ad-hoc manner under its existing executive powers of quarantine in relation to the passengers of arriving vessels.

of the COVID-19 pandemic, the country was lauded as an exemplar in its swift containment of the early waves of contagion.[17]

Be that as it may, the contemporary Singapore government did not mandate vaccination, leaving the choice to individuals. Instead, it strongly encouraged vaccination by relying on measures that it had already established in the pandemic. For example, the government banned the non-vaccinated from dining at restaurants and cafés or entering shopping malls, making daily life inconvenient for them. It also ceased its coverage of COVID-19 medical expenses for the non-vaccinated.[18] Despite establishing this range of regulations to encourage vaccinations, the reach of law remains, symbolically, limited. Perhaps mindful of the potential for non-compliance, resistance and confrontation, the postcolonial state's manifold legal interventions have focused more on securing social life and the environment through exclusions than on legal coercion.

Normalisation and Technologies of Moralisation

Governments have typically complemented their utilisation of law with other technologies that moralise and, furthermore, normalise their strategies of control. However, as the vaccination campaigns of both smallpox and COVID-19 in Singapore illustrate, such efforts at normalisation-moralisation achieved limited success, which consequently tempered the force of law.

In the case of smallpox, the colonial government and members of the mercantile elite were concerned about the potential spread of variola from 'natives' and engaged newspaper media, propaganda and surveillance to call for the legal implementation of vaccination. They treated smallpox vaccination as a beneficent act that advanced the empire's civilising project and repeatedly attributed failures in their vaccination mission to 'native prejudice'. Such jaundiced views were prevalent from the tentative beginnings of smallpox vaccination in the colony, as espoused by leading figures like Senior Surgeon Thomas Oxley who singled out the 'fatalism inculcated by the Mahomedan creed'.[19] Even after the colonial state developed and expanded its regime of mandatory vaccination through the 1915 QPDO, colonial officials continued to speak of resistance to vaccination in moralised tones. A municipal health officer, in reply to a controversial anti-vaccination letter in the local press, wrote that 'he must indeed be a bigoted individual who refuses to be convinced of the efficacy of vaccination'.[20] From such perspectives, those who

[17] Reuters, 'WHO praises Singapore's response to coronavirus outbreak' *The Straits* Times (Singapore, 2 March 2020). Available at: www.straitstimes.com/world/europe/coronavirus-who-reports-92-cases-of-human-to-human-spread-outside-china.

[18] See www.moh.gov.sg/news-highlights/details/calibrated-adjustments-in-stabilisation-phase_8Nov2021.

[19] T Oxley, 'Correspondence' *The Singapore Free Press and Mercantile Advertiser* (Singapore, 12 April 1849) 2.

[20] JAR Glennie, 'Vaccination: What is it and how does it protect against smallpox?' *The Straits Times* (Singapore, 7 November 1921) 7. In the later years of the vaccination campaign, the colonial

refused vaccination were backward and irrational. This was the dominant understanding though the grounds for resistance could be complex.

Still, despite being chastised by colonial authorities for their apparent failure to heed the government's dictates and civilising influence, various local populations continued to question and resist vaccination, not only based on religious and other beliefs but also due to their distrust of the medical technology and officials employed to deliver the vaccine. To wit, in the jurisdiction of the nearby settlement of Penang, a group of Malay petitioners wrote to the lieutenant governor and the English-language press to criticise the faulty methods used to vaccinate their children and allege that the local vaccinator was both unqualified and corrupt.[21] In this instance, officials' frequent attribution of the low success rate of vaccinations to 'native prejudice' obscured a political story of official ineptitude and corruption. To this, we add the problems that the colonial state faced with the 'vaccine virus', which regularly failed to work – success rates for vaccination fluctuated and could be as low as 50 per cent – until the adoption of calf lymph in the 1890s.[22] Notwithstanding the moral imperative that they tied to their vaccination campaign, colonial officials could be responsible for failing their 'mission', but it was much easier to moralise and blame the colonised.

In marked contrast to the colonial period, medical technology and maladministration were not impediments to achieving widespread vaccination against COVID-19 in Singapore. The government was able to purchase and effectively administer the highest quality COVID-19 vaccines for the population. Save for the minority who objected to the vaccine because of scientific doubts, religious grounds or other beliefs, the vaccination rate was high at about 90 per cent.[23] Nonetheless, faced with the seemingly relentless threat of COVID-19, the government took to twenty-first century communication technologies to help it normalise-moralise vaccination by playing up the 'socially responsible' subject constructed in earlier efforts to tackle contagious episodes: 'social responsibility' meant that individuals would strive to stay healthy, not infect others and, importantly, not become an economic burden to their families and society.

As vaccines became available, the authorities broadcast a series of catchy, multi-lingual advertisements to encourage the general population, particularly senior citizens and other vulnerable groups, to get vaccinated against SAR-CoV-2. Featuring local celebrities and sets that evoked everyday scenes in public housing estates – coffee shops, markets and provision shops – these advertisements were

government handed over the conduct of vaccination in Singapore to its municipal government with the passage of the 1915 QPDO. Empowered to conduct vaccinations, the municipality employed sanitary inspectors to check and identify unvaccinated children and prevent parents' evasion of birth registration to avoid vaccination.

[21] Editorial, 'Public Vaccinators' *The Straits Times* (Singapore, 15 January 1874) 2.

[22] Lee and Chua, 'Smallpox Vaccination' (n 9) 342.

[23] R Pazos and S Adeline, 'Tracking Singapore's Covid-19 vaccination progress' (Singapore, 29 December 2021). Available at: www.straitstimes.com/multimedia/graphics/2021/06/singapore-covid-vaccination-tracker/index.html.

filmed in vernacular languages that spoke to groups differentiated according to the official categories of race in Singapore (ethnic Chinese, Malay and Indian). The videos, widely broadcast across various media, provided accurate, up-to-date information about the vaccines, but also pointedly asked their audiences: 'What are you waiting for?' or 'Why haven't you taken your jab?'[24] Framed in this way, such tailored public-health messaging targeted those hesitant about vaccination, asking them to account for their (unnecessary) delay.

Our view is *not* that such pointed messaging is problematic – these advertisements were important in reaching communities less receptive to English-language media. Rather, we highlight the moralising dynamics of vaccination campaigns and how they compound state power by normalising the measures put in place to prevent infectious outbreaks. Contagion and its potentially fatal effects underpin the communication of the ineluctable moral necessity of GTC and its deployment of law and other technologies. Because contagion possibly concerns life and death, resistance by anybody to the legal dictates and measures of public health governance appears to be irrational, irresponsible and unjustifiable. Yet, in response, the state followed familiar patterns of social difference to pick and mete out consequences for the non-compliant and disobedient.

Inter/dysconnectedness and Rearticulation of Difference

Returning to the third theme of GTC, we reiterate the insidious side to human engagement with law and other technologies of control. Both smallpox and COVID-19 vaccination efforts in Singapore rearticulated social difference, though in ways distinct to their time and place. The governed occasionally achieved momentary success or reprieve, but their acts of resistance and reactions by government and its allies helped to reinforce existing social inequities. Over time, as contentions recurred, the counterpoints of normalisation-moralisation and resistance could compound existing structures of inequality, leading to endemic inter/dysconnectedness.

In colonial Singapore, the politics of smallpox vaccination reflected the structure of colonial rule as British officials confronted a diverse set of colonised subjects. Under colonialism, the 'rule of colonial difference' meant that local populations were categorised and subordinated as different and thus inferior to the British and other European elites.[25] Hence, despite the seeming beneficence of the colonial vaccination mission and other policies aimed at the protection of public health, colonial officials reinforced the hierarchy in their approach to governance by following the 'principle of misplaced responsibility' in attributing

[24] See www.youtube.com/watch?v=oPRv6WrPThI and www.youtube.com/watch?v=dtaSmAllwRs.

[25] P Chatterjee, *The Nation and its Fragments: Colonial and Postcolonial Histories* (Princeton, Princeton University Press, 1993); G Steinmetz, *The Devil's Handwriting: Precoloniality and the German Colonial State in Qingdao, Samoa and Southwest Africa* (Chicago, University of Chicago Press, 2007).

disease outbreaks to the deficient qualities of racially subordinated populations.[26] Not surprisingly, the first expansion of mandatory vaccination beyond children targeted stigmatised groups, whom colonial officials regarded as sources of disease. By mandating the vaccination of prison inmates, the institutionalised poor and immigrant labourers in 1915, the colonial state reinforced the racially differentiated practices of the empire.[27]

Furthermore, as discussed, since the start of the vaccination mission in the mid-1800s, 'native prejudice' remained a dominant trope among officials when they sought to account for resistance and the loss of life caused by the disease. Rarely did European elites apply to the colonised the dignified and less discriminatory term *conscientious objector*, which was used in Britain to identify and exempt those against vaccination.[28] In disrupting strategies of control and countering their technologies, including law, resistance to vaccination came with costs for the colonised. As one irate 'Father,' who was later criticized and identified as Chinese, wrote to the English-language press: 'I have been given a notice that my baby, eight months old, should be vaccinated within three days, or in default thereof, I shall be summoned, and shall be liable to pay a fine up to ten dollars.'[29] Unlike in Britain, there was no exemption available to colonised subjects who, for whatever reason, might decline vaccination. In this regard, the case of smallpox vaccination in the Straits Settlements reminds us that resistance is not liberation from power. Resistance, an important feature of GTC, can produce unintended, inequitable consequences that feed the inter/dysconnectedness already endemic in a society.

In post-colonial Singapore, the implementation of COVID-19 vaccination inadvertently reproduced existing inequities along lines of race, class and legal status. Unlike citizens and other migrant groups, migrant labourers on work permits, particularly those working in construction and other blue-collar trades, could not refuse vaccination unless they were willing to risk their jobs and their immigration status. To illustrate, between January and April 2022, the government did not allow unvaccinated employees, with exceptions for those who were medically ineligible, to enter their site of employment.[30] This requirement operated differently for white-collar professionals who could still perform their jobs from

[26] SH Alatas, *The Myth of the Lazy Native: A Study of the Image of the Malays, Filipinos and Javanese from the 16th to the 20th Century and its Function in the Ideology of Colonial Capitalism* (New York, Routledge, 2010) 205.

[27] JJG Lee, 'Plural Society and the Colonial State: English Law and the Making of Crown Colony Government in the Straits Settlements' (2015) 2 *Asian Journal of Law and Society* 229.

[28] N Durbach, *Bodily Matters: The Anti-Vaccination Movement in England, 1853–1907* (Durham NC, Duke University Press, 2004) 180–90.

[29] A Father, 'Letters to the Editor: Anti-Vaccination'' *The Singapore Free Press and Mercantile Advertiser* (Singapore, 24 May 1928) 8.

[30] See www.mom.gov.sg/covid-19/advisory-on-covid-19-vaccination-in-employment-settings.

home; for those who worked on construction sites or other similar settings, this rule meant that they had to choose vaccination or jeopardise their positions.

From the beginnings of the pandemic, the realities faced by such migrant workers reveal their dysconnectedness from the more privileged in the global city-state of Singapore. Confined to dormitories, where they lived in close proximity to one another, migrant workers were vulnerable to contagious outbreaks; however, from the perspective of the state and larger society, they were potential virus vectors whose separation needed to be maintained.[31] Consequently, should they refuse vaccination, they could be subject to more restrictive measures for not playing their part in protecting their host nation from the imminent threat of the SARS-CoV-2 virus.

Although some anti-COVID-19 measures replace the logic of difference and control from the typical lines of social inequality – for example, race, class and gender – with seemingly objective indicators of risk like case counts and clusters, GTC already operates in inequitable contexts that shape the workings of legal and other technologies. Hence, the establishment of a formally neutral vaccination requirement affected populations disproportionately, rearticulating existing patterns of inequality.[32] Moreover, the workings of law and other technologies in GTC embed dominant notions of difference. We might ask, for example, which populations are subject to generic public-health messaging and which are to be targeted based on their social identities? Tellingly, the first vaccination advertisements used Singlish, the vernacular form of English in Singapore, to appeal across all groups.[33] Although an English-speaking anti-vaccination group, whose members included a physician, was penalised for distributing misinformation and committing fraud,[34] coverage of this case focused on the offenders' actions rather than their social identities or beliefs. Despite evidence of anti-vaccination views among the English-speaking professional classes, the government did not focus on this privileged stratum for vaccine hesitancy or resistance. In sum, as a form of social regulation, GTC does not operate as a mode of power that is exceptional or exists outside endemic structures of difference and domination. What critics of the dramatic declarations of emergency in the COVID-19 pandemic miss is how GTC takes up existing relations of power, dysconnecting social actors in new but familiar ways to protect human life.

[31] Chua and Lee, 'Governing through Contagion" (n 8), 129.

[32] This is not always the case, as Nainani's (ch 2) discussion of the temporary suspension of racialised surveillance practices in the Jordan district of Hong Kong shows. Nonetheless, we note that the targeted quarantine of Jordan still overlapped with prior patterns of racial difference and did not resolve the housing problems faced by Hong Kong's South Asian population.

[33] See www.youtube.com/watch?v=Cf2T3YgyaHA.

[34] S Alkhatib, 'Healing the Divide Founder Iris Koh, Doctor, Ex-assistant Face Charges for Bogus Claims on Covid-19 Jabs' *The Straits Times* (Singapore, 28 July 2022). Available at: www.straitstimes.com/singapore/courts-crime/healing-the-divide-founder-iris-koh-doctor-and-former-assistant-slapped-with-more-charges.

Between Contagion and Power: The Future of Law in GTC

By examining the case of smallpox and COVID-19 vaccination in colonial and post-colonial Singapore, respectively, we elaborated on the mediated role of law and the insidious side of resistance in the relationships between law, contagion and power. We stressed that the formidability of GTC rests on the interconnected workings of human and non-human agents. Both humans *and* non-human creatures and non-living objects are interwoven through law's dictates into state-driven strategies of control to combat contagion. Because of their indispensable role in GTC, these diverse agents may enable as well as disrupt the way law and other technologies operate, a point that highlights the limits of legal technology and thus the contingency of state power in contagious outbreaks. Just as smallpox vaccination in colonial Singapore ran into unanticipated issues with the vaccine virus, official misconduct and the non-compliance of the colonised, law does not singularly direct how GTC unfolds in the unpredictable course of an epidemic. In the COVID-19 pandemic, states struggled to devise legal forms and regulations as new variants and characteristics of the SARS-CoV-2 virus emerged. However, despite its vulnerabilities, the power of GTC remains significant. When the governed resist the law, regardless of their success or failure, they may exacerbate embedded inequalities, fostering endemic inter/dysconnectedness within power relations.

We are cautious about offering a sweeping conclusion on the future role of law in the development of GTC. Orientated to contagion, GTC involves entangled webs of human and non-human relations. We do not know when, where and how contagions may appear. As the COVID-19 pandemic well demonstrated, policymakers (or socio-legal scholars!) cannot accurately predict the capabilities of technologies and the abilities of human actors to (re)invent the means and purposes of law. Nevertheless, the chapters in *Contagion, Technology and Law at the Limits*, as well as our analyses of smallpox and COVID-19 vaccination in Singapore, indicate that governments consistently turn to law to exert power over contagion in their complex strategies of control.

Empowered by law in this manner, state actors then respond to resistance in ways that tend to rearticulate patterns of social inequality and domination. Even in the face of the profound dislocations of contagious outbreaks, inter/dysconnectedness endures wherever power relations exist and inequities live. As a historical formation of power, GTC and its processes and effects may shrink, expand or lie endemic within a population and the state between contagious episodes. When the next contagion arrives, governments may respond by continuously altering or re-enacting the regulatory forms and diverse agencies of GTC, particularly through the authority of law.

Guided by the theoretical framing of GTC, the contributors to this book have taken the first step toward investigating the shifts in human-non-human relationships across divergent episodes of contagion. They demonstrated, as a theory, GTC is applicable across temporal and physical spaces. In future research on GTC, other scholars can modify, affirm or challenge the features and concepts of GTC based on empirical findings at their research sites. They could scrutinise and vary the emphases, relevance or degree of the three GTC themes concerned with centralised legal technology, normalisation-moralisation and inter/dysconnectedness.

They could also consider such questions as: what roles do international organisations, international law and non-governmental organisations (NGOs) play in GTC? What are the varieties of human resistance, their relation to technologies of public health governance and their implications for power relations affected by GTC? How do different viruses and bacteria, as well as other living creatures, shape the formation and trajectory of GTC in a given society over time? How do emergent infrastructures of public health surveillance and control alter the inter/dysconnectedness of social relations? How does GTC operate as a global or transnational mode of public health governance?

Contagion, Technology and Law at the Limits represents the beginning of our intellectual journey to accomplish the goal of refining and advancing GTC as a theory of public health governance and to comprehend and expose the workings of GTC as a modern socio-legal phenomenon. In the Introduction and this Conclusion, we also refer to our ongoing historical ethnography of Singapore, which tracks the long arc of GTC from its colonial origins to the present. That work will be published in due course. We hope that others will take up research on GTC across other sites and times and develop knowledge of this historical formation of power.

As an empirically informed and critical theory, GTC sheds light not only on strategies of control and their effects. Its emphasis on the non-human also compels us to reckon with our connectedness to fellow humans and creatures. Despite often being sparked by zoonotic transmission, many contagious outbreaks have been, at root, products of anthropogenic causes. It is we humans who create opportunities, whether deliberately or unintentionally, for contagion to grow, transmit or harm our fellow humans – through our interactions with nature and how we treat one another, animals and other living things. With further research on GTC, we hope that scholars will reflect upon why and how contagions have threatened human and other lives and will continue to do so as a result of human actions and practices, how strategies of control and their legal technologies often reconstruct old patterns of inter/dysconnectedness on new grounds and how human efforts to secure and sanitise their milieu, in spite of the best of intentions, can lead to the prolonged, aggravated suffering of marginalised people and non-human beings more than others. Despite the limits of law's reach, when we turn to such populations at the periphery, we see clearly the power of governing through contagion.

INDEX

Printed in the USA
CPSIA information can be obtained
at www.ICGtesting.com
LVHW020750100924
790632LV00003B/97

9 781509 970704